First Certificate PASSKEY

Teacher's Book

NICK KENNY

Heinemann English Language Teaching
A division of Reed Educational and Professional Publishing Ltd
Halley Court, Jordan Hill, Oxford OX2 8EJ

OXFORD MADRID FLORENCE ATHENS PARIS PRAGUE
SÃO PAULO MEXICO CITY CHICAGO PORTSMOUTH NH (USA)
TOKYO SINGAPORE KUALA LUMPUR MELBOURNE
AUCKLAND JOHANNESBURG IBADAN GABORONE
NAIROBI KAMPALA

ISBN 0 435 24490 6

Text © Nick Kenny 1996

Design and illustration © Reed Educational and Professional Publishing Ltd 1996

First published 1996

Permission to copy

The material in this book is copyright. However, the publisher grants permission for copies of pages to be made without fee on those pages marked with the PHOTOCOPIABLE symbol.

Private purchasers may make copies for their own use or for use by classes of which they are in charge; school purchasers may make copies for use within and by the staff and students of the school only. This permission does not extend to additional schools or branches of an institution, who should purchase a separate master copy of the book for their own use.

For copying in any other circumstances, prior permission in writing must be obtained from Heinemann English Language Teaching, a division of Reed Educational and Professional Publishing Ltd.

All rights reserved; no part of this publication may be reproduced, stored in a retrieval system, transmitted in any form, or by any means, electronic, mechanical, photocopying, recording, or otherwise, without the prior written permission of the publishers.

Designed by M Rules, London

Printed and bound in Great Britain by Thomson Litho, East Kilbride, Scotland

Acknowledgements

The author would like to thank all students and colleagues from the British Council, Milan, the International Language Academy, Cambridge, and the Cambridge Office, who have provided a source of inspiration over the years. Special thanks are due to Beth Weighill, Barbara Lewis, Margaret Twelves, and Jane Barnes for their help and advice, and particularly to my editors, Jill Florent and Xanthe Sturt Taylor.

The author and publisher would like to thank the following for permission to reproduce copyright material:
BBC Worldwide Ltd. for an adapted extract from BBC Holidays magazine p 50; Eaglemoss Publications Ltd. for extracts based on the article 'Brain Power' in Find Out More magazine © 1995 p 104; Henderson Publishing plc for an extract from Funfax p 103; Tony James for an adapted extract from his article 'Sing-a-long-a-Fax' in Flagship Air UK in-flight magazine p 102; Michael Leech for an adapted extract from his article 'Gone fishin' in Monarch Airlines in-flight magazine p 49; The National Magazine Company Ltd. for adapted extracts from articles 'Home Improvements' by Andrew Brown p 67, 'The night the lights went out' by Edward Fox p 83, 'Field of dreams' by Tim Hulse p 84 and advertisement p 33 in Esquire magazine; WH Smith Ltd. for an adapted extract from Bookcase magazine, issue 41, September 1992 p 49; Spotlight Verlag, Germany for an extract from Spotlight magazine p 18; Woman and Home magazine and a reader for her letter published in the October 1992 issue p 34

97 98 99 10 9 8 7 6 5 4

Contents

Contents map of the Student's Book *iv*

Introduction *vi*

Unit 1 First impressions *1*

Unit 2 Work for a living *11*

Revision Test 1 *18*

Unit 3 Out and about *20*

Unit 4 Crime wave *28*

Revision Test 2 *35*

Unit 5 Playing the game *37*

Unit 6 Travellers' tales *44*

Revision Test 3 *51*

Unit 7 Food for thought *54*

Unit 8 High-tech horizons *61*

Revision Test 4 *69*

Unit 9 Working out *71*

Unit 10 It's a bargain *78*

Revision Test 5 *85*

Unit 11 Our world *87*

Unit 12 Finishing touches *96*

Revision Test 6 *104*

Listening Scripts *106*

Contents Map of the Student's Book

Vocabulary	Language Focus	Help Sections	Exam Focus
UNIT ONE *First impressions* 1			
Clothes Personal information Physical descriptions *Wear/dress* Describing personality	Present simple and continuous Order of adjectives Negative prefixes *In case* Linkers for sequencing Pronunciation: Word stress	Help with word formation 1 Help with planning and writing an article	**Paper 1:** Scanning for specific information; Gapped text **Paper 2:** Planning and writing an article **Paper 3:** Word formation; Key word transformations **Paper 4:** Multiple matching; Note-taking **Paper 5:** Exchanging information; Expressing opinions **Exam practice**
UNIT TWO *Work for a living* 16			
Jobs Personal qualities and skills	*To be used to* + *-ing* Present perfect/Past simple Multi-word verbs Comparative adjectives Pronunciation: Past tense endings	Help with writing letters	**Paper 1:** Scanning for specific information; Matching information **Paper 2:** Describing jobs; Transactional letters **Paper 3:** Key word transformations **Paper 4:** Listening for specific information; Note-taking; Matching information **Paper 5:** Describing a photograph; Expressing opinions; Exchanging information **Exam practice**
UNIT THREE *Out and about* 29			
Homes and interiors Housing	Causative *have*/*Needs doing* Expressing opinions: Giving advice Genitive *'s* Verbs used in the causative *For/Since* Asking for and giving advice Pronunciation: Vowel sounds	Help with grammar: Key word transformations Help with multiple-choice questions	**Paper 1:** Reading for main points; Reading for specific information; Multiple choice **Paper 2:** Informal letters **Paper 3:** Key word transformations; Opinions **Paper 4:** Matching information; Note-taking; Short extracts; Multiple choice **Paper 5:** Expressing opinions; Asking for and giving advice; Talking about photographs **Exam practice**
UNIT FOUR *Crime wave* 47			
Types of crime Describing trends	Sequence of tenses Making deductions Relative pronouns Compound nouns Pronunciation: Stress in compound nouns	Help with guessing the meaning of words Help with writing reports	**Paper 1:** Reading for specific information; Multiple matching; Gapped text **Paper 2:** Writing reports **Paper 3:** Cloze text; Error correction; Word formation **Paper 4:** Note-taking; Blank filling **Paper 5:** Exchanging information and expressing opinions **Exam practice**
UNIT FIVE *Playing the game* 59			
Sports and games Sports equipment and skills Dividing words into groups/categories Guessing unknown words	Time linkers *Used to* Past perfect Past tenses in narrative *Before/After* *Although/Despite* Pronunciation: Intonation	Help with writing a narrative composition Help with error correction	**Paper 1:** Multiple choice; Reading for main points **Paper 2:** Writing instructions; Narrative composition **Paper 3:** Cloze text; Key word transformations **Paper 4:** Multiple matching; Listening for specific information; Multiple choice; Short extracts **Paper 5:** Expressing opinions and exchanging information **Exam practice**
UNIT SIX *Travellers' tales* 76			
Travel words Travel quiz	Compound adjectives Prepositions Directions Future time 1 Present tenses for future *So/Such that* Pronunciation: Consonants	Help with gap filling	**Paper 1:** Multiple choice; Gapped text **Paper 2:** Discursive composition; Informal letters **Paper 3:** Key word transformations; Word formation **Paper 4:** Note-taking; Listening for specific information **Paper 5:** Talking about photographs; Expressing opinions; Exchanging information **Exam practice**

Vocabulary	Language Focus	Help Sections	Exam Focus

UNIT SEVEN Food for thought 92

Food Cooking verbs Menus	Gerund/Infinitive *Too/Enough* Zero/First conditionals Preferences *If/Unless* Future time 2: Intentions, arrangements, decisions Relative clauses Comparisons Pronunciation: Vowel sounds	Help with talking about a picture	**Paper 1:** Multiple choice; Reading for specific information; Multiple matching **Paper 2:** Paragraph writing; Writing an article **Paper 3:** Cloze text; Error correction **Paper 4:** Multiple choice; Short extracts; Listening for specific information; Multiple matching **Paper 5:** Talking about photographs; Expressing opinions; Expressing preferences; Problem solving **Exam practice**

UNIT EIGHT High-tech horizons 109

Inventions and discoveries Verbs to describe a process Word formation – nouns from verbs	Passive Agents Predictions – *Will/Going to* Agreeing and disagreeing: *So/Nor* Conditionals 2 Pronunciation: /h/	Help with gapped texts Help with word formation 2 Help with writing – giving opinions	**Paper 1:** Reading for specific information; Gapped text; Multiple matching; Reading for main points **Paper 2:** Writing a report **Paper 3:** Key word transformations **Paper 4:** Matching information; Blank filling; Note-taking; Multiple choice; Short extracts **Paper 5:** Talking about photographs; Expressing opinions **Exam practice**

UNIT NINE Working out 132

Lifestyles Electrical appliances Word formation Illness and health Nouns/verbs from adjectives	Present perfect continuous Regrets Conditionals 3 Pronunciation: Word stress and *th* sounds	Help with speaking – giving opinions	**Paper 1:** Multiple matching; Reading for specific information; Reading for main points; Multiple choice; Gapped text **Paper 2:** Writing a report **Paper 3:** Key word transformations; Cloze text **Paper 4:** Short extracts; Note-taking; Matching information; Multiple matching **Paper 5:** Talking about photographs; Expressing opinions; Expressing feelings **Exam practice**

UNIT TEN It's a bargain 151

Shopping Words connected with money and trade	Obligations *Make, let, allow* Wishes Complaints Pronunciation: Word linking	Help with writing a transactional letter	**Paper 1:** Multiple choice; Multiple matching; Gapped text **Paper 2:** Writing a transactional letter **Paper 3:** Key word transformations **Paper 4:** Note-taking; Short extracts; Multiple matching **Paper 5:** Talking about photographs; Solving a problem; Expressing opinions **Exam practice**

UNIT ELEVEN Our world 168

Prepositions Parts of a car	Reported Speech Impersonal Passive Reporting verbs *It's time* Pronunciation: Shifting stress and word stress Complaints		**Paper 1:** Reading for specific information; Multiple choice; **Paper 2:** Writing a discursive composition; Writing a report **Paper 3:** Open cloze; Key word transformations **Paper 4:** Short extracts; Note-taking; Multiple matching; Multiple choice **Paper 5:** Talking about photographs; Expressing opinions **Exam practice**

UNIT TWELVE Finishing touches 187

Word formation *Alone* and *lonely* Pets Biographies Relationships	Review of tenses Question tags Future in the past Pronunciation: Contractions Uses of *do*		**Paper 1:** Multiple matching; Reading for specific information; Multiple choice **Paper 2:** Writing a transactional letter; Writing an article **Paper 3:** Word formation; Error correction; Open cloze **Paper 4:** Note-taking; Multiple matching; Short extracts; Listening for specific information; Blank filling **Paper 5:** Giving personal information; Expressing opinions; Talking about photographs **Exam practice**

Introduction

This Teacher's Book is easy to use, following the same format as the Student's Book for easy cross-referencing, and focuses on the language and skills your students need to pass the First Certificate exam. In addition to answers for exercises and Exam Practice activities and complete tapescripts, there are also detailed suggestions for setting up and exploiting activities, definitions of vocabulary from authentic readings that might cause difficulty, and six photocopiable revision tests in the exam format. The Teacher's Book includes cross-referencing to the useful Grammar Reference section at the end of the Student's Book. The Student's Book also includes a Multi-word Verb Review, a comprehensive wordlist and a table of irregular verbs.

Each unit begins with a summary of the topic, skills developed and exam strategies and techniques to be focused on. The summary is followed by sequential treatment of the Student's Book material. Every two units there is a photocopiable Progress Test which students can be given either in class or for homework. These tests are in the exam format and provide systematic practice in exam skills as the course progresses.

The First Certificate in English

The First Certificate exam is aimed at students with a good intermediate level of English in all four skills. First Certificate assesses students' general ability in English through tests of reading, writing, grammar, listening and speaking. The First Certificate in English examination was revised in December 1996.

In the revised FCE the language level and overall difficulty has not changed. The examination has 5 papers:

Paper 1	Reading	(1 hour and 15 minutes)
Paper 2	Writing	(1 hour and 30 minutes)
Paper 3	Use of English	(1 hour and 15 minutes)
Paper 4	Listening	(approximately 40 minutes)
Paper 5	Speaking	(approximately 14 minutes per pair of candidates)

Papers 1–3 are taken on a fixed date, while papers 4 and 5 are taken on various dates within two or three weeks of the written papers. In some exam centres paper 4 is taken on the same day as papers 1–3. The results arrive about 10–12 weeks after the date of the exam and students receive a grade: Grade A, B, C (Pass); D, E, U (Fail)

Each of the five papers in the examination contributes a maximum of 40 marks to the final result. To pass the exam students need to score at least 120–125 marks out of a total of 200.

Note that students do not pass or fail individual papers of FCE. Their result in the examination depends on the addition of the marks for each of the five components. This means that students who are rather weak or perhaps lacking confidence in a particular paper or papers can still be successful in FCE, as long as their marks in the other papers are sufficiently good to compensate for these weaknesses.

What's in the revised FCE

Paper 1 Reading

Time: 1 hour and 15 minutes Marks: 40/200
- There are 35 questions on 4 reading passages of between 350 and 700 words each. There is a total of about 2000 words of text.
- The passages are from authentic sources (eg from newspapers, magazines, brochures, guides, advertisements, fiction).
- Students need to use a range of reading skills to complete the tasks in the time allowed. Many students will need help with skills such as skimming and scanning and with the deduction of meaning from context when dealing with unfamiliar vocabulary.
- The instructions for each Part are as similar as possible. However, students should always read the instructions carefully because these often help them by indicating what type of text they are about to read and the topic.

For Help with guessing meaning of words see SB page 53.

Part 1 **Multiple matching**

Six or seven headings or summary sentences followed by a text of between 350 and 700 words. Students have to match a heading with something in the text. Typically this will involve deciding which sub-heading should be inserted in which gap in the text, or which summary sentence reflects which part of the text. There is one extra heading/summary sentence which students do not need to use.

Part 2 **Multiple choice**

One text of between 350 and 700 words followed by seven or eight multiple choice questions, each with four options. This is very similar to the reading tasks included in the previous FCE.

For Help with multiple-choice questions see SB page 44.

Part 3 **Gapped text**

A text of between 350 and 700 words followed by six or seven questions. The questions consist of sentences or paragraphs which have been removed from the text. Students have to decide where in the text each sentence/paragraph fits. There is one extra sentence/paragraph which students do not need to use.

Part 4 **Multiple matching**

13–15 questions followed by a text of between 350 and 700 words. Most of the questions can be answered by students scanning through the text to find the appropriate bit of information. Students have to decide which part of the text is related to which question. The final 2 questions may sometimes be about the functional meaning of the text. For these 2 questions students select from 4 multiple choice options.

Answers

For Paper 1 students are given an answer sheet which they must mark with a pencil to show their answers. This is so that the answers can be checked by a computer. Students can write on the question paper if they want to, but they must remember to copy all their answers onto the answer sheet before the end of the test – there is no extra time for this. There is an example of the answer sheet on page 210 of the Student's Book.

Marks

The four parts are weighted so that they each contribute about one quarter of the marks available for this paper, even though Part 4 has more questions than the other parts.

Paper 2 Writing

Time 1 hour and 30 minutes   Marks: 40/200
- Students write two answers, each of between 120 and 180 words.
- There is one compulsory question where an input text and some notes are provided and students must use the information in these to write a transactional letter.
  For Help with writing a transactional letter see SB page 157.
- Students answer a second question from a choice of four, which can include an article or report as well as a story, letter, composition or an answer based on one of the background reading texts.
  For Help with planning and paragraphing, see SB page 13.
  For Help with writing letters see SB page 26.
  For Help with writing reports see SB page 56.
  For Help with writing narratives see SB page 70.
  For Help with giving opinions see SB page 126.

For Part 1, (the compulsory question) students should spend 5–10 minutes reading the instructions and planning their letter, 30 minutes writing and then at least 5 minutes checking what they have written. Students should avoid copying whole phrases from the input text, and should reword the information whenever possible. Obviously, some key pieces of vocabulary included in the input text will need to be used in the answer.

For Part 2, students should spend 5 minutes selecting the question which they want to write about and planning their answer, 30 minutes writing, and then 5–10 minutes checking what they have written. Students are unlikely to have time to write a full draft of their answers and then copy it, and should be discouraged from this approach.

Answers

Typically students perform poorly in Paper 2 if their general level of language and vocabulary is inadequate or if they do not write an answer appropriate for the question. The exact length of the answer is not important. However, students who write much more than 180 words will not have their additional work fully assessed as part of their answer. Students who write fewer than 120 words are unlikely to have given an adequate answer to the question and so are unlikely to receive a good mark. Discourage students from wasting time during the examination by counting every word they have written - making a rough estimate is sufficient.

Marks

After the examination, student answers are sent back to Cambridge and marked by a team of experienced examiners. Marks are given for the quality of the language which students produce (accuracy, appropriacy, range, the effect on the target reader, etc.), and the successful completion of the task which was set.

Paper 3 Use of English

Time: 1 hour and 15 minutes   Marks: 40/200
- There are 5 parts and students answer 65 questions about grammar and vocabulary.

Part 1 **Gapped text**

A text with 15 multiple-choice questions. Students select the correct word or expression to complete each gap. The gaps focus on vocabulary knowledge.

Part 2 **Gapped text**

where students write one word only in each of 15 spaces. The gaps in this task mostly focus on grammatical words.
  For Help with gap filling see SB page 89.

Part 3 **Grammar transformation sentences**

Students are given a complete prompt sentence and the beginning and the ending of the answer sentence as well as a word (in bold type) which they must use in their answer. To complete the target sentence students must use between 2 and 5 words including the word given in bold.
  For Help with key word transformations see SB page 38.

The most common focus for transformation sentences are: active-passive; direct-indirect speech; causative *have*; conditions; Present perfect (+ *since/for*) – Simple past; *too* – *enough*; *so* – *such*; linkers (eg *although*, *in spite of*), lexical phrases and common idiomatic expressions (eg *it's high time...*).

Part 4   A text for **error correction** (find the extra word).

Students read a text with 15 lines and decide whether each line in the text is correct, or has an additional wrong word included in it. If the line is correct, students put a tick [✓], if the line has a wrong word they write the wrong word on the answer sheet. Students can probably expect between 3 and 5 lines to be correct. The additional wrong words are definitely incorrect, not optional words like an extra adjective. The wrong words are likely to be grammatical rather than lexical.
  For Help with error correction see SB page 72.

Part 5 **Word building**

A text of 10 lines each with a gap to be filled by reformulating a word given in capitals in the margin on the right of the text.
  For Help with word formation see SB pages 10 and 122.

Answers

For Paper 3, there is an answer sheet which students must mark with a pencil to show their answers. For some of the questions they must mark a letter (A, B, C or D), and for others they have to write a word or a short phrase. Students can write on their question paper if they want to, but must remember to copy all their answers onto the answer sheet before the end of the test – there is no extra time for this. There is an example of the answer sheet on pages 209/210 of the Student's Book.

Marks

There is one mark for each correct answer, except in Part 3 (sentence transformations) where for each sentence there

Introduction

is one mark for each of two distinct parts of the target answer. Correct spelling is essential for all parts of Paper 3 where students have to write a word or phrase.

Paper 4 Listening

Time: about 40 minutes   Marks: 40/200
- There are 4 parts (each heard twice) and students answer 30 questions. Listening texts may be either monologues or feature interacting speakers.

Short extracts

In Part 1 there are eight short listening passages of around 30 seconds, each with one multiple-choice question. To help students in this part the questions are recorded on the tape as well as printed on the question paper. Students choose the best alternative from three options to show understanding of gist, main points, specific information, or deducing the meaning from the context.

For Help with multiple-choice questions see SB page 44.

Note-taking/blank filling

In Part 2 students must write a word or short phrase to complete 10 questions based on a longer listening text of around three minutes. Some questions take the form of incomplete notes, while others are summary sentences with blanks to be filled. Where blanks are part of complete sentences, the key must fit grammatically, otherwise note form is acceptable. Generally, students do not need to write more than two or three words in each gap.

Multiple matching

In Part 3 students hear 5 short listening passages all about the same topic and match what they hear to a list of prompts on the question paper. There is one extra prompt which students do not need to use. Task focus is the same as in Part 1.

Selecting an answer

In Part 4 there are 7 questions based on a listening passage of around three minutes. Questions ask students to choose between two or three alternative answers, (eg true/false, multiple choice).

Answers

During the Listening test students must write their answers on the question paper as they listen. At the end of the test they have five minutes to copy these answers onto an answer sheet. There is an example of the answer sheet on page 210 of the Student's Book.

Marks

There is one mark for each correct answer in Paper 4. In Part 2, where students have to write a word or phrase, incorrect spelling is not penalised as long as the answer can be clearly understood.

Paper 5 Speaking

Time: 14 minutes (per pair of candidates)   Marks: 40/200
- The usual format is two students with two examiners – one examiner talks to the students, the other examiner just listens (in a few places there may be examinations with one student and one examiner, but students cannot choose to do the test in this way – if you are in any doubt about whether to prepare your students for a one-to-one or paired oral format contact your local centre for advice).
- Students will be asked to talk about themselves and their everyday life, family, hobbies, etc.; and also talk to a partner and discuss some photographs, solve a problem or give their opinions.
- Each of the four parts of the test lasts 3–4 minutes.
In Part 1, students are asked to give personal information. While this can be thoroughly practised in class, students should avoid preparing a set speech which may sound very unnatural and wooden on the day of the examination.
For Help with giving personal information see SB page 187.
In Part 2, each student is asked to compare and contrast two pictures. It is useful to know some of the language for talking about a picture, but students are not supposed to give a full description of the pictures. Students should be taught to paraphrase unknown vocabulary and speculate about what may or may not be happening/how the people pictured feel about it, etc.
For Help with talking about a picture see SB page 103.
In Part 3, students are asked to talk to each other about a given topic. This will not relate to the subject of the pictures in Part 2, but students are given visual and word prompts to help them. Students should discuss various alternatives before coming to an agreement or decision. Students should be able to complete Part 3 co-operatively without the intervention of the examiner, but the discussion rather than conclusion is the important element and if students 'agree to differ' this is an acceptable outcome.
For Help with speaking about opinions see SB page 126.
In Part 4, one of the examiners leads a discussion which develops the topic covered in Part 3.

In the case of one-to-one speaking tests, the student discusses the photographs and topics with the examiner. Exceptionally, there are speaking tests with three candidates and two examiners. Examiners are trained and provided with specially designed material for these tests. The procedure is similar to above, but the test is slightly longer.

Marks

Students are assessed on their grammar, vocabulary, pronunciation, communicative ability and their achievement of the tasks they are asked to do (this does not mean they actually have to complete the task - see Part 3 above).

Answers

It is very important for students to remember that they can only be assessed on the language which they produce, and therefore to give full answers. If students do not understand the instructions they are given, or what their partner is trying to say, they should ask for clarification and are not penalised for this.

UNIT 1

First impressions

TOPIC	HELP SECTIONS	Paper 5
Clothes, appearance and personality	Help with word formation 1	Exchanging information
VOCABULARY FOCUS	Help with planning and writing an article	Expressing opinions
Clothes	**EXAM FOCUS**	**EXAM PRACTICE**
Personal information	**Paper 1**	Open cloze
Physical descriptions	Scanning for specific information	Discursive writing
Wear/dress	Gapped text	Word formation
Describing personality	**Paper 2**	
LANGUAGE FOCUS	Planning and writing an article	
Present simple and continuous	**Paper 3**	
Order of adjectives	Word formation	
Negative prefixes	Key word transformations	
In case	**Paper 4**	
Linkers for sequencing	Multiple matching	
Pronunciation: Word stress	Note-taking	

READING 1 Page 1
Giving personal information

Pre-activity: Write **Pen-friend** on the board and elicit the meaning. Ask: Have you ever had a pen-friend? Can you describe your pen-friend? eg age, nationality, interests (to get brief descriptions of pen-friends they have now or have had). If your students have not had a pen-friend, ask: What are the benefits of having a pen-friend?
Divide the class into groups and ask them to decide on the characteristics of the ideal pen-friend. Give them a few minutes to discuss, helping with vocabulary as necessary, then ask for brief details from a few groups. Tell students that they are going to read some extracts from a magazine in which people who are interested in finding pen-friends describe themselves.
Students read and answer questions 1–3 as quickly as possible. Set a time limit for reading (3 minutes) before checking the answers.

Key

1 Lars   **2** Louisa   **3** Lars

Ask students to make their choice and to underline the main points which attracted them to a particular pen-friend.
Once students have discussed this, ask for examples of the pen-friends selected and the reasons for the choice.

5 Students complete the grid taking information from the descriptions. Tell them not to complete the last two columns yet.

Key

	Louisa	Lars	Akemi
Age	19	26	25
Nationality	Italian	Swedish	Japanese
Occupation	Student	Trainee manager	Shop assistant
Interests	Cinema Environment-	Skiing Water sports	Theatre Cinema Classical music/ Opera

UNIT 1 *First Impressions*

SPEAKING 1 Page 2
Exchanging personal information

1 Now get students to work in pairs and ask each other the questions to complete the last two columns of the grid.

2 Key

How old are you?
Where do you come from?
What's your job/What do you do?
What are your interests/hobbies?

The Present simple tense is used to talk about states. In the descriptions of pen-friends there are also examples of the Present simple used to talk about habits and routines.

3 If possible, get students to move around the classroom as they ask the above questions. Insist that they change partner frequently so that they speak to a lot of different people in the class. Otherwise, get them to work in groups of four or six and to ask the questions to the people sitting near them.

4 Complete in class or for homework. As a follow up, read a selection of the descriptions to the class, omitting the name, and ask your students to guess the identity of the writer.

GRAMMAR 1 Page 2 (GR p 215)
Present simple and continuous

To introduce this section, read two or three of the following sentences aloud, or write them on the board, and ask students to tell you whether they relate to usually, always or now. Then refer students to the grid before returning to more of the examples below.

a He's tall and thin. (always)
b He's waiting for a bus. (now)
c He drinks coffee for breakfast. (usually)
d She's wearing jeans. (now)
e Wool comes from animals. (always)
f She's got brown eyes. (always)
g She drives to work. (usually)
h My birthday's in July. (always)

Note that in c and g students might want to say *always*. Point out that in this activity *always*, *usually* and *now* are used to mean:
always something which is fixed and cannot be changed.
usually something repeated regularly.
now something happening at the moment (and will change).
If necessary, explain that we might say: *He always drinks coffee for breakfast,* but we mean that this is something that happens very regularly, not that this is a fixed situation which cannot be changed.
Before completing the exercise, refer students to the Grammar Reference section if they have difficulty.

Key

1 wears, is wearing
2 gets/wakes up, goes/drives
3 wears/buys, wears/buys
4 lives, is staying
5 trusts/respects
6 goes, is taking/is going in

Further Practice: Get a large picture or a number of pictures from a magazine or newspaper which show people doing different things. Ask students to say what the people are doing (eg he's playing football), describe the scene and make sentences about the lives of these people (eg he works in a bank). Elicit some sentences using each of the target forms, then get students individually or in pairs to write their own sentences about the pictures. Students then compare sentences in pairs/groups. Write some of the examples they produce on the board.

VOCABULARY 1 Page 2
Clothes

Pre-activity: Show students some pictures from magazines to elicit basic clothing vocabulary and as an introduction to the topic. Write this clothes vocabulary on the board.

1 Input vocabulary as required by your students.
2 Particularly with a monolingual class encourage students to explain in English any words on their list which their partners do not know.
3 You may need to make suggestions, eg clothes you wear on holiday, for playing sports, for special occasions.
4 The lists which students produce might be organised according to material, purpose, place, climate, etc. Stress that there is no single 'right' answer in this activity. Any groupings are acceptable if they can be justified.
5 If students have not been able to make groupings with all the words, their partners can suggest possible titles.
6 The words are all either simple or compound adjectives which are often used to describe clothing.
7 Students can work together in pairs for this activity.

Further practice: Hold up pictures of (or real) items of clothing so that only part of the class can see them. Get those who can see the picture/item to define it for the others, who guess its correct name. (eg You wear it round your waist and it holds up your trousers = a belt.)

GRAMMAR 2 Page 3 (GR p 215)
Order of adjectives

1 Tell students to keep their books closed. Write the words *waterproof* and *long*, in the top right and bottom left corners of the board. Ask: What do these words

First impressions **UNIT 1**

describe? (a coat). Write *coat* in the middle of the board and get students to order the adjectives to form *a long waterproof coat*. Ask: It's long, for who? (the person wearing it). It's waterproof, for who? (everyone). Then refer them to Student's Book Page 3 exercise 1.

2 The adjectives nearest the noun are the most objective, with the colour usually coming before the type of material. The adjectives furthest from the noun are more subjective (eg 'loose-fitting' depends on who is wearing the pullover, and 'beautiful' refers to someone's personal opinion).

3 Possible answers

1 She's wearing a light brown skirt and top with a dark brown jacket and flat brown sandals.
2 She's wearing a red skirt and white blouse with a short grey woollen coat and scarf and high-heeled brown shoes.
3 He's wearing jeans and a T-shirt with black trainers and a white jumper with navy stripes.
4 She's wearing a grey raincoat and checked scarf with black leather gloves and high-heeled brown leather shoes.

4 Key

a – 1, 2, 4   **b** – 3   **c** – 3   **d** – 2, 4   **e** – 1
f – 1   **g** – 4   **h** – 1, 4   **i** – 3   **j** – 2, 3, 4

Note that *blonde* refers to women, *blond* to men. The pronunciation is the same.

5 Possible answers

1 She's carrying a large brown leather shoulder bag. She's wearing a watch.
2 She's carrying an umbrella. She's got a brown shoulder bag.
3 He's got his right hand in his pocket. He's smiling.
4 She's holding a large green umbrella. She's carrying a shoulder bag.

LISTENING 1 Page 3
Describing people

1 Introduce the listening by getting students to read the sentences they have written describing the people in the previous exercise. Before you play the tape, set the scene by saying that they will hear part of a radio news programme in which a woman suspect is described. Tell the class that the police want to find this woman because she has robbed a post office and stolen £10,000. Tell students that they will hear the tape twice.

Key

Picture 2 most closely resembles the description on the tape.

2 Key

The words to be underlined are: *brown* (eyes), *long, flat, beige, early, Liverpool*.

3 You may wish to get students to do both of these things, one in class and one for homework.

4 Either ask students to read out their descriptions (perhaps at the beginning of the next lesson, in order to revise descriptions and clothes vocabulary), or collect and redistribute all the descriptions and ask students to read and identify the person described. Finally ask students to write a description of themselves.

VOCABULARY 2 Page 4
Wear/Dress

Pre-activity: Divide your board into four sections and write *clothes* and *dresses* as titles for two of the sections. Elicit an example sentence for each word, then ask students to write two or three more sentences. Do the same for *to wear* and *to dress*.

1.1 Refer to students to the sentences in 1 as they discuss the difference between *clothes* and *dresses*.

Key

Clothes: the plural form of 'an item of clothing'. A general word to describe what people wear.
Examples
He's a film star, so he's got lots of expensive clothes.
Felicity wants to buy some new clothes for the summer.
If you go skiing you need special clothes to keep you warm.
Dresses: the plural form of a particular item of clothing worn by women.
Examples
Judy usually wears jeans, but she's got a few dresses that she keeps for special occasions.
The bride wore a beautiful long white wedding dress.
Some people say it's better for a woman to wear a dress at a job interview, and not a pair of trousers.

1.2 Follow the same procedure for *to wear* and *to dress*.

Key

To wear: to have clothes (and jewellery or glasses) on your body.
Examples
'Sorry, I can't open the door – I'm not wearing anything!'
The thief was wearing a grey raincoat and a hat.
Roger usually wears glasses when he goes to the cinema, but he doesn't need them for reading.
To be worn out: Clothes which have been used so much that they need to be replaced.

3

UNIT 1 First Impressions

To dress:
a Used to describe styles of clothing (often followed by 'in').
Examples
She often dresses in bright colours.

b The action of putting on clothes.
Example
Andy must have dressed very quickly – he was wearing one green sock and one white one.
To get dressed is an alternative form.

2 Add the above definitions to the grid on the board before students complete the gap-fill exercise.

Key

1 wearing 2 wearing 3 dresses 4 worn 5 dress
6 dressed 7 dresses 8 dress, wearing 9 dressed
10 wear

LISTENING 2 Page 4
Note-taking

1 **Pre-activity:** Show a couple of pictures of non-famous people and ask students to guess what their personalities are like. Start them off by asking questions like, "Do you think he/she is ... eg easy-going/lively/vain/bossy/friendly, etc.?" Use some of the words from the Key to exercise 2 below, so that the students are familiar with them before they listen. Then get students to discuss 1.1 and 1.2 in pairs. Ask a few students to report back on what they decided about 1.2, and why.

2 **Pre-activity:** Get students to read through the incomplete notes and explain any unknown vocabulary to them. Ask students to predict before they listen whether each feature (eg Round Face, Square Face) will be described in the discussion in negative or positive terms. Point out that they will hear a discussion from a radio programme, and ask them how many voices they expect to hear (in fact, in this discussion they hear two people, a man and a woman).

Key

1 home-loving   6 selfish
2 practical   7 friendliness
3 successful   8 independent
4 lively   9 sociable, warm
5 bossy   10 easy-going
                   11 vain

VOCABULARY 3 Page 4
Describing personality

1 **Pre-activity:** Elicit some of the words in the box by showing pictures of famous people and asking students to talk about their character. (With weaker students the pictures can be used to check the meaning of words in the box.)
Set up the activity by reading out a few words from the box while the class tell you if they are positive or negative qualities. Tell students to work in pairs and when they have decided, indicate + to mean positive or – to mean negative qualities. If they are not sure they put a ?.

Key

+ = positive, – = negative, ■ = word-stress when speaking.

+ sensible   – dull   + reliable
+ amusing   – stupid   – cold
+ strong   + charming   + helpful
+ intelligent   – bossy   + lively
– silly   + responsible – fussy
+ patient   + sensitive   + friendly
+ entertaining + careful   + honest
– nasty   – lazy   + independent

2 Ask students to circle four adjectives which describe themselves and to underline four adjectives which they think describe their partner. Get them to compare choices.
3 Students can continue to work in pairs to add to the list.
4 Before students do this activity, elicit or present the range of prefixes used in the exercise: un-, im-, dis-, in-, irr-.

Key

unamusing, unselfish, unintelligent, impatient, untrustworthy, irresponsible, insensitive, unreliable, impractical, unhelpful, unobservant, unfriendly, dishonest.
Note that the opposite of sensible is *silly* or *stupid*.

Extra activity: Get students in pairs to decide on the opposites of the other words in the box. Tell them to concentrate on opposites which relate to character.

Possible answers

sensible–silly/stupid; boring–exciting; strong–weak; silly–sensible; entertaining–dull/boring; nasty–nice; dull–bright/exciting; stupid–intelligent/sensible; charming–unpleasant/dull; foolish–sensible; bossy–passive; careful–careless; lazy–hardworking; cold–warm; lively–quiet/dull; fussy–easy-going; independent–dependent.

READING 2 Page 5
Reading for specific information

Pre-activity: Start the activity with Student's Books closed. Introduce the idea of fingerprints by drawing a huge one on the board, or finding a suitable example on your classroom wall. Ask students the name for this and write 'Fingerprint' on the board.

1 Ask students to predict the answers before they read.

1.1 Key

Fingerprints identify criminals (= villains).

1.2 Before they read, get students to briefly describe how they might take fingerprints.

Possible answer

First, find an ink pad.
Next, press your fingertip against the pad.
Finally, press firmly on a piece of paper, rolling the fingertip from side to side.

1.3 Key

Because they can reveal things about a person's character.

1.4 Encourage students to work quickly on this by setting a time limit of five minutes to complete the task.

Key

whodunnits (n) = murder stories
convicted (vb) = proved to be guilty
unwary (adj) = not aware of danger, not careful
swirls (n) = parts of circles in fingerprints
unique (adj) = of which there is only one
irrefutable (adj) = that cannot be doubted
ascribe (vb) = link to
decipher (vb) = work out the meaning
smudging (vb) = making unclear

2 This is a split reading activity. Students read different parts of the same article, answer questions and then exchange their information with their partners. First, divide the class into two and identify each person as student A or B. Do this by going quickly round the room saying A-B, A-B etc. Check that everyone is following by going back occasionally and asking students at random: What letter are you? Explain to students that they will each read about the same topic, but the information they read will be different. They must read *only* their section (A or B) and answer questions about it. They will then have to explain their answers to a partner in the other group.

2.1 Key

Words to underline are:
Student A – The Whorl
fixed, inflexible attitude
artistic
creative
quiet, deep thinkers
slow to respond
Student A – The Composite
an ability to appreciate all points of view
confused
Student B – The Arch
practical, sensible attitude
realists
common sense
trustworthy and reliable
find it difficult to express emotions/feelings
Student B – The Loop
flexible, adaptable and versatile
open-minded and tolerant
excellent communicators
creativity
open, amenable approach

2.2 Key

Adjectives from the box are:
The Whorl – independent, creative, thoughtful
The Composite – understanding, analytical, indecisive, fair
The Arch – realistic, helpful, unemotional, reserved
The Loop – enthusiastic, adventurous, communicative, sociable

2.3 Key

The Whorl: ring finger = artistic, creative appreciation
little finger = quiet, a deep thinker
The Composite: not important
The Arch: not important
The Loop: not important
Point out that the headings for each of the reading sections are very specific vocabulary used by fingerprint experts. They are not important for students to learn.

2.4 After students have exchanged information ask for some sample answers about different types of fingerprints.
2.5 The instructions for taking fingerprints are given at the beginning of the reading. If you wish, get students to make their own fingerprints at home, or to photocopy their hands, to make notes about themselves from the information in the article. In the next class they can then explain their own fingerprints to their partners.

PRONUNCIATION Page 6
Word stress

1 Get your students to decide in pairs how many syllables are in each word. Don't ask them to decide where the syllable boundaries are – the spelling/pronunciation relationships are complex and probably not very helpful to students. Quickly check through the list of words. Where students are not sure of the the number of syllables, either say the words or play the list on the tape and ask them to confirm the answers.
2 Tell students to indicate which syllable is stressed in each word as they listen. Pause the tape after the first three or four words and check the answers before continuing.

UNIT 1 *First Impressions*

Key to 1 and 2

- sociable (3)
- unemotional (5)
- realistic (4)
- helpful
- independent (4)
- reserved (2)
- religious (3)
- communicative (5)
- thoughtful (2)
- creative (3)
- understanding (4)
- analytical (5)
- indecisive (4)
- adventurous (4)
- enthusiastic (5)
- imaginative (5)
- idealistic (5)
- lazy (2)
- fair (1)

3 First replay the tape and get the class or individuals to repeat, then read out the words yourself in random order, then get students to read the words to each other.

4 Complete in class (pairing students who have the same fingerprint patterns) or for homework.

Key

The Whorl	The Composite	The Arch	The Loop
individual (4)	composite (3)	practical (3)	represent (3)
inflexible (4)	ability (3)	sensible (3)	flexible (3)
attitude (3)	appreciate (4)	attitude (3)	adaptable (9)
artistic (3)	occupation (4)	conversation (4)	versatile (4)
creative (3)	necessary (4)	usually (3)	individuals (5)
appreciation (5)	understand (3)	everyday (3)	tolerant (3)
majority (4)	situation (4)	material (4)	character (3)
difficult (3)	advantage (3)	thoroughly (3)	variety (4)
opinions (3)	personal (3)	trustworthy (3)	excited (3)
information (3)	decision (3)	reliable (4)	stimulated (4)
consider (3)	definite (3)	excellent (3)	everyday (3)
considering (4)	difficult (3)	activities (4)	
alternatives (4)	repressing (3)	challenges (3)	
analysing (4)	emotions (3)	opportunities (5)	
complicate (3)	excellent (3)		
totally (3)	communicators (5)		
environment (4)			
creativity (5)			
indicates (3)			
amenable (4)			

Point out that the Student's Book has a list of selected FCE-level vocabulary on Page 225, but students may want to keep their own lists of words which are new to them, or of particular interest to them, or difficult for them.

LISTENING 3 Page 7
Note-taking

Pre-activity: (Note that this is a change of topic and is used to practise *if* and *in case* in the following grammar section.) Ask students what they would take with them on a walking holiday. Then refer students to the grid and give them plenty of time to read it. Before they listen ask where the walking holiday will take place (in Scotland). Students may be able to predict some of the answers before they listen. Play the tape twice.
Vocabulary: sleeper (n) = a train with beds
rucksack (n) = nylon bag which you carry on your back
packed lunch (n) = food prepared in advance, wrapped and taken on a trip
rough country (n) = land where it is difficult to walk around because there are no paths or roads
glucose tablets (n) = a type of sugar which gives people an energy boost when walking or doing sports

Key

1 train **2** coach **3** hostels **4** small, waterproof bag/rucksack **5** full-length **6** hood (= a cover for the head attached to a coat or jacket) **7** socks **8** pullovers **9** skiing **10** old/comfortable (ones) **11** (casual) shoes **12** first-aid kit **13** chocolate

GRAMMAR 3 Page 7 (GR p 215)
In case

1 Focus on the example sentence and elicit the answer to 1.1 from the class.

1.1 Key

The time referred to is the future. Verb forms used are the imperative and present simple.

1.2 Get students to discuss this in pairs.

Key

In case is used because the weather may be bad or it may be good, but we take the anorak because we are not sure.
If is used to show that we should only take the anorak in the event of bad weather – in the event of good weather we do not take the anorak.

1.3 Before you play the tape again, point out to students that there will not be enough time to write very much, and they should concentrate on picking out **Key** phrases

First Impressions **UNIT 1**

which they can use after listening to make complete phrases with *in case*.

Key

in case it gets lost, in case you get wet feet, in case they rub or hurt your feet, in case your boots get wet and dirty, in case you have an accident, in case you get lost or exhausted.
In case is followed by the present simple tense in each example.

2 You may prefer to get students to write out the transformations on a separate piece of paper, or in an exercise book.

Key

1 In case the car breaks down at night, you should take a torch.
2 In case it rains, take an umbrella.
3 In case you decide to do some shopping, you should take a large bag.
4 In case you cut yourself, put some plasters in your bag.
5 In case you get cold, pack an extra pair of warm socks.

3 Tell students that this type of exercise, which involves transforming sentences using a word which is given in bold and up to four other words, is always found in the Use of English part of the FCE exam (see Introduction).

Key

1 in case it gets lost
2 should take an anorak because
3 in case you want to
4 because you might get
5 because you might have to

4 Ask students to read the instructions and tell you what they think *properly dressed* means in these circumstances, and what a *packed lunch* might consist of. Students can then use dictionaries to help them with the vocabulary matching exercise.

4.1 Key

1 = penknife
2 = box of matches
3 = whistle
4 = chocolate

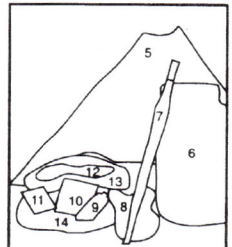

5 = tent
6 = rucksack
7 = umbrella
8 = rope
9 = water bottle
10 = first aid kit
11 = map
12 = extra pair of socks
13 = an extra pullover
14 = a sleeping bag

4.2 When students have discussed this, ask them to tell you what they have selected, using *in case*.
4.3 Students can write these sentences in class or for homework.

READING 3 Page 8
Gapped text

1 Give the class a couple of minutes to talk about the picture in pairs and then elicit a description of what seems to be happening in the photograph and your students reaction to it. Ask them what they think of tattoos and how they react when they see people with them. Explain that while a tattoo is permanent, what they see in the picture is produced by using henna (a natural colouring) and it wears off after a few weeks.

2 This helps students to find out about longer texts without having to laboriously read through every word. Emphasise that you want them to find the answers quickly and treat each heading (eg parts of the body) as a separate exercise. Give the group a time limit to find and underline as many parts of the body as possible - a couple of minutes is enough. Check their answers then repeat the procedure for the other headings. To vary the activity slightly you can tell them, for example, that there are 6 names to find.

Key

parts of the body
legs, foot/feet, shoulders, ankle, arm, hands, fingernails, toes, skin, legs
(words to describe) **parts of the world/nationalities**
Arabian/Arabic, Indian, Egyptian, Asian, Kuwait, Britain, British, Europe
names of people
Jane, Karen, Lorraine, Sarah, Jackie, Aileen, Lynne
jobs
photographer, financial consultant, clothing designer

3 Key

3–6 weeks	the time it takes the design to wash off (line 12)
an hour	the time it takes for the henna to dry /fall off (53/4)
two days	the time it takes the full colour to develop (56)

4 Before students attempt this exercise draw their attention to the example (0). Ask them what *they* in the example sentence (J) refers to (the women meeting at Sarah's home) and what *It* in the following sentence refers to (the designs made with henna). Then get them to decide which sentence fits into the first gap (1) and to explain why:
They come from Halawa Henna suggests that the missing sentence will include a mention of people. *The women ...*

7

UNIT 1 First Impressions

are waiting in the previous paragraph indicates that something is going to happen, and *It is time to make decisions* suggests that something has happened. Therefore the sentence which best fits the gap is (I) *The specialist body painters have arrived*.

Get students to complete the rest of the exercise, tell them that if they cannot decide between two answers, to write down both. As they complete the exercise the number of possibilities will reduce. Then ask students to check their work in pairs, and to decide on their final answers.

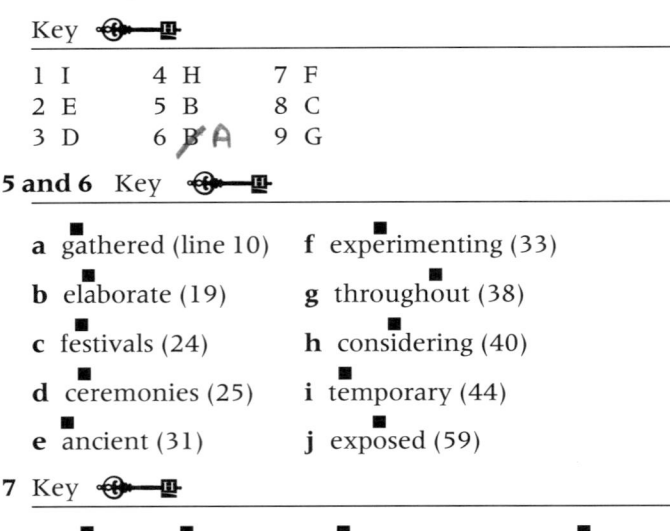

Key

1 I	4 H	7 F
2 E	5 B	8 C
3 D	6 A	9 G

5 and 6 Key

- a gathered (line 10)
- b elaborate (19)
- c festivals (24)
- d ceremonies (25)
- e ancient (31)
- f experimenting (33)
- g throughout (38)
- h considering (40)
- i temporary (44)
- j exposed (59)

7 Key

uncrosses, nervously, photographer, financial consultant, complicated, Indian, Arabian, charity, mineral, Arabic, difference, Halawa, Manchester, decisions, designer, Islington, elaborate, fiance, centuries, decorate, recently, cosmetics, fingernails, Egyptian, specialist, receiving, invitations, exotic, secretly, fabulous, usually, underneath, develop, definitely, temperatures

HELP WITH WORD FORMATION 1 Page 10

This is one of several 'help' sections throughout the book which focus students on exercise types which they will meet in the exam, and help them with exam strategies. It is important for students to be able to use word formation to build their vocabulary, and word formation is also specifically tested in the Use of English paper of FCE.

1 Key

1 helpless	5 helper
2 unhelpful	6 helped
3 help	7 helpfully
4 helpful	

3 Key

1 adjective	5 noun
2 adjective	6 verb
3 noun	7 adverb
4 adjective	

5 Key

1 psychology – noun (subject of study) → noun (person)
   choice – noun → verb
   strong – adjective → adjective (superlative)
   one – noun → pronoun
   cover – verb → verb (negative)
   hide – verb → verb (past participle)

Note that in this exercise and the following one the stem words have no context, therefore in some cases they can be understood to represent more than one part of speech. Get students to concentrate on the form of the word which has been produced from the stem, rather than the stem word itself.

Key

5.2
(1) chosen — verb → past participle
(2) importance — adjective → noun
(3) arguments — verb → noun
(4) co-operation — verb → noun
(5) completely — adjective → adverb
(6) unusual — adjective → negative adjective
(7) eagerness — adjective → noun
(8) sometimes — noun → adverb
(9) limitless — noun → adjective
(10) lively — adjective → adjective

5.3
(1) someone
(2) carefully
(3) misunderstand
(4) whatever
(5) exactly
(6) friendship

WRITING 1 Page 12
An article

1 Use the pictures to elicit 'school uniform' and recycle clothes vocabulary. Ask what your students wore (or still wear) for school.
   Additional vocabulary: skirt, trousers, tie, shirt, socks, blazer/jacket, cardigan, pullover/sweater, dress/pinafore, badge.

2 By discussing the advantages and disadvantages, much of the relevant vocabulary will already have been covered before students listen in the next activity. Draw two columns headed *Advantages* and *Disadvantages* on the board and ask students to copy and make notes as they listen:

First Impressions UNIT 1

3 Key

	Advantages	Disadvantages
st.1		horrible colours and styles no choice
st.2	you know which schools students are from	
st.3	they look smart	
st.4	everyone looks the same – you can be proud of your school – common identity	
st.5		expensive – poor families can't afford them

Ask students to discuss whether they agree with the opinions on the tape, and then refer them to the example article. The content of the article should now be very familiar to them, so they can concentrate on how it is organised.
Get students to tell you why this is a good article:
a) it answers the question
b) it is clearly laid out using proper paragraphs
c) it has an introduction and conclusion and paragraphs which include advantages and disadvantages
d) it uses linking words and expressions to introduce or connect ideas.

4 Tell students that they have only a couple of minutes to complete this.

Key

be the correct size = fit
be the same colour or style = match
of an untidy appearance = scruffy
be the right colour or style for someone = suit
tidy and attractive = smart

HELP WITH WRITING Page 13
Planning and paragraphing

1 Students can discuss these points in pairs or groups.

Key

1.1 A paragraph consists of a number of sentences grouped together. A paragraph can have only one sentence (typically at the beginning or the end of a letter), but it is more common for a paragraph to consist of two to four sentences. In handwritten English, the first line of a paragraph is indented (ie a space is left blank at the beginning of the line). A gap of one line is often left between paragraphs.

1.2 A paragraph includes information or ideas which together form a unit (eg advantages), or it can form an introduction or conclusion.

1.3 Possible titles: Paragraph 1 = Introduction
Paragraph 2 = Advantages
Paragraph 3 = Disadvantages
Paragraph 4 = Conclusion

2 Ask: What do you do before you begin to write an article? (select a title/topic, think about content, make a plan.)

Key

2.1 Paragraph 2: **b** looks smart
c students feel equal
Paragraph 3: **b** some people always look scruffy
c horrible colours and designs

2.2 The introduction includes some background information and establishes that there are arguments for and against.

2.3 The conclusion gives a summary of the existing situation.

2.4 The question does not ask for the writer's opinion and therefore no opinion is given (although we can imagine that the writer is probably anti-uniforms as these arguments seem stronger).

2.5 Point out that where no opinion is requested in the title, students must include arguments for and against, even when they have strong feelings about the topic. The next section helps students to concentrate on developing the content of this type of writing rather than focusing only on their opinion.

3 The words in italics give structure to the article and help to connect the ideas. They make the composition easier to read and understand.

Planning

1 Ask students to remind you of the qualities of a good article or composition, which they identified earlier. Point out that these can be summarised under the three headings:
Subject matter
Layout
Language
and that the first two of these certainly require some thought before students begin writing. Stress that to write successfully, preparation is essential.

2 Either get students to select from the titles given, or choose one title yourself for the whole class to work on.

3 Get students to think individually for a few minutes and make some notes in 2 columns before you ask them to discuss the advantages/disadvantages with a partner or another group, and select the most important points. Students complete the skeleton plan. Point out that they need to make a plan of this type every time they complete a piece of writing.

Students can either write individually and then compare their introduction with a partner, or pairs can work together on the introduction.

UNIT 1 *First Impressions*

4 The article can be completed in class or for homework. If it is done in class, ask students to select another title from the list to write about at home, keeping in mind the approach to writing suggested here and particularly the need to make a plan.

EXAM PRACTICE 1 Page 15

1 Key

1 to	4 both	7 not	10 they	13 only/just
2 common	5 that	8 who	11 way	14 of
3 and	6 as	9 not	12 wrong	15 at

3 Key

1 majority	6 unlucky
2 daily/everyday	7 pessimistic
3 themselves	8 noticeable
4 relationships	9 shyness
5 fortunate	10 successful

UNIT 2

Work for a living

TOPIC Work	HELP SECTIONS Help with writing letters	Note-taking Matching information
VOCABULARY FOCUS Jobs Personal qualities and skills	**EXAM FOCUS** **Paper 1** Scanning for specific information Matching information	**Paper 5** Describing a photograph Expressing opinions Exchanging information
LANGUAGE FOCUS *To be used to + -ing* Present perfect/Past simple Multi-word verbs Comparative adjectives Pronunciation: Past tense endings	**Paper 2** Describing jobs Transactional letters **Paper 3** Key word transformations **Paper 4** Listening for specific information	**EXAM PRACTICE** Key word transformations Open cloze Error correction Discursive article Transactional letter

SPEAKING 1 Page 16
Expressing opinions

Pre-activity: Focus attention on the pictures of the workplaces on page 16. Get students to identify the places (airport, hotel, hospital).
1 Ask if anyone has had experience of working in these places, or would like to work in these places and why, then get students to discuss the questions in pairs.
2 Input vocabulary as required by students. The job list for each place (ie not just the jobs shown in the pictures) might include:
   Airport: security guard, customs officer, ground crew, pilot, air traffic controller.
   Hospital: doctor, nurse, cook, ambulance driver.
   Hotel: porter, lift attendant, receptionist, bell-boy, cleaner, waiter/waitress, chef, cashier.
3 If it is not practical in your classroom to get students to move round and find a partner who has selected the same place, ask them to work with a new partner sitting near them and to compare jobs in different places. Students discuss this briefly in pairs or groups of three. Select one of the pictures and elicit some jobs from the lists which students have made in 2 above.
4 Ask students which job they would be good at and why.

VOCABULARY 1 Page 16
Skills and qualities

Pre-activity: Using some of the jobs selected by students in the previous exercise, ask: What skills are necessary for (name of job)? Explain that *skills* = a practical ability with which we learn to do something specific, and refer students to the *Skills* column. Then ask: What qualities are necessary? Explain that *qualities* = aspects of a person's character or general behaviour, and refer students to the *Qualities* column.
1 Get students to match some of the skills and qualities with the jobs on their lists, and then to form sentences as in the example.
2 Ask students to think of other skills and qualities which may be required for these jobs, and get them to combine skills and qualities from the box and the additional ones they have thought of.

WRITING 1 Page 17
Describing jobs

1 Get students to read the passage and the decide with a partner which job is being described, and the reason for their decision.

Key

The job described is a **police officer**.

UNIT 2 Work for a living

2 and 3 Students write a paragraph in class or for homework. If they write in class, they can select the job and produce the paragraph with a partner. This may give confidence to weaker students and encourage students to correct each other. You can select some example paragraphs and read them out to the class, omitting the name of the job so that students can guess what it is.

SPEAKING 2 Page 17
Expressing opinions

1. Tell students to give reasons (both positive and negative) for their choice.

2. Possible answers

   Restaurant: you meet lots of different people; you get tips, but the hours are long and you have to stand up all the time; if you work in the kitchen it is very hot.

   Food factory: probably rather like any other factory - rather boring and repetitive; might put you off food; could be interesting if you could try the food.

   Supermarket: people always in a hurry and they don't talk to you; some jobs probably rather boring; usually a clean environment.

READING 1 Page 17
Reading for specific information

1. This is a scan-reading exercise to identify specific information. Tell students they should read quickly and concentrate only on finding the information to answer the questions. They will have time later to read in more detail. Check each of these exercises with the whole class before students continue with the following exercise.

   Key

   1 Marks & Spencer   3 sample chocolates
   2 Confectionery Selector   4 15 years

   Additional vocabulary:

   title: (proper noun) = a company which has more than 300 shops in Britain and abroad, specialising in good quality food and clothes at reasonable prices; chocoholic (n) = a person who cannot stop eating chocolate (from *alcoholic*, there are also expressions like *workaholic*)
   in the course of duty – lines 5/6 (n) = part of the responsibility of the job
   range – line 13 (n) = type of product
   went off – line 13 (vb) = when food decays and becomes inedible (inf. *to go off*).
   how come? – line 16 = why/why not?
   in the business – line 20/21 = Marks & Spencer (the head office of which is in Baker Street in the centre of London – also famous as the fictional home of Sherlock Holmes)
   Mars Bar – line 27 (proper noun) = a chocolate product, very popular in the UK
   worn off – line 29 (vb) = the desire or effect reduced (Inf. *to wear off*)

2. Get students to do this exercise in pairs.

   Key

   1 a binge   3 entire   5 airy
   2 sample   4 tasting   6 overwhelming

3. Ask students to attempt this individually. Then tell them that there are three false and two true answers. Ask them to check their answers again, this time with a partner.

   Key

   1 false   2 true   3 false   4 false   5 true

4. Students should be able to complete the missing information on the grid before you go through it with them.

   Key

   Qualifications: 'A' levels
   Work experience: banking (1 year)
                              Harrods buyer (8 years)
                              Marks & Spencer (since 1987)
   Present responsibilities: – developing new lines
                                (product and packaging)
                              – overseeing production
                              – doing comparative shopping
                                and visiting food fairs

   Additional vocabulary:
   'A' levels (n) = examinations taken by students at the age of 17 or 18 before they leave school or go to university
   my niche = a job which was particularly suitable for me
   fast turnover = products which sell very quickly in the shop have a fast turnover
   new lines (n) = new types of products
   overseeing (vb) = supervising
   comparative shopping = buying products from other shops to evaluate them.

GRAMMAR 1 Page 18 (GR p 215)
To be/get used to + ing

1. Check that students have understood that in each pair of sentences:
   a has a verb in the Present simple tense
   b has *used to + -ing*.

Key

Used to + *ing* (or + noun) is for something we are accustomed to doing; something which is a normal part of life at present and does not involve any unexpected difficulty. It tells us about both the activity and about the person and his/her experience.
Note that *to get used to* + *ing* is used to talk about the process of becoming accustomed to something.
The Present simple tense only tells us about the activity.

2 Go through the first comment and questions with the whole class as an example. Then get students to discuss the other statements and questions in pairs before you check their answers.

Key

(They may be expressed differently.)
1 Now she quite likes eating potatoes every day, but she didn't when she first arrived. She is used to eating the food.
2 He didn't understand very well but now he understands more. He's used to listening to English.
3 It was too cold for him. It was difficult for him to adapt to the cold weather. Ronaldo was able to adapt – now Ronaldo's used to the weather.

3.1 Focus on the examples of *used to* from the previous exercise and elicit some information about things which people might find it difficult to get used to in your students' home country or countries. Then ask students to write down example sentences in pairs.

3.2 Get students to discuss in pairs after exchanging information about each other's countries.

4 **Key**

1 used to driving
2 not used to having/eating
3 used to getting
4 not used to drinking
5 get used to
6 getting used to
7 not used to queueing for
8 not used to
9 used to eating
10 getting used to wearing

LISTENING 1 Page 19
Note-taking

Pre-activity: Ask students to read the introduction, then ask: How old is Carole? (22); What sort of company does she work for? (a large company); Where is she now? (at her old school); Why is she there? (to talk about her work experience); Who is she talking to? (students in their last year of school); What is her job? (we do not know)

1 Use the picture to encourage guesses about her job, but do not confirm what it is at this stage.
2 Refer students to the form on page 19 and ask them to guess what questions she will be asked. Accept all suggestions and write them on the board (eliciting corrections as necessary).
Play the tape and get students to compare and complete answers. After the first listening get students to confirm her job (a holiday company courier), and to decide which, if any, of the questions on the board they heard. This part of the exercise requires quite a lot of writing, so get students to collaborate. (eg first they listen and note the questions, then compare with a partner, finally they listen and complete the notepad.)

Key

The questions are:
How did you get your present job?
Were the subjects you studied at school useful in your work?
Did you apply for many different jobs?
Did you have to have an interview?
How much training did they give you when you started?
What have you got out of the job?
What hours do you work?
What's the worst crisis you've had to deal with?
What about the salary? Is it worth it?

3 Note that students will probably be able to complete the name of the job before they listen for the other information.

Key

Her job: holiday company courier
Her original ambition: to be a translator/interpreter
Qualifications: Spanish, French
Other languages: (understands) Italian
Training: 2 months in London / at head office
Skills developed: problem solving, interpersonal skills (= dealing with people), language skills
Hours worked: no fixed hours
Things which cause problems: strikes, people getting ill
Pay: average

GRAMMAR 2 Page 19 (GR p 215)
Present perfect/Past simple

1 **Key**

1 In the time since Carole started working.
2 Present perfect tense.
3 Because these things have happened in a period of time which has not finished (Carole at work).

2 **Key**

1 When Carole was at school

UNIT 2 Work for a living

2 Past simple tense
3 The events happened during a time period which has now finished (Carole at school).

Focus on the time-line diagram and establish that the events happened in the past, and that there is a division when Carole left school. Point out again that **Carole at school** is a period in the past which has completely finished, while **Carole at work** is a situation which includes the past and present. For the first situation the Past simple tense is used, for the second Present perfect.
Note that the grammar explanation in this section covers the three main uses of the Present perfect tense in more detail. When students have studied the examples, read the sentences below to the class and get them to tell you **when** and **which tense**. If necessary write some of the sentences on the board.
I've never been to the USA. (in my life = Present perfect)
I went skiing last winter. (last winter = Past simple)
He visited his cousin at Christmas. (at Christmas = Past simple)
I've played tennis this week. (this week = Present perfect)
She started a new job last January. (last January = Past simple)
She's started learning Japanese this year. (this year = Present perfect)
We've just done that exercise. (Just [in this period of time] = Present perfect)
I've read that book already. (in my life = Present perfect)
She's flown around the world twice. (in her life = Present perfect)
It snowed in Moscow yesterday. (yesterday = Past simple)

3 With a strong class, elicit one example of each type of expression, then ask students to close their books while you read out the other time expressions and students decide if they are present or past.

Key

Present	Past
for the last 3 weeks	last week
this month	when I was a child
since I left school	at Easter
since Christmas	last Tuesday
in recent weeks	last month
this century	two weeks ago
	an hour ago
	in February

4 Students complete these sentences individually and then compare answers with a partner.

Key

1 passed	**6** has worked
2 met	**7** has been
3 learned	**8** haven't had
4 has been	**9** has seen
5 phoned	**10** became

PRONUNCIATION Page 21
Past tense endings

1 Write the endings on the board and and get students to repeat the three examples before playing the tape. Play once and get students to compare answers with a partner. Then play the tape again.

Key

/d/	/ɪd/	/t/
robbed	printed	helped
lived	decided	asked
described	waited	worked
answered	included	dressed

3 Key

'ed' is pronounced /d/ when it is added as the past tense ending to a word finishing with a vowel or a voiced consonant. If a word already finishes with a /t/ or a /d/ sound, the 'ed' ending is pronounced /ɪd/. If a word finishes with a voiceless consonant the pronunciation when 'ed' is added becomes /t/.

4 Key

/d/	/ɪd/	/t/
arrived	needed	helped
tried	sounded	packed
turned	disappointed	discussed
listened	educated	washed
skilled		passed
trained		

LISTENING 2 Page 21
Selecting an answer

Pre-activity: Elicit from students different ways of finding a job. Focus on the role of a job agency (= a company which specialises in matching job vacancies to people who are looking for work).
Before you play the tape get students to read through the application form. Ask: Is this an application form for a permanent job? (No, it's for a temporary job or a job for a student.)

Key

1 Bennett	**4** Yes	**7** No	**10** Yes	**13** No
2 15	**5** No	**8** Yes	**11** No	**14** No
3 Italian	**6** Yes	**9** Yes	**12** Yes	

SPEAKING 3 Page 22
Exchanging information

1 Ask students to decide with a partner what type of job they think is particularly suitable for Lucy. Refer them to the job advertisements and tell each pair to select one appropriate job.

Work for a living UNIT 2

2 and 3 Either get students in pairs to decide who is A and who is B, or quickly go round the room naming students A–B, A–B, etc. Explain that student A should think about the questions which Lucy might ask about the job they have selected, and B will have to invent information to answer student A's questions.
Further practice: When students have practised both roles ask them to select another job, this time for themselves, and to repeat the same process.

Additional vocabulary:
seasonal vacancy = a job for part of the year only
to work under pressure = to work hard and quickly
long hours = starting early and finishing late
tips = small amounts of extra money given by customers to the waiter or waitress at the end of a meal
would suit = would be appropriate for
kids = children

LISTENING 3 Page 22
Matching information

Pre-activity: Before students listen get them to focus on the information included in the short decriptions of the people and their previous experience by either asking these questions or writing them on the board. Treat it as a quiz – with the answers to be found as quickly as possible. Students do not have to read every word of every decription to find the answers.

Quiz
Which person
– is the youngest? (F)
– wants to work in an office? (B)
– wants to have more contact with people? (A)
– has recently done some training? (C. F has just left school, which might also be considered training)
– is looking for her first job? (F)
– used to work in the food industry? (B and D)

Play the tape once, get students to compare their answers with a partner, then play again for them to check their answers.

Key

1 C 2 E 3 D 4 A 5 F

READING 2 Page 23
Multiple matching

1 and 2 Either use the photos included in the article or provide a few photos of glamorous models (preferably male as well as female) to encourage discussion of 1 – 4. Elicit some opinions about these discussion points before asking students to read Part One of the article to see if they were correct or if they can add anything.

3 Get students to work in pairs to complete the information.
Key

1 Sam   6 Emma/Jo
2 Jo   7 Hannah
3 Sam   8 Emma
4 Emma   9 Jo
5 Jo/Emma   10 Hannah

4 Key

1 to get into   – to enter (a new career)
2 to make it   – to succeed (finally)
3 to get sorted   – to organise (yourself)
4 to get spotted   – to be noticed
5 to be out and about – to travel
6 to tag along   – to follow
7 to put on hold   – to postpone

5 Key

1 person whose job is to find new models – booker
2 something which makes things more difficult – hindrance
3 photographic session – shoot
4 which never looks old-fashioned – classic
5 very thin – skinny
6 very confused – chaotic
7 very strange – weird
8 something which makes things easier – bearable

LISTENING 4 Page 24
Note-taking

Pre-activity: Ask students to read the job advertisement. Check their understanding by asking:
What is the job? (conference organiser)
What skills and qualities are essential? (common sense, administrative and communication skills, team work, word processing, driving)
What skills is desirable but not essential? (computer graphics)

1 Get students to listen twice to this conversation and give them time between and after listening to compare answers.

Key

	Strong points	**Weak points**
Terry	conference experience good personality (good with people)	appearance no computer graphics
Pattie	computer graphics calm and sensible, smart	can't drive very young little conference experience
Jack	smart, older, lots of conference experience enthusiastic	bad reference very nervous

15

UNIT 2 Work for a living

2 Key

1 Terry/Pattie	4 Pattie/Jack
2 Pattie/Terry	5 Pattie/Terry
3 Pattie/Jack	6 Terry/Pattie

Further practice: Get students to look back at the advertisements on page 22. Put students into groups of three people who all selected the same job, and ask them to think again about the skills and qualities required. Then get each student to explain to the others how they are suited to the job.

Each group makes a grid like the one they completed in the listening exercise. Finally students write sentences about the people in their group, using the comparative forms.

GRAMMAR 3 Page 25 (GR p 216)
Comparatives

1 Key

more + adjective	adjective + ier	adjectiv + (e)r
enthusiastic	tidy	calm
reliable	dirty	young
responsible		old
nervous		smart
sensible		
able		

If possible elicit these rules from students:
a) Adjectives with one syllable usually form the comparative with + *er* (eg calm→ calmer).
   So do adjectives with two syllables ending in a vowel sound (eg narrow→ narrower, clever→ cleverer). Remind students of the common exceptions: good→ better, bad→ worse.
b) For two-syllable adjectives ending in *y*, the *y* is replaced by + *ier* (eg tidy→ tidier).
c) Most other two syllable adjectives become *more + adjective* (eg enthusiastic→ more enthusiastic).
d) All longer adjectives become *more + adjective*.

2 Possible answers

1 Terry is more able than Pattie.
2 Pattie is younger than Jack.
3 Jack is tidier than Terry.

3 Point out that for negative comparisons we use *as + adjective + as* in the negative (eg She isn't as tall as her sister) and this can be used with all adjectives. *Less + adjective* is not widely used and is incorrect with some adjectives (eg less old is not correct.)
Refer students to the information about Paul and Susie, and elicit some negative comparisons from the whole class before they write sample sentences.

Possible answers

1 Paul is not as tidy as Susie.
2 Susie is not as enthusiastic as Paul.
3 Paul is not as experienced as Susie.
4 Susie is not as talkative as Paul.
5 Paul is not as reserved as Susie.
6 Susie is not as sociable as Paul.

4 Key

1 have as much experience as
2 isn't as punctual as
3 is better qualified than
4 as polite as her sister
5 wasn't as long as / was shorter than
6 hasn't got as much
7 wasn't as nervous as
8 were smarter than
9 seem as reliable as
10 wasn't as enthusiastic as

HELP WITH WRITING Page 26
Letters

Pre-activity: List these reasons for writing a letter and ask students to decide which are likely to require a formal letter and which an informal letter.

- thanking a friend for a birthday present (informal)
- congratulating someone who's just had a baby (informal)
- complaining about public transport in your town (formal)
- inviting someone to a party (informal)
- asking for information about a language course (formal)
- apologising for not meeting someone at the cinema last week (informal)
- telling someone about your holiday plans (informal)
- enquiring about a bag which you left on a bus (formal)
- applying for a holiday job (formal)

1 Possible answers (in addition to the above)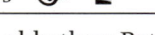

A formal letter – to order something by post, to complain about something you bought which does not work properly, to book a hotel room.
An informal letter – to greet a friend you have not seen for a long time, to thank a relative who sent you a present, to invite a friend to come and visit you, to congratulate a relative on passing an examination.

3 Key

1 a formal letter
2 to apply for a job
3 it includes a variety of tenses including present continuous for actions at the moment (*I am writing*), past

Work for a living **UNIT 2**

simple (*I left college*), present perfect (*I have worked*), present simple (*This involves talking to people ... / I enclose a copy*), and polite forms (*I would be interested to know...*).

4   a   for his job – on business
    b   book his tickets – organise his travel arrangements
    c   when he's away – in his absence
    d   using – operating
    e   get better at – improve
    f   tell me – I would be interested to know
    g   it's in the envelope – I enclose
    h   answer me soon – I look forward to hearing from you

5   They are formal words and phrases, appropriate to a letter applying for a job.

4   Students will always have to write a letter in the first part of the Writing paper and there will be no choice of topic in this part. The letter will always be for a specific purpose with exact instructions provided, but the purpose given might require a formal or an informal letter. In this case, a formal letter is required.
    Points to note:
    - students should read the instructions carefully.
    - they should include the specific information requested.
    - they should avoid copying from the prompt material - using Key vocabulary is acceptable, but not complete sentences or phrases.
    - although the instructions say 120-180 words, they should try to write around the maximum, not the minimum required.
    - students should not worry about the exact number of words they write, but they should have an idea of how many words are in, say, half a page in their normal handwriting.

5.1   Students should form questions focusing on the circled information. For example, possible questions might be:
    When does the job begin?
    How long will the job last?
    How many hours per week will/would I have to work?
    Will/Would I have to travel?
    Which languages will/would I need to know?
    How much will/would I be paid?/What is the salary?/How much will/would I earn?

5.2   Students should say why they are writing and give some personal information, including:
    age
    qualifications
    any relevant experience
    their interests and hobbies
    any other relevant details

5.3   Ask students to look back at the model letter in 2 and the tenses used there.

5.4   Similarly, students will find some useful words and phrases in the model letter.

Weak students can use the model letter as a template for their own work, changing the information to fit the task given. Stronger students can be encouraged to plan their own letters without further reference to the model. NB Remember that there is a convention that formal letters beginning 'Dear Sir/Madam' finish with the salutation 'Yours faithfully', whilst letters beginning with 'Dear Mr/Mrs etc. +name of person' finish with the salutation 'Yours sincerely'.

EXAM PRACTICE 2 Page 27

1   Key

1 haven't been to	6 in case you have to
2 not as well paid as	7 last time I saw Greta
3 doesn't usually wear	8 used to going
4 n case it gets	9 doesn't usually eat
5 not used to having	10 is more talkative than

2   See Student's Book page 18 for the Key.

3   Key

1 for	4 only	7 a	10 ✓	13 made
2 she	5 ✓	8 every	11 your	14 ✓
3 ✓	6 might	9 of	12 ✓	15 can

REVISION TEST 1

1   Key

1 than	5 about/on	9 in	13 rather
2 from	6 as	10 the	14 has
3 were	7 although/while	11 so	15 at
4 which	8 since	12 because	

2   Key

1 always wears strange	6 is not as tidy as/is not tidier than
2 in case you get	7 is bigger than
3 is used to eating	8 last time I spoke
4 have already seen	9 in case lunch is
5 have lived in this city	10 not as smart/neat as

3   Key

| 1 will | 2 would | 3 one | 4 them | 5/6 their | 7/8 are |
| 9 go | 10/11 how | 12 too | 13 to | 14/15 for | |

4   Key

1 manager	2 equipment	3 different	4 various
5 generally	6 sales	7 marketing	8 tiring
9 teacher	10 twice		

Note that for 3 and 4 you can get students to check their own work against the original texts in the Student's Book on pages 13 and 1.

REVISION TEST 1

1 Fill each of the numbered blanks in the following passage. Use only one word in each space.

Story of an Island

In the summer there are five times more people (0) *on* the Greek island of Castellorizo (1) _____ live there in the winter. Most of the visitors come (2) _____ Australia and most of them (3) _____ born on Castellorizo. Although more than 30,000 Australians are of Castellorizan descent, today there are no more than 190 people living on the island, (4) _____ has an area of only nine square kilometres. The Australian historian Nichola Pappas, who recently wrote a book (5) _____ the island and its history, says that as many (6) _____ 10,000 people are thought to have lived on Castellorizo in the 19th century. According to Pappas, (7) _____ most Greek-Australians emigrated after the Second World War, Castellorizans have been moving to Australia (8) _____ the 1880s. Most of them settled (9) _____ Sydney, Perth or Darwin, and some of (10) _____ wealthiest people in Perth today are of Castellorizan origin. No one is sure why (11) _____ many people from the island have decided to move to Australia. Pappas thinks it is (12) _____ the islanders were traders and shipbuilders (13) _____ than farmers, and this background (14) _____ made them less afraid of distances and able to feel (15) _____ home more easily in new places.

2 Complete the second sentence so that it has a similar meaning to the first sentence. Use the word given and other words to complete each sentence. You must use between two and five words. Do not change the word given.

1 She's always dressed in strange clothes.
   wears
   She _____ clothes.

2 Take a map with you because you may get lost.
   case
   Take a map _____ lost.

3 Sandy eats chocolate every day in her job.
   used
   Sandy _____ chocolate every day in her job.

4 I saw that film recently.
   already
   I _____ that film.

5 I arrived in this city two months ago.
   lived
   I _____ for two months.

6 Lucy is tidier than Jeff.
   not
   Jeff _____ Lucy.

7 John's car is not as big as Mark's.
   than
   Mark's car _____ John's.

8 I haven't spoken English since June.
   time
   The _____ English was in June.

9 Have a big breakfast because lunch may be late.
   case
   Have a big breakfast _____ late.

10 Bill is scruffier than his brother.
   as
   Bill is _____ his brother.

REVISION TEST 1

3 Read this text and look carefully at each line. Some of the lines are correct and some have a word which should not be there. If a line is correct put a tick (✓). If the line has a word which should not be there, write down the word. There are two example lines at the beginning.

School uniforms

The main advantage of them school uniforms is that	0 *them*...............
they give common identity to the school. Even when	00 ✓..................
the students are on their way home, everyone will knows	1 ....
which school they go to. This is important if would the students	2 ....
misbehave, for example. Another one advantage is that if all	3 ....
the students in a school wear the same type of them clothes	4 ....
in matching colours and styles, then they tend to look	5 ....
smart when they are all together. Finally, students whose their	6 ....
parents can't afford nice clothes look the same as everyone	7 ....
else and so don't feel inferior.	
Most students are don't agree with school uniforms, however,	8 ....
for a number of reasons. Firstly, when you have to go wear	9 ....
the same clothes as everyone else, you don't have a chance	10 ....
to develop personal taste in the way how you dress. Moreover,	11 ....
people who look scruffy usually look too scruffy in their uniforms	12 ....
too and you can always tell the people who to come from poor	13 ....
homes because their uniforms are not as new or don't fit	14 ....
properly. Lastly, the main reason for why most students don't	15 ....
like school uniforms is because most schools choose such	
horrible colours and styles, that don't suit young people at all.	

4 Use the word given in capitals at the end of each line to form a word that fits in the space.

Pen-friend

My name's Lars. I'm 26 years old and I come from	
Malmo in Sweden. I'm a trainee (**1**) _____ in a	MANAGE
a company which sells office (**2**)_____. I spend	EQUIP
one week of each month in a (**3**) _____ department	DIFFER
so that I learn (**4**) _____ aspects of the work. I	VARY
(**5**) _____ spend at least one day per week out	GENERAL
of the office as my job involves (**6**) _____ and	SELL
(**7**) _____. My job's very interesting but rather	MARKET
(**8**) _____ I get up early each morning and drive ten miles to my	TIRE
office but I still find the time to study English, because a (**9**)_____	TEACH
comes to the company (**10**) _____ a week. In my	TWO
spare time I like to go skiing and I enjoy all water sports.	

UNIT 3

Out and about

TOPIC Staying at home and visiting friends **VOCABULARY FOCUS** Homes and interiors Housing **LANGUAGE FOCUS** Causative *have*/*Needs doing* Expressing opinions Giving advice Genitive *'s* Verbs used in the causative *For*/*Since* Asking for and giving advice Pronunciation: Vowel sounds	**HELP SECTIONS** Help with grammar – Key word transformations Help with multiple-choice questions **EXAM FOCUS** **Paper 1** Reading for main points Reading for specific information Multiple choice **Paper 2** Informal letters **Paper 3** Key word transformations Opinions	**Paper 4** Matching information Note-taking Short extracts Multiple choice **Paper 5** Expressing opinions Asking for and giving advice Talking about photographs **EXAM PRACTICE 3** Key word transformations Word formation cloze Multiple-choice cloze

READING 1 Page 29
Reading for main points

1 **Pre-activity:** Before students look at their books explain the idea of exchanging homes as a type of holiday. Find out if anyone in the class has tried it and what your students think about swapping homes as a holiday idea. Let them discuss questions 1 and 2 before they read the first part of the magazine article.

Key

1 Advantages mentioned are:
you have more freedom than in a hotel
you find out what life is really like
the accommodation costs nothing
both houses are occupied
you are part of a community
you might make friends with other families

2 No, although it's better to pack away valuable items.

Additional vocabulary:
a change (is) as good as a rest = an English proverb
a package (n) = a package holiday, when you buy a holiday, inclusive of transport and accommodation, from a travel agency
daunting (adj) = discouraging
the most reasonable = the cheapest

vandals (n) = people who damage things intentionally
soulless (adj) = without individual character
have the run (of something) (vb) = have permission to use it
firm friends = very good friends
subsequent (adj) = later

3 This is a split reading in three parts. Students read one of the three sections (A, B or C), make notes and then report back to students who have read the other two parts.
Either divide the class into groups of A, B and C and ask them to prepare the answers for their section together, **or** get students to work individually on one of the three sections and then group them with students who have read the same section so that they can check their answers before **finally** students get into groups of three (A, B and C) and tell each other the information they have found. In this phase make sure that the listening students are making notes about the information they hear. Tell them that they will need this information to complete the next activity.
Alternatively, you can treat the exercise as a normal reading which happens to be in three parts. if you decide to do it this way, take each part in turn and check the answers before moving on to the next part. Note that students will only be able to complete the final writing

activity in this section once they have read the whole article.

Key

Student A (PART A)
- Privately or through a specialist agency.
- Money, information about your home, photographs, preferences.
- Put you in touch with other families, inspect properties, match your requirements, arrange air travel.

Student B (PART B)
- Write quickly to make contact. Establish a relationship by post or phone, exchange information. Prepare an information folder.
- Emergency phone numbers, details of shops, instructions for pets and equipment, brochures about things to do.

Student C (PART C)
- Someone to meet them, leave some food (not too much), insurance and petrol for the car, information about bills.
- Leave the house as they find it, leave some flowers and a thank-you note.

Additional vocabulary:
Student A: set about (vb) = begin
vet (vb) = check

Student B: well in advance = a long time before
and so on = etcetera
stately homes = old country houses belonging (or which used to belong) to aristocratic families. They are sometimes open to the public

Student C: failsafe (adj) = which cannot go wrong
Co-op (proper noun) = a chain of supermarkets
settled up (vb) = paid

WRITING 1 Page 31
Summary

2 This guided writing activity can be completed in class or for homework using the additional information which students collected during the split reading.

VOCABULARY 1 Page 32
Housing

Pre-activity: In pairs students can select the home that they most like, give reasons and decide which picture looks like their own home. A few minutes' discussion will be enough to introduce the topic.

Focus on the short descriptions of homes on this page. Students look at them quickly and suggest why they were written. (As advertisements).

1 Key

1 d   2 e   3 f   4 b   5 c   6 a

2 Key

a flat
b detached house
c semi-detached house
d country cottage (a cottage is any small house of traditional design in the country)
e terraced house
f bungalow (a bungalow is any one-storey house, it does not refer specifically to holiday homes)

Additional vocabulary:

a resident porter = an attendant who also lives in the block
b mature garden = a well-established garden with fully-grown trees and plants
c double garage = a garage with space for two cars
e Victorian = from the time of Queen Victoria (1837–1901)
f needs some modernisation = this usually means that the house needs completely rebuilding

3 Key

a one   b the   c been   d has   e much   f for

Further practice: Ask students to describe their own homes to each other using the adverts to help with vocabulary. Students can write short descriptions in class or for homework. With a strong class ask students to prepare an advertisement which will make their home sound as attractive as possible.

LISTENING 1 Page 33
Part One
Selecting an answer

Pre-activity: Brainstorm names of rooms in a house or flat. Refer students to the four diagrams and give them a short time to identify the differences between the pictures. Explain the situation before they listen: Sharon has found a new flat and is phoning her mother to tell her about it.

1 Key

Flat C

Play the tape again.

UNIT 3 Out and about

2 Key

	yes	no	not mentioned
lift	✓		
balcony	✓		
phone			✓
shower	✓		
bath		✓	
garage			✓
cooker	✓		
fridge		✓	
central heating		✓	

LISTENING 1
Part Two
Note-taking

Pre-activity: Ask students to imagine that they have arrived home to find that the washing machine has broken down and there is soapy water all over the floor. What do they do? (Switch off the electricity, clean up the mess, call a plumber or electrician to come and fix the machine.)

Establish that some things they will do themselves and other things they will ask another person to do. Point out that we use *to have something done* for the latter situations. This is further practised in the Grammar section after the listening. Introduce the listening by explaining that Sharon has now moved into her flat and is telling her mother about the work which needs doing. Students must complete the missing information. Play the tape twice before checking the answers.

Key

things that need doing	do it myself	have it done
bathroom needs cleaning	✓	
windows need (1) *washing*	✓	
(2) *lock* needs changing	✓	
(3) *kitchen walls* need repainting	✓	
light switches need (4) *replacing*		✓
(5) *central heating* needs (6) *servicing*	✓	
(7) *towel rail* needs (8) *putting up*	✓	

Further practice: Ask students to discuss as a class or in pairs what needs doing in their home/school environment.

GRAMMAR 1 Page 34 (GR p 216 and 217)
Causative have/Needs doing

1.1 Sharon is not going to do the work but will ask another person to do it for her. (A person who fits locks is a locksmith.) Read some of these examples to students or write them on the board and ask: Who is going to do the work?
I'm having my hair cut (the hairdresser/barber)
I'm having my shoes repaired (the shoe repairer)
I'm having my coat dry-cleaned (the dry cleaner)
I'm having my room painted (the painter/decorator)
Now ask students what changes must be made if you are doing the same work yourself:
I'm cutting my hair
I'm repairing my shoes
I'm dry-cleaning my coat
I'm painting my room

1.2 Get students to match the information individually and then compare their answers with a partner.

Key

A	B	C
1	6	11
2	8	9
3	7	10
4	5	12

2 Ask: What can you do to a dog? (to elicit the activities illustrated). Then get students to match the pictures and words.

Key (from left to right)

feed; exercise; clip; groom; wash; train

Vocabulary:
feed = to give food to (usually a child or animal)
clip = to cut an animal's fur
groom = to brush an animal's fur
The things you attach to a dog when you take it for a walk are a collar and lead, and possibly a muzzle to cover its mouth.

3 Key

1 grooming 2 washing 3 clipping
4 exercising 5 training

4 Pre-activity: Ask students to look at 'Dogsbody'. Ask them what sort of text it is (an advertisement), and what it is advertising (a canine beautician and pet service).

Additional vocabulary:
breed = (n) category of dog or other animal
(to breed (vb) past form and past participle = bred)
show ring training = training for animals which will take part in competitions

Key

You can have your dog – exercised, cared for (looked after), clipped, groomed, trained.

5 Students may need some help with the garage words: eg you can have the oil changed, the tyres checked, the exhaust replaced.

Further practice: This is a list of other people who do things for you. Write some of them on the board and ask students what you can have done by these people:

optician	gas fitter
dentist	engineer (eg heating)
painter	gardener
interior decorator	builder
plumber	beautician
electrician	

6 Key

1 had my vacuum cleaner
2 had my car washed
3 am having the broken window
4 had her clothes made
5 is taking my photograph
6 has had her hair coloured
7 am having my house
8 have had one of my
9 am having my kitchen painted
10 mother is making her

Note that the agent (eg **4** *by a famous designer*) is only used when this person is specified, ie 'by someone' is not used; when 'someone' is the original subject the agent is usually omitted.

SPEAKING 1 Page 35
Expressing opinions

1 Let the class discuss these points in pairs for a few minutes, then elicit some opinions before moving on to **2**.
2 Students compile lists separately as A and B and then compare. Students then write lists of correct rules of behaviour as a warm up to Reading 2.

READING 2 Page 36
Multiple choice

1 Key

1 C
2 C
3 B
4 A

2 Key

changing – adapting
pleasant – agreeable
not very often – rarely
improbable – unlikely
makes you angry – annoying
makes you feel pleased – appealing
really – genuinely
ask – enquire
look at – examine
being polite – courtesy
brothers and sisters – siblings
answer (noun) – response
answer (verb) – reply (NB reply can also be a noun)
things which you own – belongings
things which you own – possessions
given – provided
ready – prepared
results – consequences
inconvenient or embarrassing – inopportune

3 Key

■ adapting   ■ siblings
■ agreeable   ■ response
■ rarely   ■ reply
■ annoying   ■ belongings
■ appealing   ■ provided
■ genuinely   ■ prepared
■ enquire   ■ consequences
■ examine   ■ inopportune
■ courtesy

GRAMMAR 2 Page 37 (GR p216)
Genitive 's

2 Key

See GR page 216.

3 Key

a Ask "How many friends are there? One, or more than one?"
If friend is singular the sentence should read:
… at my friend's house tonight.
If there is more than one friend, then the sentence should read:
… at my friends' house tonight.

UNIT 3 Out and about

b correct
c ... the children's new toys.
d correct
e correct
f ... Rosie's holiday
g correct
h ... parents' car. (i.e. two parents)
i correct
j ... her blue coat.
k ... a cinema ticket.
l correct

LISTENING 2 Page 37
Listening for specific information

Pre-activity: Ask students to imagine they receive a phone call from someone they have not heard from or seen for a very long time. What questions would they ask? What tense would they use? Elicit a few possible questions. It does not matter if the questions are different to the ones in the listening exercise – this is just a warm-up activity to focus students on the situation before they listen to the tape.

1 Key

New Address: 15 Valentine Road
Type of house: (4-bedroomed) detached
Reason for moving: got married
How long has Margaret lived there? – two weeks
How long has Peter lived there? – three months
How long has Margaret known Peter? – since New Year's Eve

2 Key

For is used with periods of time.

Since is when we talk about a specific moment in time or a particular day, month, year, season or event.

GRAMMAR 3 Page 37 (GR p217)
For/Since

1 Key

1 for	2 since	3 since
4 for	5 for	6 since
7 since	8 since	9 for
10 since		

2 Key

It's ages since I saw him is different to the others – It's ages + since + past tense. Note that Present Perfect is also possible: It's been ages + since + past time.

Dictate –

Further practice: Put the following words and expressions jumbled up on the board and get students to say if they are used with *for* or *since* and make appropriate sentences with them.

for	*since*
a long time	my birthday
three months	1990
an hour and a half	last year
ages	Monday
a decade	they got married
twenty-five years	this morning
a fortnight	I met you

HELP WITH GRAMMAR Page 38
Key word transformations

There are always 10 Key word transformation sentences in the FCE Use of English paper. See page vi.

2 Key

1 The subject and word order have changed – and so the focus of the sentence changes from the person to the period of time. Ago has changed to *since*.
2 The time period has not changed, and the phrase *she left school* is given. It is not necessary to change these.
3 *ago*
4 *since*

3 Key

1 The meaning is close to the original, although the the phrase *than I am able to do* is not very elegant. However, the gap has been filled with 7 words, when the limit in the instructions is 5 words including the Key word given. In the examination, this answer would get no marks.
2 Correct – the meaning is similar and the gap has been filled with 4 words in total. Remind your class that contractions count as two words.
3 Wrong – the Key word is *like*, not *likes* and students cannot change the Key word given. The correct answer is She <u>did not like Cambridge</u> as much as London.
4 Correct
5 Wrong – the answer given asks for a reason rather than making a suggestion. The correct answer is Why <u>don't we go</u> and have a swim?
6 Correct

4 Key

1 not received a letter for
2 months since I ate
3 had my dog washed by
4 ages since the newspaper was
5 had her house cleaned

Out and about **UNIT 3**

SPEAKING 2 Page 39
Talking about photographs

Suggested answers

Bride and groom after their wedding ceremony – guests throwing confetti
Bride and groom cutting their wedding cake at the wedding reception (the party after the wedding)

LISTENING 3 Page 39
Giving advice

1 Play the tape once, then get students to compare answers. Play the tape again for them to check their answers.

Key

1 no 2 yes 3 no 4 no 5 yes 6 no

2 In this exercise you need to stop the tape after each problem has been explained (there is a pause on the tape to indicate this), and allow students to note the problems and discuss what advice they would give. You may find it easier to check the answers to each section as it is completed, before you go on to play the next part of the tape.

Key

Part 2
Problem: Is it a good idea to make a list of presents?
Expert's advice: Yes

Part 3
Problem: Do you take a present to a wedding or send it by post?
Expert's advice: Traditionally presents are sent but nowadays they are often taken to the reception.

Part 4
Problem: Do you return engagement presents if the wedding is cancelled?
Expert's advice: Yes, if the presents are expensive. No, if the presents were not expensive and were given at a party.

SPEAKING 3 Page 39
Asking for and giving advice

Pre-activity: Get the class to brainstorm some topics that they might ask about before getting them to complete this activity in pairs.

READING 3 Page 40
Reading for specific information

1 Use the discussion points 1–4 to introduce the topic of the reading by encouraging students to give their opinions. Also personalise the introduction more by asking students to tell you, or each other in groups, about letters they have written and situations where they have received completely unsuitable or horrible presents.

2 Key

1 It was too big and a horrible mix of colours.
2 Because it was too honest.
3 Saying 'please' and 'thank you' and giving up your seat on the bus.
4 When presents come by post.
5 Letters (or notes) are special, grandparents like to receive them or show them to friends, writing focuses your thoughts.
6 Let children choose a picture postcard; put on the address and stamp for them; small children can just write 'thank you' or draw a picture.

3 Key

1 jumper
2 wool(s)
3 needless to say
4 to put pen to paper
5 altered
6 knit
7 where do we stand
8 re (reread)

PRONUNCIATION Page 41
Vowel sounds

1 and 2 Key

/ɜː/	/ʊ/	/ɒ/	/uː/	/aʊ/	/ɔː/	/əʊ/
girl	good	got	room	how	more	know
heard	could	block	choose	found	sure	own
first	would	lock	groom	house	ought	phone
church	should	off	group	sound	door	though
work	cook		move	now	bought	only
					floor	don't

WRITING Page 42
An informal letter

2 Key

You may need to give students the first two phrases. Point out that the punctuation will help them. The correct order is c-f-h-d-a-g-b-e.

3 and 4 Remind students that they must write a letter with the address of the sender and date, a greeting (note that 'Dear Friend' is not a usual beginning to a letter in English), and suitable close (the end of the letter). The letter should be divided into paragraphs. Students

UNIT 3 Out and about

frequently ignore this aspect of letter writing and it should be pointed out that one important difference between letters and other types of writing is the layout. The letter at the bottom of page 42 is deliberately printed in this way to focus on the layout.

READING 4 Page 43
Multiple choice

1 **Pre-activity:** Ask 'What subjects do foreign students come to your/our country to study?' and 'What subjects do students from your/our country study abroad?'.

1.3 Possible answers

Advantages
experience of studying abroad
chance to meet people from different countries
because the facilities are better
opportunities to learn/improve a foreign language

Disadvantages
away from family and friends
language difficulties
different habits and food
expensive

1.4 Students read quickly to answer these questions.
Key

- Hotel and Catering Management
- a four-year-sandwich course (two years study, one year work, one year study)
- restaurant/kitchen design

Additional vocabulary:
pending (adj) = she expects to get her qualifications in the near future
polytechnic (n) = rather like a university (polytechnic does not mean 'science university' as in some languages)
currently (adv) – line 1 = at the moment
in her year – line 4 = in her class at the polytechnic
placement (n) – line 18 = period of training in a company

2 Key

to take up = accept
arduous = difficult
dropped out = gave up (stopped studying)
hence = therefore
award = prize

3 Key

1 D   2 B   3 C   4 B

HELP WITH MULTIPLE-CHOICE QUESTIONS
Page 44
Reading texts

This section is designed to encourage students to think about their approach to multiple-choice questions like those they will meet in the FCE exam.
Younger or weaker students tend to select superficially attractive answers which repeat some key words used in the passage. Point out the danger of this approach and how test designers prepare the 'wrong' answers to multiple-choice tests with this in mind.
The approach suggested here concentrates on the student's understanding of the information in the passage, and encourages learners to check the answers they select for possible traps.

Listening texts

3 Key

1 It is routine and can be tedious.
2 Finding work that can be done at home.

4 Key

1 B   2 B

LISTENING 4 Page 45
Short extracts

Point out that for this section only the instructions and each question is recorded on the tape (as in the examination) to help students follow the task. (See page vi.)

Key

1 C   2 B   3 B
4 C   5 B

EXAM PRACTICE 3 Page 45

1 Key

1 had her bicycle repaired
2 too weak to do
3 is better qualified than
4 first time I have spoken
5 are having our house repainted
6 has got more experience than
7 not been cleaned yet
8 in favour of living
9 two months since I went
10 have not seen him for

Out and about UNIT 3

2 Key

1 somebody	5 included	9 stricter
2 rarely	6 something	10 finally
3 likely	7 misbehave	11 possessions
4 annoying	8 immediately	12 suitable

3 Key

1 B	2 C	3 D	4 A	5 D
6 D	7 C	8 A	9 D	10 C

UNIT 4

Crime wave

TOPIC	HELP SECTIONS	Paper 4
Crime	Help with guessing the meaning of words	Note-taking
VOCABULARY FOCUS	Help with writing reports	Blank filling
Types of crime	**EXAM FOCUS**	**Paper 5**
Describing trends	**Paper 1**	Exchanging information and expressing opinions
LANGUAGE FOCUS	Reading for specific information	**EXAM PRACTICE**
Sequence of tenses	Multiple matching	Open cloze
Making deductions	Gapped text	Error correction
Relative pronouns	**Paper 2**	Word formation
Compound nouns	Writing reports	Discursive article
Pronunciation: Stress in compound nouns	**Paper 3**	Narrative composition
	Cloze text	
	Error correction	
	Word formation	

SPEAKING 1 Page 47
Exchanging information

Pre-activity: Write 'Crime' on the board and ask for some names of crimes (eg murder, robbery) and some descriptions of crimes (eg taking things from shops), as well as a definition of the word 'Crime' itself. This is sufficient to focus students' attention on the topic area of this unit and begin to activate some relevant vocabulary.

1 Get students to suggest a general definition of crime (doing something which the law does not allow). Then ask them in pairs to match the descriptions with the names of crimes in the box. Check this activity before you move on to exercise 2.

Key

1 shoplifting	6 forgery
2 murder	7 mugging
3 theft	8 robbery
4 burglary	9 kidnapping
5 assault	10 minor offences

2 Extend the discussion by asking which crimes create the most problems/people are particularly concerned about in students' own countries or in Britain. Do your students think that crime is increasing or decreasing? Which crimes in particular?

3 Point out the difference between *rob* and *steal* before beginning this activity.

to rob = to attack a person or a place with the purpose of taking something which does not belong to you (eg The post office was robbed last week. My neighbour was robbed when he was on holiday.)

to steal = to take something which does not belong to you (here the emphasis is on the thing which is taken (eg The bank was robbed and £20,000 was stolen. The thieves stole a gold watch and some cash.)

Refer students to the chart and check their understanding of the types of crime by asking for an example of each type of crime or of what might be stolen in the different types of theft. Remind students of what the chart shows. (It compares crime last year and this year.) Elicit one or two examples of the language of trends in the box and then get students to practise this language using the information on the chart.

Further practice: Students write sentences describing trends either in crime or in other areas (eg prices, population changes, etc.) in their country.

READING 1 Page 48
Multiple matching

1 **Pre-activity:** Students predict the answers to this activity before they go on to read the passage and check their answers. Introduce the passage by telling students that it

is from a booklet about crime prevention which aims to encourage people to do more to reduce crime.

Key

| 1 true | 2 false | 3 false | 4 true | 5 true |
| 6 true | 7 false | 8 false | | |

Additional vocabulary:
we are all aware (part 1) = we all know that …
play a part (part 1) = participate
thrive on (part 2) = grow as a result of
a sitting target (part 3) = something which is easy to attack
bother (part 3) = make an effort
householder (part 3) = owner, or person who lives in a house
tackling (part 4) = dealing with (a problem)
coping (part 4) = dealing with (a situation)

2 Key

| 1 C | 2 E | 3 A | 4 D |

VOCABULARY 1 Page 48
Crimes and criminals

1 Key

Verb	**Noun** (crime)	**Noun** (person)
to steal	stealing/theft	thief
to rob	robbery	robber
to burgle	burglary	burglar
to commit an offence	offence	offender
to mug	mugging	mugger
to murder	murder	murderer
to forge	forgery	forger
to shoplift	shoplifting	shoplifter
to kidnap	kidnapping	kidnapper

2 Key

1 robbery
2 burgled/stolen
3 burglar
4 thefts (or robberies)
5 mugger
6 thief
7 robber
8 shoplifting
9 forgeries
10 offences

LISTENING 1 Page 49
Blank filling

Pre-activity: Ask if anyone has been burgled and what happened. What was stolen? Did they contact the police? What did the police do? Refer students to the police form and play the tape.

Key

1 Anna Webb
2 52 George Street
3 afternoon (after 2 pm)
4 traveller's cheques
5 $250
6 First National Bank
7 passport
8 D531087, red cover, new
9 gold watch
10 £125
11 lock broken

GRAMMAR 1 Page 49 (GR p 217)
Sequence of tenses

1 Key

1 Past simple tense: to talk about events in sequence
2 Past continuous/Past simple to describe one action interrupted by another
3 Past continuous/Past simple: to describe one action interrupted by another
4 Past simple/Past continuous: to describe one action which took place during a longer period

2 Key

1 was phoning/rang
2 was living/happened
3 was raining/decided
4 didn't hear/was sitting
5 broke/were staying
6 did/went
7 went
8 arrived/was playing/was reading
9 was sitting/stole
10 was watching/heard

READING 2 Page 50
Gapped text

1 Key

| 1 G | 2 C | 3 I | 4 B | 5 H | 6 A | 7 E |

2 and 3 Key

take quickly	grab (1 syllable)
easy to carry	portable (3 syllables)
collect	pick up (2 syllables)
appear	show up (2 syllables)
in a convenient place	to hand (2 syllables)
connect	link (1 syllable)
easily damaged	delicate (3 syllables)
things you own	possessions (3 syllables)

UNIT 4 Crime wave

maker
which you can trust
put in
easy to attack

manufacturer (5 syllables)
reliable (4 syllables)
install (2 syllables)
vulnerable (4 syllables)

SPEAKING 2 Page 51
Exchanging information and expressing opinions

Get students to work in pairs or groups of three or four. For each phase, ask a few students to report on their discussions to the rest of the class. Use the discussion questions as warm-up for reading the passage which follows.

READING 3 Page 51
Reading for specific information

This is another extract from the crime prevention booklet (see page 48).

1 Give students just a few seconds to scan the passage and identify the numbers.

Key

- 460,000 cars are reported missing in Britain each year.
- Many car criminals are under 20 years old.
- Car thefts and thefts from cars are ¼ of all recorded crime.

2 This exercise can be completed individually or in pairs.

Key

1 cost of police time
  cost of the criminal justice system
  (the courts, prisons, etc.)
  cost of increased insurance premiums
2 they are never recovered
  (never returned to the owner)
  they are damaged by thieves
  they are involved in accidents
3 they are sometimes drunk
  they are unskilled petty criminals
  they are under 20

Additional vocabulary:
vulnerable (adj) (title) = easy to attack or damage
drastically (adv) (paragraph 3) = by a large amount
petty (adj) (paragraph 4) = minor, unimportant

LISTENING 2 Page 52
Note-taking

Pre-activity: Ask students to read the introduction and information. Then check their understanding by asking: Is this a conversation in the street? (No, a radio phone-in.) Who do we hear speaking on the programme? (A security expert, two people phoning in, plus the interviewer.)
Is the first caller going to talk about a murder? (No, a theft.)
Is the second caller going to talk about a mugging? (Possibly, we do not know.)

Key

1 a clock
2 his house
3 keep doors locked
4 get window locks
5 a bag (with credit cards and tickets)
6 a restaurant (in Paris)
7 never put your bag on the floor
8 don't trust strangers
9 don't put all documents and money in one bag

GRAMMAR 2 Page 52 (GR p217)
Making deductions

1 Key

All the sentences use the past form of a modal verb to refer to unspecified past time.

2 *might have* and *could have* refer to one possible explanation (possibility), *must have* and *can't have* are used to talk about the only possible explanation (certainty).

3 **Pre-activity:** Ask students to glance at exercise 3 and tell you if the text is from an advertisement, a novel or a newspaper. (A novel.) What type of novel is it from? (a detective story or 'whodunnit').
Explain that students must read the extract and try to work out from the clues who the murderer must be.

Additional questions to ask when students have read the passage:
Who was murdered? (Keith Thurbold)
What's the name of the police inspector? (Inspector Skea)
When was the body discovered? (at 9pm)
Was the body found in the town? (no, in some woods)
How far was the body from the town? (12 miles = about 19 kilometres)
When did Keith die? (between 6–7 pm)
How many of the suspects had a car? (all of them)
How long does it take to drive from Raybury to the woods? (20 minutes)
What was unusual about the night of the murder? (it was foggy)

Get students to tell you what they think are the most important pieces of information. Elicit the three crucial facts and write them on the board:

Crime wave **UNIT 4**

Key facts

1 Keith died between 6–7 pm
2 the body was found at 9 pm
3 the car journey to Raybury must have taken much more than 20 minutes because of the fog

4 Write 'Alibi' on the board and get students to tell you what it means (alibi = a claim by a suspect that when a crime was committed the suspect was in a different place), then explain that all the suspects have alibis but one of them must be the murderer.
There is a lot of detail for students to handle in this activity. If you want to make the task seem easier **either** divide the class into four groups, each group to examine one alibi before reporting back to the class, **or** get students to check the information in pairs, then combine the pairs into groups of four for students to compare their conclusions.

WRITING 1 Page 52
Giving and justifying opinions

If students are to complete the writing follow-up for homework, make sure that they have detailed notes to help them remember which pieces of information are relevant to which paragraph.

Possible answers

1 In my opinion Marilyn can't have been the murderer because she was with a friend from 5.30–9.30.
2 I think Derek might have been the murderer because he could have killed Keith between 6.00–6.30 and taken the body to the woods between 8.00 and 8.40.
3 I think Daphne could have been the murderer because she had time to kill Keith before 6.15 pm, and could have taken his body to the woods before she went to the theatre.
4 I think Agnes must have committed the murder because she could have killed Keith before 6.15 and disposed of the body after 8.00 pm.

When students think they have found the murderer, or if they are unable to decide, give the 'Super Clue' below.
Super Clue:
These are the questions that Inspector Skea wanted to ask **one** of the suspects:
1 What did you eat for dinner that evening?
2 Where was your car parked that evening?
3 Where does your friend live?
Students should now be able to identify the murderer.
Read the next part of the novel to them.
'It was quite simple,' said Inspector Skea, 'Keith went to his sister's house after leaving Derek Morecott in the city centre. Agnes had invited him to dinner. She had invited him many times over the years since their quarrel but he had always ignored her letters. Now she got her revenge by feeding him on poisoned chocolate mousse (his favourite!). Then she transferred the body to her car boot before her friend arrived. The car was in the garage next to the house and a door leads from the house directly into the garage, so no one saw her. Agnes's friend, Mrs Jay, lives on the edge of Raybury – on the road to the woods. When Agnes drove her home, the body was **already** in the boot.'

HELP WITH GUESSING THE MEANING OF WORDS
Page 53

Making accurate guesses about unknown vocabulary is an essential skill in learning any language and one which students will need for the FCE examination. Note that although the ability to guess the meaning of unknown words is not directly tested in FCE, dictionaries may not be used in the exam and students will certainly come across difficult words. This section helps students to develop a strategy for dealing with such words. So, do not allow students to use dictionaries to help in this section.

1 Stress that *'spreg'* does not exist as a word in English. It is an invented word which has a different meaning each time it is used in the passage.

Key

	Word Type	General Meaning	Possible Words
2	noun (plural)	things seen in a zoo	animals
3	verb	something people do	visited, been to
4	adjective	qualifies 'interested in'	very, quite
5	noun (plural)	type of animal	lions, gorillas
6	adjective	zoo animal	lion, gorilla
7	verb	activity which people do	arrived
8	noun	time	time
9	verb	something done to animals	fed, washed
10	adjective	something positive	great, magic

READING 4 Page 54
Dealing with difficult vocabulary

1 **Pre-activity:** Before students read the article focus attention on the headline and ask students what the story is about. Ask: Why might someone be described as a wolfman? They might recognise 'Wolfman', but if necessary tell students that a wolf is an animal rather like a large wild dog which lives in mountains and forests and attacks and eats other animals. From this your students should be able to suggest that a wolfman (or werewolf) is a man who sometimes becomes a wolf.
Ask for suggestions about why 'wolfman' is in inverted

UNIT 4 Crime wave

commas in the headline. (Because the story is not about a genuine wolfman.) If none of your students has any ideas about 'gory riddle' tell them to ignore these words for the moment and point out that when reading foreign newspapers it is often necessary to read the story to find out what the headline is about.

Key

1 true   2 false   3 false   4 true   5 false

2 Key

1 b/a   2 a/a   3 b/b   4 b/c

Note: The mention of Sherlock Holmes and a 'three-pipe problem' refers to the fictional detective and his habit of smoking a pipe to help him concentrate on solving mysteries.

Additional vocabulary:
In the headline:
gory (adj) = with lots of blood
riddle (n) = mystery
(Both words are typical of newspaper headlines.)

3 Key

Word	Type of Word	Meaning in Text
faded (7)	adjective	lost colour as a result of the sun or washing
scoured (12)	verb	searched very carefully
enigmatic (23)	adjective	mysterious
re-traced (24)	verb	recreated (his movements)
footstep (24)	noun	place where he had been
tracker (25)	adjective	(dog) capable of following a scent
combed (25)	verb	looked very carefully in
spotted (26)	verb	saw, noticed
dishevelled (27)	adjective	untidy
jigsaw (33)	noun	picture cut into many pieces
rolls (37)	noun	lists of people
discarded (40)	verb	taken off and abandoned

4 Key

1 a   2 b   3 c

GRAMMAR 3 Page 55 (GR p217)
Relative pronouns

1 Key

1

2 Key

1 Detectives are people who investigate crime.

2 Residents are people who live somewhere on a permanent basis.
3 Frogmen are swimmers who work under water.
4 Lakes are areas of fresh water surrounded by land.
5 A market town is a town where there is a regular market which people visit from the surrounding area.
6 Sheds are small buildings, usually made of wood, which are used for storing things.
7 A car park is a place off the street where cars can park.
8 Search parties are groups of people who look for missing people.
9 Tracker dogs are dogs which are trained to find people or things using their sense of smell.
10 A jigsaw puzzle is a picture which has been cut into pieces.

3 Key

Compound nouns are: frogmen, market town, car park, search parties, tracker dogs, jigsaw puzzle

PRONUNCIATION Page 55
Compound nouns

1 and 2 Key

ṕassport
ṕenknife
ńewspaper
śuitcase
gúidebook
first-áid kit
shóplifter
líght switch
h́airdresser
v́acuum cleaner
ẃalkman
tŕavellers' cheques

3 Get students to repeat the words as they listen.

4 Possible answers

A passport is a document which allows you to travel abroad.
A penknife is a small folding knife which you can keep in a pocket.
A newspaper is large sheets of paper which have news and information printed on them.
A suitcase is a bag which you can use to carry your clothes in when you travel.
A guidebook is a book which gives information for tourists or visitors.
A first-aid kit is a container which has basic medical

Crime wave **UNIT 4**

equipment for immediate use when someone is injured.
A shoplifter is a person who steals things from shops.
A light switch is a switch which is used to turn electric lights on or off.
A hairdresser is a person who cuts, washes and styles people's hair.
A vacuum cleaner is a machine which cleans carpets and floors.
A walkman is a personal tape recorder or radio which you can use to listen to music without other people hearing.
Travellers' cheques are cheques which you can buy at a bank and change into foreign currency when you visit another country.

SPEAKING 3 Page 55
Exchanging information

Pre-activity: Ask students to suggest what they take with them apart from clothes when they go on holiday or are staying in a hotel. Then set the scene by explaining that each pair of students is staying in the same hotel. Student B is at the hotel at the moment, and there is a problem, so he/she phones student A who is somewhere else in the same town (perhaps at a school or visiting a conference) to tell him/her about the problem and to ask some questions.

HELP WITH WRITING Page 56
Reports

Point out that a report should be organised in a logical way and should include a statement that it is a report – either as a title (eg *Report on a Theft at the Grand Hotel*), or at the begining of the report (eg *This is a report on a theft at the...*). It will not look like a letter with addresses and expressions like *Dear X* and it could be organised using sub-headings and numbering. There is no single correct way to present a report – the important thing at FCE level is that the content is properly organised.

1 Key

The following would probably be included in a report:
- date and time of the theft
- list of the stolen items
- description of the stolen items
- who discovered the theft
- who might have stolen the items
- who you are and how you are involved

2 Key

1 Personal information: who you are and how you are involved

2 What happened: date and time of the theft; who discovered it
3 What was stolen: list and description of stolen items;
4 Any other important information: who might have stolen the items

LISTENING 3 Page 56
Blank filling

1 Key

to log on – to get entry to a computer system
database – software which holds large amounts of information which can be extracted very quickly
keyboard – the part of a computer with rows of letters and numbers to press
network – a system which allows more than one computer terminal to communicate via a central computer

2 Possible answers

computer hacking; theft

3 Key

1 many qualifications
2 telephone
3 to damage
4 be arrested
5 an office/a big organisation
6 old-fashioned
7 the systems manager
8 locked out
9 young staff/women
10 experienced

EXAM PRACTICE 4 Page 57

1 Key

1	the	9	used
2	For	10	when
3	have	11	off/away
4	of/were	12	Next
5	them	13	where/when
6	spent	14	which
7	with/through	15	at
8	Despite		

2 Key

1	of	6	a
2	the	7	✓
3	to	8	its
4	✓	9	to
5	which	10	by

33

UNIT 4 Crime wave

11 ✓
12 them
13 age
14 is
15 go

3 Key

1 networks
2 information
3 criminals
4 forgeries
5 fingerprints/fingerprinting
6 detection
7 developments
8 invention
9 powerless
10 prevention

REVISION TEST 2

1 Key

1 for	2 a	3 of/from
4 and	5 to	6 of
7 made	8 had	9 be
10 by	11 to	12 used/had
13 on	14 while/but	15 it

2 Key

1 needs cleaning/needs to be cleaned
2 had my CD player mended
3 has had her hair cut
4 haven't seen Tim for
5 arrived too late
6 can't be the
7 must have seen
8 swims faster than
9 never eaten a better
10 thank your host before leaving

3 Key

1 the	2 a	3 ✓
4 to	5 ✓	6 of
7 for	8 where	9 it
10 and	11 ✓	12 too
13 them	14 ✓	15 with

4 Key

1 valuable	2 happening	3 prevention
4 advice	5 security	6 reliable
7 installation	8 jewellery	9 electrical
10 hidden		

REVISION TEST 2

1 Fill each of the numbered blanks in the following passage. Use only one word in each space.

Shaving Past and Present

The average man has 30,000 small hairs (**0**) <u>on</u> his face and shaving accounts (**1**) _____ about ten minutes of his time each day.

The first man to shave used (**2**) _____ sharpened shell to remove unwanted facial hair and the first razors were made (**3**) _____ heavy bronze or iron, making shaving difficult (**4**) _____ painful. The ancient Greeks preferred the clean-shaven look (**5**) _____ beards. For them it was a sign (**6**) _____ noble birth and status. Alexander the Great always (**7**) _____ sure his soldiers (**8**) _____ shaved before commencing battle, thus ensuring the enemy would (**9**) _____ unable to grab them (**10**) _____ their beards. In 17th century Russia, Peter the Great imposed a beard tax (**11**) _____ encourage shaving, while the British navy (**12**) _____ to reward bearded seamen with a few pennies a day in an effort to conserve water.

These days the average man in Britain spends about three hours a week (**13**) _____ his personal appearance, (**14**) _____ the average woman spends three and a half hours. Over 50% of men, however, say that they hate shaving because (**15**) _____ leaves their skin dry and sore.

2 Complete the second sentence so that it has a similar meaning to the first sentence. Use the word given and other words to complete each sentence. You must use between two and five words. Do not change the word given.

1 Someone should clean the bathroom this morning.
 needs
 The bathroom _____ this morning.

2 A shop mended my CD player for me.
 had
 I _____ at a shop.

3 Her hairdresser has cut her hair really short.
 had
 She _____ really short.

4 It's years since I saw Tim.
 seen
 I _____ years.

5 He didn't arrive in time to get a good seat.
 too
 He _____ to get a good seat.

6 It's impossible that Mary's the murderer.
 be
 Mary _____ murderer.

7 I'm sure that someone saw her take the money.
 must
 Someone _____ her take the money.

8 Lisa doesn't swim as fast as her sister.
 than
 Lisa's sister _____ she does.

9 This is the best beefburger I've ever eaten.
 better
 I've _____ beefburger.

10 You shouldn't leave the party without thanking your host.
 before
 You should _____ the party.

REVISION TEST 2

3 Read this letter and look carefully at each line. Some of the lines are correct and some have a word which should not be there. If a line is correct put a tick (✓). If the line has a word which should not be there, write down the word. There are two example lines at the beginning.

Taken for a Ride

A strange thing happened to me the other day.		
I was standing in our local town square, quite close	0	✓
to a group of 'bikers'. These such tall, unshaven young	00	such
men with long hair were dressed all in the leather and looked quite threatening.	1	....
Suddenly, an elderly gentleman, who was wearing a smart	2	....
and brightly polished shoes walked up to the group	3	....
and started to watching them with a kind of nervous	4	....
interest. As I watched, he moved towards one particularly	5	....
magnificent large black machine and started to touch of it.	6	....
As the owner of the bike noticed, and started for to	7	....
walk towards where the elderly gentleman, I began to	8	....
worry about what it was going to happen. I couldn't	9	....
hear what they said to each and other, but I	10	....
watched in amazement as the biker offered the	11	....
man a crash helmet and too helped him onto the	12	....
motorbike. They then drove them into the traffic and off into the distance.	13	....
Five minutes later, they reappeared. The man was	14	....
helped off the bike by the group and, after with shaking hands	15	....
with the bike's owner, left the group with an enormous smile on		
his face. For five minutes he had once again been 'one of the boys'.		

4 Use the word given in capitals at the end of each line to form a word that fits in the space.

Burglary

Someone is burgled every two minutes in the UK.
A (**0**) <u>burglar</u> can enter your house, grab the   BURGLE
most (**1**) _____ items and escape. So what   VALUE
can you do to stop this (**2**) _____ to you?   HAPPEN
A police crime (**3**) _____ officer will call   PREVENT
and give you free (**4**) _____ on such measures   ADVISE
as (**5**) _____ locks, timing light switches and   SECURE
alarm systems. He may also recommend (**6**) _____   RELY
firms who will take care of the (**7**) _____ .   INSTALL
You should also keep a list of such things as (**8**) _____ JEWELS
and (**9**) _____ equipment, with photographs, if   ELECTRIC
possible. This list, however, should be kept (**10**) _____ , so   HIDE
that the thieves don't find it.

UNIT 5

Playing the game

TOPIC	HELP SECTIONS	Paper 4
Sports and games	Help with writing a narrative composition	Multiple matching
VOCABULARY FOCUS	Help with error correction	Listening for specific information
Sports and games	**EXAM FOCUS**	Multiple choice
Sports equipment and skills	**Paper 1**	Short extracts
Dividing words into groups/categories	Multiple choice	**Paper 5**
Guessing unknown words	Reading for main points	Expressing opinions and exchanging information
LANGUAGE FOCUS	**Paper 2**	**EXAM PRACTICE**
Time Linkers	Writing instructions	Multiple choice cloze
Used to	Narrative composition	Key word transformations
Past perfect	**Paper 3**	Word formation
Past tenses in narrative	Cloze text	Narrative composition
Before/After	Key word transformations	Article containing narrative
Although/Despite		
Pronunciation: Intonation		

SPEAKING 1 Page 59
Expressing and justifying opinions

Pre-activity: Ask students what leisure activities they do and elicit the names of some sports and games. Write the names of one or two sports on the board and ask students in pairs to think of three other sports which they have tried and three sports which they have not tried, but would like to try. Give them a couple of minutes to complete their lists then ask for some sample answers or allow everyone to contribute, but students only add the names of sports which have not already been mentioned by someone else.

Key 🔑

1 *Picture 1:* Football. Equipment: football. Aim: to score goals against an opposing team. *Picture 2:* Fishing. Equipment: fishing rod, bait, fishing line. Aim: to catch fish. *Picture 3:* Tennis. Equipment: racket and ball. Aim: to score points by hitting the ball over a net so that it lands inside the opponent's court but out of the opponent's reach. *Picture 4:* Chess. Equipment: chess pieces and chessboard. Aim: to achieve 'checkmate' (immobilise the opponent's king).

2 Sport (can be countable or uncountable) = a leisure (or professional) activity involving an element of physical skill or effort. It may be played in a team (eg football), or against one or more opponents (eg tennis), or practised simply as a way of relaxing and taking exercise (eg jogging).
Game (a countable noun) = a competitive activity with fixed rules which must be followed. Some (not all) sports are also games (eg football, tennis and golf), other games do not involve any particular physical skill and so are not sports (eg cards, chess and backgammon).

Sport and games: Grammar

When we talk about sports which are not games, we use only the verb formed from the name of the sport (eg *swim, ski*), or the verb *to go* + the name of the sport (eg *to go sailing, to go running*). For games, we use the verb *to play* + the name of the game (eg *to play golf, to play cards*).

3
Sports	Games	Sports/Games
swimming	billiards	squash
fishing	Trivial Pursuit	basketball
rollerskating	Scrabble	golf
parachuting	chess	hockey
skiing		rugby
		tennis

37

UNIT 5 *Playing the game*

You may need to point out that although the things labelled *sports* can be competitive (eg a skiing championship), the element of competition is not essential to the activity – you can ski alone if you want to – but it is impossible to have a game of tennis without a partner.

LISTENING 1 Page 60
Multiple matching

Pre-activity: Write *Trivial Pursuit* and *Scrabble* on the board and ask students to think of some more board games and add to the list. Then get them to talk in pairs about the discussion points in **1**.

2 Focus on the instructions and ask if students have ever heard of (or been to) somewhere like this. Play the tape once and then get students to compare answers with a partner before you play the tape for the second time.

Key

| 1 D | 2 C | 3 H | 4 A | 5 F |

GRAMMAR 1 Page 61 (GR p 217)
Time linkers

Pre-activity: On the board, write the name of a game which your students will know (eg basketball, football, tennis, backgammon). Ask for some facts about how to play the game (eg number of players, objectives, time required, area/place of play). Make a distinction between interesting extra information (eg tennis balls are usually white) and information essential for the game (eg each tennis player holds a racket).
Write **Scrabble** on the board and ask students if they know this game. You may need to elicit or teach some Scrabble vocabulary. Use the picture on page 60 to pre-teach *Scrabble board, bag and tiles*. Stress that it is not important for this activity if students do not know the game. Students who know Scrabble must imagine that they have to explain the rules to someone who has never played. Students who do not know Scrabble must imagine that they are playing for the first time.
Get students to select the essential information from the box. Give them a few minutes to make initial individual choices, then students can compare and discuss in pairs. If time allows group students into fours and ask them to agree on the 10 most important facts.

1 Key

Although students may be able to justify including other sentences, the most significant pieces of information are probably:
Scrabble can be played by two to four players.
The first word must cover the star.
Scrabble is played using small tiles.
Each tile has a number to indicate its value for scoring.
Each player must taken seven tiles from the bag.
Covering the coloured squares on the board gives extra points.
On each tile there is a letter of the alphabet.
The game ends when the bag is empty and one player has used all his or her tiles.
Each new word must use one letter from a word already on the board.
As letters are used they must be replaced from the bag.

2 Students complete the text, which describes how to play Scrabble. Students need to use these expressions when they are writing narratives, but they are also useful when writing instructions.

Key

2 Firstly	3 Then	4 After that
5 either	6 or	7 As soon as
8 so that	9 until	10 While
11 During	12 Lastly	

Note that *then* is interchangeable with *after that*.
While and *during* are similar (meaning *at the same time*), but *while* is followed by a gerund or subject and verb; *during* is followed by a noun.
During is used to say that something happens inside a particular period of time; *while* is used to connect two actions happening at the same time.

WRITING 1 Page 61
Instructions

1 Students can use the game discussed in the pre-activity or another game. If you prefer, elicit four or five games and ask students to select one from the list.
2 Ask students to compare their information and the order they have decided on with a partner before they complete 3.

READING 1 Page 62
Multiple choice

Pre-activity: Get students to focus on the photograph and ask them to discuss these questions:
• Where was the photo taken?
• Who is in the picture?
• What is she doing?
• How does she feel?

Explain that the picture shows Leslie Scott, who invented the game the game in the photograph, Jenga. The article mainly describes the development of Jenga. If any of your students recognise the game, ask them to describe it and how it is played to the rest of the class (in English). If they do not know the game, ask them to guess from the picture how the game is played and how you win at Jenga.

Focus on the article and ask students to find out what the word Jenga means and what language it comes from by looking through it as quickly as possible (answer: it is Swahili for 'to build').

Ask them to look through the article quickly again and find and explain these numbers:
- millions (the number of copies of Jenga sold)
- £15,000 (the amount of money Leslie borrowed from the bank)
- 30 (the number of countries where Jenga is played)
- 39 (Leslie Scott's age)

Get students to answer questions 1 – 7. Then compare their answers with a partner's.

Key

| 1 D | 2 B | 3 A | 4 C | 5 B | 6 A | 7 D |

SPEAKING 2 Page 64
Sports quiz

Allow students to try to complete the quiz in groups before they look in a dictionary. Encourage informed guessing followed by dictionary checking.

Key

| 1 d | 2 b | 3 c | 4 c | 5 d | 6 c |
| 7 a | 8 a | 9 c | 10 c | 11 b | 12 c |

Additional vocabulary:
Avoid focusing attention on the 'wrong' answers unless you feel that some of the vocabulary is of particular interest to your students. If you get a lot of questions about the 'wrong' answers, then ask students to look up the words in a dictionary after the class or at home.

badminton:	a game rather like tennis played over a high net with rackets. Instead of a ball, a small weight called a shuttlecock is used. This originally had bird feathers attached, but is now usually made of plastic.
javelin:	a sport which involves throwing a sharp stick (called a javelin) as far as possible.
shot put:	a sport which involves throwing a heavy metal ball (called a shot) as far as possible.
pole vault:	a sport which involves jumping over a high obstacle with the help of a long pole.
discus:	a sport which involves throwing a plate-shaped metal weight (called a discus) as far as possible.
tobogganing:	a winter sport which involves travelling down a snow-covered hill while sitting on a wooden platform (a toboggan).
archery:	a sport which involves using a bow to fire an arrow at the centre of a target.
croquet:	a game played on grass in which players use large wooden hammers to push coloured balls through metal rings pushed into the ground.
dominoes:	an indoor game played with many small rectangular pieces of plastic or ivory, each piece divided into two sections and marked with dots representing the numbers from zero to six.
darts:	an indoor game in which small arrows are thrown with one hand at a target.
abseiling:	a sport which involves 'walking' down a vertical rock face using a system of ropes.
rowing:	a sport which involves making a boat move forwards by repeatedly pushing a piece of wood (an oar) through the water.
snorkelling:	an underwater activity which involves using a short plastic tube to breathe air while swimming under the water.
lacrosse:	a team game from North America in which players each use a stick with a net to catch and throw a small hard ball in order to score goals.

Note the alternative spellings; *racquet* and *racket* – both forms are correct.

LISTENING 2 Page 65
Selecting an answer

1 Key

  1.1 They are all games and they all require special equipment to play them.

  1.2 Get students to work in pairs for this and the following exercise. Ask the class for suggestions about how these might be grouped, and if necessary give some help in suggesting possible ways of grouping the sports.

  Possible groupings include

  team sports/individual sports
  ball-only games/stick, racket or bat games
  sports with a net/sports without a net

  1.3 Possible groupings include:
  Usually played outside / usually played inside / played inside and outside
  racket games / kicking and carrying games / bat and ball games
  hard ball / soft ball / other type of ball

  1.4 The actual groupings which students have decided on are not important as long as they can justify them to the rest of the class.

  1.5 Explain that students will hear a radio discussion between two people who are talking about the history and development of sports. The first time they listen,

UNIT 5 Playing the game

students should write down the names of all the sports they hear. Warn students that the interview is quite fast so they will need to write quickly **and** listen for the next sport at the same time.

Key

The sports mentioned are:

cricket	squash
football (soccer)	American football
tennis	baseball
rugby	badminton
baseball	windsurfing
hockey	skateboarding

2 Ask students to look at the multiple-choice questions, then play the tape once or twice more.

Key

1 B 2 B 3 A 4 C 5 A

GRAMMAR 2 Page 65 (GR p 218)
Used to

1 Ask students to study the explanation and answer the questions 1–3.

Key

1 In the past.
2 No. They happened continually over a period of time.
3 No.

2 Key

1	used to play / played	6	used to smoke
2	go	7	play
3	used to be	8	used to travel
4	went	9	used to go/watches
5	used to take	10	got

SPEAKING 3 Page 66
Exchanging information

Tell the class briefly about one or two sports you play or used to play before asking them to talk about the discussion points in pairs. Ask some of the class to report back on their conversations.

LISTENING 3 Page 66
Selecting an answer

1 Key

1	which/that	5	of	9	this
2	for	6	that	10	just/only
3	been	7	as	11	into
4	least	8	how	12	by

2 **Pre-activity:** Introduce the topic of the listening by asking students if they have ever skied and if they enjoyed it. What problems did they have the first time they went skiing? If your students have not skied, is it because they do not want to? What problems might they have the first time? This should elicit some of the drawbacks to skiing which are included in the listening exercise.

Key

Students tick these problems:
- expensive equipment
- language difficulties
- too many people
- cost of lessons

GRAMMAR 3 Page 66 (GR p 218)
Past perfect

1.1 The tense used is the Past perfect. Before students go any further you may feel it is necessary to point out the non-contracted form (ie I'd never tried = I had never tried).

1.2 The Past perfect is typically found in narratives, that is as part of a longer story or description of things which happened in the past. Point out that the moment when the story begins is described using the Past simple form, but for everything which happened **before** the beginning of the story we use the Past perfect form.

2 Key

1	had started	6	became
2	had not played	7	had never dived
3	won	8	had taken part
4	had heard of	9	had won
5	had arranged	10	presented

Further practice: Ask students to think about a particularly good or bad experience they have had. Suggest some possibilities – trying a new sport and feeling excited and enthusiastic or arriving home exhausted and injured; visiting a particular place (Disneyland, Epidaurus, Stratford upon Avon, etc.).

Students describe their experience starting with the moment they arrived home (eg 'I was tired but happy when I got home …' or 'I arrived home wet, tired and depressed…'), and then use the Past perfect form to talk about the earlier events. Give an example from your own experience. The explanation and your example will help students to remember and think about their own experiences. Then get students in pairs to tell their stories to each other. If you have time, ask them to change partners and repeat the same story but with more details. Listen for some of the more unusual

Playing the game **UNIT 5**

experiences described, and get those students to repeat their stories for the whole class.
Students then write up their stories for homework.

WRITING 2 Page 68
Narrative

1. There are many different ways of ordering the pictures to make a logical story, and it is not important if students do not select the order which is described in 2. Elicit one or two different stories from students.

2. Key

    4, 2, 5, 1, 3.

3. Now ask students to close their books before discussing possible endings. Encourage as many different endings as possible before students read the final section on page 69.

4. Key

    1. Students should be able to describe a paragraph (see Unit 1 page 13 in Student's Book, page 9 in this book).
    2. The writer begins a new paragraph when he or she begins a new part of the story.
    3. Possible titles are:
       Paragraph 1 – Introduction
       Paragraph 2 – Plans for the day
       Paragraph 3 – Exploring the mountain top
       Paragraph 4 – A change in the weather
       Paragraph 5 – Lost on the mountain
       Paragraph 6 – A safe arrival
       Paragraph 7 – Conclusion
    4. The fact that it was a terrible experience.

5. Key

    1. Most of the story was in the Past simple tense.
    2. There are also examples of the Past perfect tense (in paragraph 2 before the true moment of the 'start' of the story when they arrive at the top of the mountain and in other places when events are described out of order).
    3. Ask students to identify and underline the Past perfect verb forms and discuss with partners why these forms are used.

6. Key

    1. The words and phrases in bold print are all linking expressions which help the reader to understand the relationship between events in the story. Using expressions like these makes narratives easier to understand and more sophisticated.
    Note that there is nearly always an opportunity to write a narrative-type composition in the FCE exam and students can produce much better narratives by using some of these expressions.

    2. *After* is followed by mention of at least two events. The pattern is:
    After + first event + second event
    When we use *after* we are indicating that the events happened in the order in which they are mentioned.
    Afterwards is used when an event previously mentioned happened first. The pattern is:
    First event. *Afterwards* + second event
    Afterwards is followed by a sentence (subject + verb).

    3. When *before* is used at the beginning of a sentence it indicates that the two events which are mentioned are in reverse order. The pattern is:
    Before + second event + first event
    eg Before I paid the bill I checked the total to make sure it was correct.
    However, when *before* is used between two events the order of the events is:
    First event + *before* + second event
    eg I checked my change before I left the shop.

7. *Although* and *despite* are to be used to indicate contrast.
    Although is followed by a subject and verb
    eg Although it was early in the season, the skiing resort was crowded.
    Despite is followed by **either**
    the fact that + subject + verb
    eg Despite the fact that it was so cold, there was no heating in the hotel.
    or
    noun (or gerund)
    eg Despite the cold weather, we decided to climb the mountain.
    Despite feeling cold, we decided to climb the mountain.

    Key

    1. Although we felt cold we kept walking.
    2. Despite the sun/the sunny weather, I felt quite cold.
    3. Although it was snowing I felt warm.
    4. Although there was a large amount/a lot of snow we had our picnic.
    5. Despite having/the fact that we had a map, we got lost.

PRONUNCIATION Page 70
Intonation

1. Key

    1. The intonation is rising.
    2. The intonation is falling.

    If the intonation rises, it indicates that the sentence will

41

UNIT 5 *Playing the game*

continue, whereas if it is falling, the sentence is coming to an end.

2 Key

| 1 rising | 2 rising | 3 falling | 4 rising | 5 falling |
| 6 falling | 7 rising | 8 rising | 9 rising | 10 falling |

HELP WITH WRITING Page 70
Narrative

Emphasise to students once again the importance of planning a composition before beginning to write. In the FCE examination candidates are instructed to write between 120 and 180 words. Here, a narrative composition of 180 words is recommended because of the difficulty of telling a good story using fewer words. Tell your students that for the purpose of writing a narrative composition they should aim at the maximum number of words. Get students to complete one of the compositions for homework. You may decide to ask them to show you their composition plans too, or these can be prepared in class, checked, and then the stories written for homework.

READING 2 Page 71
Reading for main points

1 Before students discuss these points, ask them what, in their opinion, is the most fashionable designer label for sports wear at the moment. Then get students to look at the reading passage and establish that it is from a magazine about TV programmes and is about a programme called *Family Matters*.

2 Key

| 1 true | 2 false | 3 true | 4 false | 5 true |

Dealing with difficult vocabulary

3 Key

Word	Line	Type of word	Possible meaning
swept	2	past participle	spread quickly
slashed	9	past tense	cut
trendy	11	adjective	fashionable
gear	12	noun	clothes
targets	13	noun	objects of attack
taking the mickey	28	gerund + noun	making unpleasant jokes about someone
recalls	29	present tense	remembers
pauper	31	noun	person with no money
scratched	35	past tense	cut
taunt	42	infinitive	deliberately annoy
picked on	43	past participle	attacked for no good reason

Additional vocabulary:
shell suits (line 18) = colourful lightweight shirts and sports trousers made of nylon. They were originally worn by athletes but are now very common in Britain as casual clothes.
make (line 23) = label/name of manufacturer
casualty (line 36) = hospital first-aid department
contusions (line 37) = bruises (when the skin becomes blue or yellow because it has been damaged)
spine (line 38) = backbone
In my day (line 40) = when I was younger

LISTENING 4 Page 72
Short extracts

Allow students to read through the questions/options before you play the tape twice. Remind them that in this section of the Listening test only they will hear each of the questions recorded on the tape.

Key

| 1 B | 2 B | 3 A | 4 C | 5 B | 6 C |

HELP WITH ERROR CORRECTION Page 72

The aim of this section is to raise awareness in students about how to approach this part of the Use of English test. The main points for them to remember are that the words they have to identify as wrong additional words are likely to be grammatical words rather than lexical words. They will not be randomly inserted nonsense words, but will resemble a correct structure or expression. They will also be definitely wrong – optional extra words (eg adjectives in a description will not be targeted here). Students should also be reminded that in the exam there are likely to be between 3 and 5 correct lines where there is no extra wrong word. (See page vii of this book for more details.)

1 Key

1 preposition
2 article
3 conjunction
4 word used before infinitive
5 preposition

2 Key

| 1 will | 2 she | 3 in | 4 be | 5 the |
| 6 of | 7 to | 8 yet | 9 up | 10 much |

3 Key

1 the/article
2 of/preposition
3 by/preposition
4 in/preposition
5 to / word used before infinitive
6 much/quantifier
7 from/preposition

8 a/article	11 most/quantifier	
9 the/article	12 that/conjunction	
10 up/preposition		

4 Key

1 it	2 there	3 all	4 also	5 to
6 ✓	7 going	8 a	9 can	10 ✓
11 else	12 ✓	13 ✓	14 got	15 the

Point out that the answer to **11** is slightly different from the others in that to identify the additional wrong word students have to show that they understand the meaning of that part of the text, rather than simply identifying a structure or expression which is incorrect.

EXAM PRACTICE 5 Page 74

1 Key

1 B	2 D	3 A	4 C	5 A
6 C	7 A	8 C	9 A	10 D
11 C	12 B	13 D	14 A	15 C

2 Key

1 used to be
2 years since I wore/I've worn
3 is more frightening than
4 don't we go
5 am having my racket repaired
6 first time I've played
7 the fact that it
8 after they had finished
9 before you go
10 he was injured/ had been injured

3 Key

1 Successful
2 highest
3 activity
4 preparation
5 central
6 skilful
7 competitors
8 fitness
9 efficiency
10 strength

UNIT 6

Travellers' tales

TOPIC	HELP SECTIONS	Paper 5
Travel	Help with gap filling	Talking about photographs
VOCABULARY FOCUS	**EXAM FOCUS**	Expressing opinions
Travel words	Paper 1	Exchanging information
Travel quiz	Multiple choice	**EXAM PRACTICE**
LANGUAGE FOCUS	Gapped text	Open cloze
Compound adjectives	Paper 2	Error correction
Prepositions	Discursive composition	Word formation
Directions	Informal letters	Informal letter
Future time 1: Present tenses for future	Paper 3	Narrative composition
So/Such that	Key word transformations	A report
Pronunciation: Consonants	Word formation	
	Paper 4	
	Note-taking	
	Listening for specific information	

SPEAKING 1 Page 76
Talking about photographs

Pre-activity: If appropriate, ask students how they usually travel to the class or to school. Do they enjoy the journey? Why (not)? What would make the journey more enjoyable or more comfortable? If this introduction is not suitable because all your students live close to the school and walk to class, then ask them about their favourite journey or favourite means of transport. Get some students to explain their choice to the rest of the class or to their group.

1 Use the pictures to elicit as much vocabulary as possible before students discuss them using the where, why and how prompts. Point out that these are the types of questions which candidates can expect to be asked during the speaking test (Paper 5) of the FCE exam, before they go on to discuss the topic more generally.
Possible vocabulary: commuters, day trip, picnic, convertible, map, motorbike, economy class, luggage rack, aisle.

Give students a few minutes to talk about the photos, then elicit some possible answers.

2 This kind of activity is often found in parts 3 and 4 of the Speaking test.

When students have prepared their lists, elicit a few items from them before they talk to new partners.

READING 1 Page 76
Multiple matching

Pre-activity: Ask students to brainstorm games which they would suggest playing eg on a beach, in a car, on a wet day at home during a holiday. Then get them to complete the reading task. Point out that it is not necessary to read through the entire article before starting to answer the questions. Give them a time limit and then ask them to compare answers with a partner (it does not matter if they have not finished at this point) before they continue and complete the task.

1 Key

1 G	2 C	3 A	4 B	5 C	6 H
7 B	8 A	9 D	10 C	11 F	12 E

Note: Answers to 5/6, 7/8/9 and 10/11/12 are interchangeable.

2 Key

1 triangle, circle
2 fold/unfold, bottom/top, up/down, on/off, over/under, tie/untie
3 shallow
4 eyes, back, thumb
5 let go of
6 sink (sank/sunk), throw (threw/thrown)
7 whoever
8 tricky

9 spot
10 (to) cross off
11 entire

LISTENING 1 Page 78
Note-taking

Pre-activity: Focus on the notepad where students will write their answers. Get them to read through the notes and to predict the type of answer and some possible answers for each gap, eg **1** will probably be a name like Club or Executive or First, **2** is likely to be a sum of money, etc. Do not comment on the accuracy of the answers given, but indicate whether the suggestions about the type of answer seem likely. Then play the tape twice and get students to compare their answers.

Key

1 Superior
2 a few pounds
3 leg-room
4 (choice of) hot food
5 check-in
6 October 1st *
7 daily
8 weekend
9 5 times
10 flight bag
11 discounts (on shopping)

(*Note that in **writing** the date, in the UK people usually put the day before the month while in the USA the opposite is true. This can be very confusing when the date is expressed as a number only – 6.7 = 6th of July in UK, and 7th June in USA. In the FCE Listening test, it is not important how the information is recorded, as long as the answer is clear.)

PRONUNCIATION Page 78
Consonants

This can serve as a useful diagnostic exercise for your students. A wide range of typical problems is represented on the list. Some of them are particularly problematic for certain first-language groups.

1 Key

1 B–flight	6 A–west	11 A–train	16 A–joke
2 A–fryer	7 A–leaf	12 A–fright	17 A–off
3 B–flee	8 B–view	13 B–road	18 A–ice
4 B–vet	9 A–price	14 B–back	19 B–lose
5 A–fan	10 B–yet	15 A–sock	20 A–rate

READING 2 Page 79
Mutiple choice

Pre-activity: Write the headline of the article ('Fury on the 22') on the board and ask students if they can explain it to you. At this stage they probably will not be able to identify 'the 22' even if they know that fury means anger. Ask for suggestions about the meaning of 'on the 22' – it is not important if students guess the correct answer or not at this stage. Accept all reasonable suggestions, then tell students that the article contains several other numbers, and write these numbers on the board in random order:
22, 24, 75, 10, 3
Tell students to read paragraphs 1 and 2 quickly and find out what the numbers refer to. After one minute ask them to check their understanding of the numbers with a partner.

Key to pre-activity

22 = the number of the bus
24 = Tracy Lewis's age
75 = the number of minutes Tracy had to wait for the bus
10 = Tracy offered the driver a £10 note
3 = the correct fare was £3

Check that everyone has understood the meaning of the numbers. This sets the scene for reading the rest of the article. Tell students to read the whole article more carefully, and answer the multiple choice questions 1–3.

Key

1 A   2 C   3 C

Additional Vocabulary:
(para 1) change (n) = when you pay for something with a note or coin of a larger value than the price you get some money back, which is called change
(para 3) caught out (vb) = trapped because they did not know about the change
(para 4) due notice = information given to people a suitable period before something happens
(para 4) vending machines = machines which sell tickets, cigarettes, drinks, etc.

GRAMMAR 1 Page 79 (GR p218)
Compound adjectives

1 **Pre-activity:** Ask students: How long did Tracy have to wait for the bus?', and write **seventy-five** on the board. Then ask 'When did the bus come?', to elicit 'After a seventy-five minute wait'. Point out that **minute** is singular in this expression because it is part of an adjective phrase.
For further practice before students attempt the transformation exercise, read these phrases to your class and

UNIT 6 Travellers' tales

get students to make the numbers into adjectives:
A wait of thirty minutes (= A thirty-minute wait)
A fare of two pounds fifty (=A two-pound-fifty fare)
A journey of forty-five minutes (= A forty-five-minute journey)
A tour of two weeks (= A two-week tour)
A reduction of ten pounds (= A ten-pound reduction)
A course of ninety hours (= A ninety-hour course)
A discount of two pounds (= A two-pound discount)
Note that a hyphen (-) is used to join two or more words when they form a single adjective before the noun. Compound numbers (eg twenty-six) are always hyphenated.

2 Key

1 only a five-minute walk.
2 lasted/was for nine months.
3 a twenty-four-hour flight.
4 a two-year contract.
5 a five-thousand-pound car.
6 costs three hundred pounds.
7 a two-hour ferry crossing to the island.
8 coach tour takes/lasts twelve days.
9 a three-hour train journey.
10 twenty-dollar tickets.

WRITING 1 Page 80
Discursive composition

Pre-activity: Ask your class if they ever enter competitions or do quizzes in magazines or newspapers. Has anyone ever won a prize? Ask students to look at the quiz and to read the introduction. Ask 'What prize is offered?' (a four-week round-the-world trip for two). Get students to complete quiz questions 1–9 in pairs.

1 Key

| 1 b | 2 b | 3 d | 4 d | 5 a |
| 6 c | 7 d | 8 c | 9 d | |

10 Brainstorm possible reasons why a round-the-world trip would be a good experience, then ask students to write their answer in about 150 words either in class or for homework. Ask the class what would be a good way to begin, and elicit an introduction eg 'I think a round-the-world trip would be a good experience for me because …'.

VOCABULARY 1 Page 81
Travel and holidays

1 Key

cruise – countable noun or verb
trip – countable noun
journey – countable noun
flight – countable noun
travel – verb or uncountable noun
crossing – countable noun
fly – verb
sight-seeing – uncountable noun

Note that *trip, journey* and *travel* are often confused. The most important difference is that *trip* and *journey* are countable nouns, while *travel* is an uncountable noun. In addition, *trip* usually suggests pleasure or entertainment or another specific purpose (eg a business trip): The school is organising a trip to the theatre next month.
trip is often used in expressions like: a day trip, a round (= return) trip, an over-night trip:
A day trip to Oxford is included in the cost of the course.
A *journey* can be for pleasure or work/study, and is used when we emphasise the fact of travelling rather than the reason:
My journey to school takes half an hour.
Travel is an uncountable noun and can be for pleasure or work:
Travel broadens the mind.
It is more commonly used as a verb:
I travelled around the Greek islands for a month last summer.

1 journey	6 sight-seeing
2 trip	7 crossing
3 flight	8 fly
4 cruise	9 trip
5 travel	10 Crossing

2 Key

| 1 package | 2 packed | 3 packed |
| 4 packing | 5 to pack | |

3 Key

| 1 at | 2 off | 3 for | 4 away/out | 5 for |

SPEAKING 2 Page 81
Expressing attitudes and opinions

Pre-activity: Refer students to the fax message and check that they have understood the information it contains by asking:
How long is the trip? (four weeks)
How many people can go? (two people)
When is the trip? (February next year)

1 Ask your students which countries they would particularly like to visit, their preferred method of transport and what additional information they would require before they finally decide (about the weather, cost, places to see, etc.). Then get students to make individual lists.

2 Either get each student to select a partner, or quickly go

around the class naming alternate students A and B. Students then discuss their plans together, and should agree on a maximum of five countries to visit. They can then report to the class, or write about their proposed trip for homework.

Further practice: If possible obtain some travel brochures and posters from a local travel agent, and arrange them in the classroom so that groups of 3 students, A, B and C can act out a situation, where the 2 customers find out answers to the information they need for their trip from an 'agent'. You can decide on how much/what information they should ask for, depending on time available and what brochures you have. The 'agents' should be given time together to look at the brochures and know where to find the information.

READING 3 Page 82
Gapped text

1 If you have time and your students are interested, get them to discuss the things listed here with their partners. Otherwise just elicit a few opinions from the class as a whole.

2 Introduce the article by reading the first sentence with your students. Then tell them to look very quickly through the rest of the article and the option sentences A – H and underline all the names of places mentioned (cities, suburbs, continents, islands, etc.).
The places are: Richmond (a suburb of London), London, New York, California, Australia, Hong Kong, Bali, Singapore, Thailand, Southern India, Europe, Brooklyn, the Far East, Jakarta, Melbourne.

Give students enough time to select some of the answers, then ask them in pairs to compare their answers and to justify their choices if they are unsure or disagree.

Key

| 1 C | 2 G | 3 A | 4 F | 5 B | 6 D |

Get students to identify the problems experienced by Carole and Berry. Encourage them also to discuss any unknown vocabulary and to make guesses about probable meanings. Elicit some (not all) of the information under each of the headings in exercise 1.

3 Key

1 fled	6 shabby
2 leisurely	7 perspective
3 misgivings	8 style-conscious
4 break	9 vital
5 came to a head	10 in very good shape

4 On the board, draw a table, with the headings **word**, **type of word**, and **meaning**. Get students to complete the table with, say, ten words they have selected from the article.

Additional vocabulary:
nest (n) = where birds live, here meaning a comfortable and safe home where the children grew up
rickshaws (n) = means of transport common in some parts of the Far East consisting of a large chair on wheels pulled by a man on a bicycle
pass over (vb) = not mention, (used here ironically because the writer **does** describe what happened when his wife lost her passport)
giving up (vb) = leaving (as used here)
a rhetorical question = a question asked not for the answer, but only for dramatic effect
let (vb) = allow another person to live in your home in exchange for payment
our near and dear ones = our family and friends
pressure points = problem areas
floor space = the size of a room (here meaning a large room)
begging (vb) = asking for gifts (usually meaning gifts of money from strangers)
escapist (adj) = done in order to forget the present situation.
inoculated (vb) = given a weak form of a disease as a protection against that disease
alien (adj) = foreign or strange
a filling (n) = the material used by a dentist to fill a hole in a tooth

LISTENING 2 Page 83
Selecting an answer

Pre-activity: Focus students on the situation (customer in travel agent asking about insurance. Get the class to suggest reasons why people buy holiday insurance (in case of accidents, robbery, loss, delays, etc.). Then play the tape twice while students decide if the statements are true or false.

Key

| 1 true | 2 true | 3 false | 4 false |
| 5 false | 6 false | | |

GRAMMAR 2 Page 84
Prepositions

1 Key

| 1 by | 2 on | 3 by | 4 in |

By is used when the means of transport is mentioned without the addition of an article (a/an, the), ie in the general sense:
We came by car (not by bus).

UNIT 6 Travellers' tales

Compare this with:
We came in the new car (not in the old one).

2 Key

1 by	2 by
3 on	4 on
5 on	6 by, in
7 to, on	8 on, by

9 by, at, by, from, to, on
10 by, from, between, by (the Scilly Isles are a group of small islands off the South West coast of England)

LISTENING 3 Page 84
Directions

Pre-activity: Introduce the topic area by asking for some simple directions about how to get from the school to places nearby, or from one landmark in your town/city to another. This should elicit some examples of the three types of sentence described in the next section (Grammar) of the Student's Book: Those with imperatives, prepositions and *will*.

Get students to look at the map of a part of London and before you play the tape, ensure they have all identified Walthamstow (pronunciation: /ˈwɔːlθəmstəʊ/) Central Station, where the directions on the listening begin. After listening once, allow students to compare their answers with a partner, then check by getting students to give you the directions while you draw a sketch map on the board.

1 Key

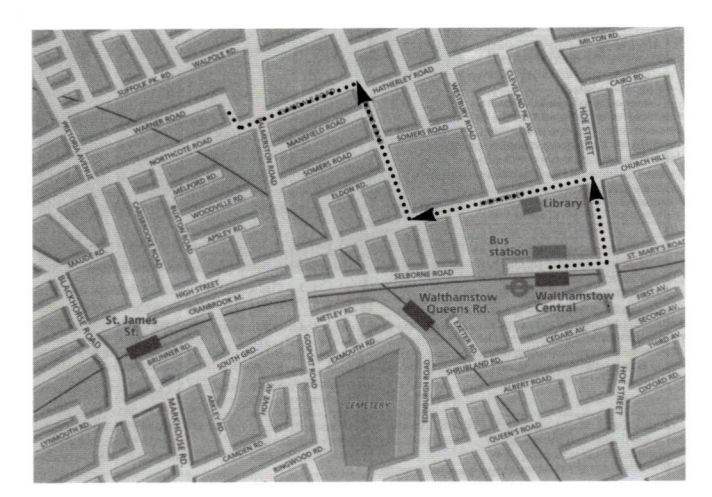

Further practice: Play the tape again and ask students to write down four of the expressions used to give directions.

This is the complete list of phrases:
turn right ... and go up a hill
you'll come to a main road ...
turn left along Hoe Street
walk as far as the High Street
turn left into the High Street
the library is on your left
keep walking ... as far as Erskine Road ...
it's the third turning on your right off the High Street
walk along Erskine Road
take the fourth turning on your left
go down Elmsdale Road
at the bottom you come to Palmerston Road
just cross it
as soon as you're in Northcote Road, turn right immediately into Warner Road

GRAMMAR 3 Page 85
Giving directions

1 When students study the language of giving directions, stress that if they follow the patterns suggested they will avoid many typical mistakes.

2 If your class are already quite good at giving directions, this activity can be completed orally with the whole class.

Key

sentences 1, 2, 3, 4 are type **1**
sentence 6 is type **2**
sentence 5 is type **3**

3 Key

1 Turn – right *at* the crossroads.
2 Walk *down* the road as far as the library.
3 Turn – left *at/into* Forest Road.
4 The shop is *opposite* the bus station.
5 My house is *in /on* Palmerston Road.
6 Go straight *on* at the traffic lights.
7 Turn – left and then – left again.
8 It's the third house *on* the left.
9 Take the third turning *on* the left.
10 At the roundabout, turn – right.

SPEAKING 3 Page 85
Exchanging information

If you feel your group needs a lot of controlled practice, both students in each pair give the two sets of directions. You can elicit some of the directions and write them on the board and/or get students to write one of the sets of directions when they have completed the oral practice.

Travellers' tales **UNIT 6**

WRITING 2 Page 85
Informal letters

Pre-activity: Establish with the class what arrival points there are in your town or city for someone travelling in by public transport. Ask students to select one of the arrival points and, before they begin writing, get students to tell a partner about the friend they are writing to, the arrival point they have selected and what reason they will give for not meeting the friend. Finally remind the class that this is an informal letter and therefore it must follow the pattern described in Unit 3 page 42.

LISTENING 4 Page 85
Note-taking

Pre-activity: Before you play the tape ask students to look at the notepad and tell you what type of information is required in each space:
Gianna arrives at (name of airport) airport on flight number (a number) from (a city or country) at (a time) on (a day or date).
Tell the class that Gianna and Angelo are flying to London and, if possible, elicit the names of the three London airports (Heathrow, Gatwick and Stansted). Then brainstorm some names of Italian cities and make sure that Florence and Pisa are both mentioned.

Key

1 Gianna arrives at *Stansted* airport on flight number *UK 927* from *Florence* at *1520* on *Thursday*.
2 Angelo arrives at *Heathrow* airport on flight number *BA603* from *Pisa* at *1640* on *Thursday*.
3 Gianna's fax number is *01039 2 8934617*.

GRAMMAR 4 Page 86 (GR p 218)
Future Time 1

1 Key

Gianna is talking about future actions but uses the Present tense because she is referring to a timetable – something to which she must conform because she cannot change it.

2 Key

1 right
2 wrong
3 right
4 right
5 right
6 right
7 wrong
8 right (a leap year = a year which includes 29th February)
9 right
10 wrong

3 Ask students to compare:
I'm *going to do* some shopping after school.
School *finishes* at four o'clock this afternoon.
The shops *are* open until late this evening.
I'm *meeting* Tim at seven o'clock and going to the theatre.
The play *starts* at seven-thirty.

Key

Either *going to* or *-ing* are possible. The difference is that:
going to is used to express personal intention – when we have already decided to do something, but have made no definite arrangements.
-ing is used to talk about arrangements – when we have planned an event in detail, usually with other people (eg fixed a time, bought tickets, etc.)

4 Key

sentences 2, 4 ,6, 7 and 10 express arrangements (with *-ing*)
sentences 1, 3 , 5, 8 and 9 express intention (with *going to*)

5 Key

1 am coming   4 is meeting
2 arrives   5 are eating/are going to eat
3 am staying   6 am going to visit

READING 4 Page 87
Gapped text

1 The activities shown in the photographs are: hang gliding, flying a microlight aircraft, parachuting and ballooning.

2 Key

| 1 E | 2 A | 3 B | 4 H | 5 D | 6 C | 7 G |

3 Key

1 ambition   2 full of anticipation
3 adjacent   4 previously
5 whatsoever   6 rapidly
7 essential   8 roared
9 unique

4 Key

| 1 C | 2 B | 3 D | 4 A |

GRAMMAR 5 Page 88 (GR p 219)
So/Such that

1 Key

The words are all adjectives.

UNIT 6 Travellers' tales

2 Key

Each adjective is followed by a noun.

3 Key

Both are used with *that* to provide a link with resulting actions but *so* is used with adjectives and *such* with adjective and noun combinations.

4 Key

1. about to
2. so cold that
3. happened to meet
4. such a quiet voice
5. is supposed to arrive
6. such a rude man
7. am keen to
8. was so dirty
9. about to leave
10. (really) looking forward to going

HELP WITH GAP FILLING Page 89

1 Key

By looking at the context, not just the words which come immediately before and after the gap, but the whole sentence or paragraph or the whole passage.

2 Key

a verb	sleeps, walked
a noun	pencil, happiness
an adjective	green, quick
an adverb	slowly, usually
a preposition	into, such, behind
an article	the, an
a pronoun	myself, whose
one other type of word	and (conjunction)

3 Key

Type of word	Answer
2 pronoun	her
3 noun	scarf
4 conjunction	and
5 article	a
6 pronoun	us
7 adverb	carefully
8 adverb (frequency)	never
9 preposition	under
10 adjective	lovely

4 Key

Type of word	Answer
1 infinitive	to
2 article	the
3 preposition	by
4 modal	will
5 preposition	in
6 pronoun	There
7 noun	lots
8 pronoun	its

9 pronoun   which
10 adjective   best

EXAM PRACTICE 6 Page 90

1 Key

1 own	2 are	3 to
4 as, since, because	5 can	6 who
7 making	8 long	9 in, during
10 from	11 its	12 before
13 main, annual	14 out	15 up

2 Key

1 up	2 can	3 much
4 get	5 the	6 it
7 so	8 ✓	9 on
10 ✓	11 down	12 now
13 ✓	14 you	15 ✓

3 Key

1 helping	2 arrived	3 specialise
4 representatives	5 solution	6 traveller
7 package	8 flight	9 choice
10 additional		

REVISION TEST 3

1 Key

1 C	2 D	3 A	4 B	5 C	6 D
7 A	8 D	9 B	10 A	11 B	12 D
13 A	14 C	15 C			

2 Key

1 for	2 that	3 most	4 take
5 go/try	6 while	7 an	8 others/some
9 order	10 them	11 look	12 there
13 have	14 up	15 give	

3 Key

1. despite the fact that
2. drinking our coffee we left
3. a five-hour
4. met Louise by chance
5. is supposed to arrive
6. can't wait to see
7. used to be
8. although there was/had been
9. first time I've played
10. might have been left

4 Key

1 if	2 in	3 ✓	4 with
5 of	6 have	7 not	8 ✓
9 the	10 it	11 ✓	12 time
13 what	14 out	15 come	

REVISION TEST 3

1 Read the text below and decide which word A, B, C or D best fits each space.

Write On

Beautiful handwriting (or calligraphy) is within everyone's (0) __A__. With a few basic tools, and even fewer basic techniques, you can (1) _____ everyday writing into something really rather beautiful.

Ever since the ancient Egyptians first developed a system of symbols for writing (2) _____ words, calligraphy has been one of the our simplest and most beautiful art (3) _____ . The continued popularity of calligraphy is not (4) _____ to understand. Almost everyone learns how to write as a child, and calligraphy is (5) _____ a way of making your writing more beautiful.

With care, attention, and just a little practice you can (6) _____ the different styles and give your letters real elegance. Beginners will find that in a relatively (7) _____ space of time they can (8) _____ invitations, greeting cards and a host of other items.

But perhaps the (9) _____ reason for the popularity of calligraphy is how easy it is to get (10) _____ . Besides paper and a good flat surface on which to work, the only tools you really (11) _____ are ink and a (12) _____ pen. If you're looking (13) _____ a hobby that's not only cheap and practical, but will also (14) _____ lovely gifts for family and friends, then why not (15) _____ out more about calligraphy?

0	A grasp	B hold	C grip	D hand
1	A switch	B swap	C turn	D exchange
2	A along	B across	C through	D down
3	A forms	B types	C ways	D manners
4	A tough	B hard	C strong	D heavy
5	A easily	B directly	C simply	D readily
6	A conquer	B defeat	C overcome	D master
7	A short	B slow	C small	D slight
8	A project	B propose	C progress	D produce
9	A grand	B main	C large	D full
10	A started	B set	C off	D away
11	A refer	B require	C request	D rely
12	A singular	B peculiar	C unique	D special
13	A for	B after	C out	D over
14	A display	B perform	C provide	D distribute
15	A look	B bring	C find	D carry

2 Fill each of the numbered blanks in the following passage. Use only one word in each space.

Gone Fishing

At this very moment, all (0) *over* the world, thousands of people are just waiting (1) _____ work or school to finish so (2) _____ they can head for favourite spots on riverbank, seashore or bobbing boat.

Fishing is, in fact, the world's (3) _____ popular sport and, of course, it can (4) _____ many different forms – children with bamboo sticks can (5) _____ fishing in the local stream, (6) _____ more experienced sports people may prefer fly-fishing for trout in highland rivers or big-game fishing in the open ocean. For some, it's (7) _____ exciting sport, something to set the heart racing, while for (8) _____ it's pure relaxation. Many people fish in (9) _____ to wind down after a hard week of work or study and for (10) _____ actually catching fish is not the most important aspect of the sport. Others (11) _____ forward to going home with the makings of a meal, and many people would argue that (12) _____ is nothing more delicious to eat than fresh fish you (13) _____ caught yourself.

If you are interested in taking (14) _____ fishing there is no shortage of helpful books to read which will (15) _____ you good advice about when and where to begin and the equipment you will need.

© Nick Kenny 1996 Published by Heinemann English Language Teaching. This page may be photocopied and used within the class.

REVISION TEST 3

3 Complete the second sentence so that it has a similar meaning to the first sentence. Use the word given and other words to complete each sentence. You must use between two and five words. Do not change the word given.

1 Although it was sunny, I felt quite cold.
   fact
   I felt quite cold _____ it was sunny.

2 We drank our coffee before leaving the bar.
   left
   After _____ the bar.

3 The match lasted five hours.
   a
   It was _____ match.

4 I happened to meet Louise at the bus stop.
   chance
   I _____ at the bus stop.

5 The train should arrive in ten minutes.
   supposed
   The train _____ in ten minutes.

6 I'm really looking forward to seeing his new film.
   wait
   I _____ his new film.

7 Originally, skis were made of wood.
   used
   Skis _____ made of wood.

8 We left on time in spite of the heavy snowfall.
   although
   We left on time _____ a heavy snowfall.

9 I haven't played Scrabble before.
   time
   It's the _____ Scrabble.

10 It's possible that the doors were left unlocked.
   might
   The doors _____ unlocked.

4 Read this letter and look carefully at each line. Some of the lines are correct and some have a word which should not be there. If a line is correct put a tick (✓). If the line has a word which should not be there, write down the word. There are two example lines at the beginning.

A holiday which went wrong

Going on holiday with a large group of them people is	0	*them*
not an experience I would like to repeat. I wanted a	00	✓
relaxing two weeks in the country and if the arrangements	1	....
some friends had made seemed fine. There were in eight of	2	....
us altogether staying in a farmhouse in the middle of nowhere.	3	....
I only knew two of the group well, but as with everyone knew	4	....
someone, I thought we would get along.		
I was wrong. For a start, there was only one of car between	5	....
us, so if we went anywhere, three people have had to stay	6	....
behind and there was not nothing to do in the farmhouse	7	....
except sitting about reading. No one minded if Tom went out	8	....
on our day trips because it was his car, but the his girlfriend	9	....
never offered to give it up her seat. She always wanted her	10	....
own way. In the middle of a beautiful old city, she was only	11	....
interested in shopping. In the farmhouse time and in the car,	12	....
we always had to listen to the music what she wanted. When	13	....
we looked for something else to put on, we found out our	14	....
tapes hidden down the back of the sofa. By come the end of	15	....
the holiday I knew I never wanted to see her again.		

UNIT 7

Food for thought

TOPIC	HELP SECTION	Multiple matching
Food, drink and cooking	Help with talking about a picture	Selecting an answer
VOCABULARY FOCUS	**EXAM FOCUS**	**Paper 5**
Food	**Paper 1**	Talking about photographs
Cooking words	Multiple choice	Expressing opinions
Menus	Reading for specific information	Expressing preferences
	Multiple matching	Problem solving
LANGUAGE FOCUS	**Paper 2**	**EXAM PRACTICE**
Gerund/Infinitive	Paragraph writing	Open cloze
Too/Enough	Writing an article	Key word transformations
Zero/First conditionals	**Paper 3**	Descriptive composition
Preferences	Cloze text	Discursive writing
If/Unless	Error correction	Word formation
Future time 2: Intentions, arrangements, decisions	**Paper 4**	
Relative clauses	Multiple choice	
Comparisons	Short extracts	
Pronunciation: Vowel sounds	Listening for specific information	

SPEAKING 1 Page 92
Talking about photographs

Pre-activity: Ask your class to think about a meal which they particularly remember. Tell them to think about the food, the people they were with, the place, and why they remember this particular meal so well. Ask a few people to describe the scene they are thinking about. This will activate some food, eating and restaurant vocabulary.

1 Focus students on the three pictures and ask them to talk about the discussion points with a partner. When they have had an opportunity to talk about the pictures, ask for some sample opinions from the class. Encourage students to speculate and use their imagination if they feel that the answers are not clear from the pictures.

2.1 The discussion on types of food will obviously depend partly on the age of your students, but they should at least be able to talk about the food of their home country, and will probably have ideas about food in Britain and the USA.

2.2 If your class are not particularly interested in the topic, do not allow the discussion to go on very long. If necessary, concentrate the discussion on what is good or bad about the food of each country mentioned.

READING 1 Page 93
Reading for specific information

Pre-activity: Continue the previous discussion, when students have established what they think are the bad aspects of the food of different countries, and how things could be improved. Refer students to the article about improving the British diet, and get them to name the foods illustrated. Which of these foods are recommended and which should be avoided? (fibre – toast or bread – is recommended, fat, salt and sugar should be avoided).

1 Get students to read Part One of the article and decide in pairs if the advice is relevant to people in their countries.

2 Key 🔑

1 single   6 build up
2 supply   7 unnoticeably
3 narrower   8 affect
4 eventually   9 lower
5 blocked

Additional vocabulary:
cholesterol (n) = chemical which causes arteries to become blocked

54

blood vessels = arteries
saturated fat = a type of fat which is particularly damaging to arteries
pulses (n) = seeds which you can eat (eg peas, beans)

3 This discussion activity is about student's own eating habits. Introduce it by asking if your students think they eat too much salt and sugar at the moment.

4 Divide students into pairs, Student A and Student B. Before they start to read the separate parts of the article, tell them to make brief notes in answer to the questions to help them remember the answers later. After they have read, made notes on and then explained their half of the article to their partner, quickly go through the answers to the questions in each section.

Key

Part Two **Sugar**
1 You are less likely to become obese, which means less risk of heart disease.
2 Drink unsweetened tea and coffee.
Eat fresh fruit or natural canned fruit for dessert.
Eat fewer sweets, chocolates and biscuits.
Use less sugar in cooking.
Avoid foods which contain a lot of sugar.

Additional vocabulary:
obese (adj) = very overweight
all too easy = very easy (with a negative sense)
cut down = reduce the quantity
tend to (vb) = have the habit of
syrup = fruit juice with added sugar
go easy = do not eat a lot
meringues (n) = a dessert made from egg whites and sugar, cooked in the oven

Part Three **Salt**
1 Reduces blood pressure which causes heart disease.
2 Use less salt in cooking and measure your salt.
Use other food flavourings instead of salt.
Do not use salt at the table.
Eat fewer salty snacks.
Do not eat canned or packet soups.

Additional vocabulary:
not nearly as much = much less than
in turn = in succession
high in salt = contain a lot of salt

5 Students write about either sugar or salt (the part which they have studied), using only the notes which they made in the previous activity.

GRAMMAR 1 Page 94 (GR p 219)
Gerund/Infinitive

There is no easy way to learn which verbs are followed by a gerund and which by an infinitive. Encourage students to keep a list of examples they come across when reading and listening.
Refer them to the Grammar Reference section on page 219.
Remind students that there are four possibilities:
infinitive only (eg I want to go …)
gerund only (eg I enjoy reading)
both possible – same meaning (eg I like to go shopping/I like going shopping)
both possible – different meaning (eg he stopped eating ice cream/He stopped to eat an ice cream.)
Also remind students not to confuse *it needs doing* with *need to do it*. Point out that *needs doing* is a special form (see page 34). In most other sentences *need* is followed by the infinitive. *Need* can also be used as a modal verb, often in the negative (eg *I needn't go*, see page 155).

Key

1 reading   6 going
2 to go   7 to go
3 to reduce   8 to give up
4 to cut down   9 to become
5 changing   10 buying

LISTENING 1 Page 95
Multiple choice

Pre-activity: Ask students to remind you about some of the comments they made about British or US food in the first part of this unit. Elicit *junk food* by asking 'What is the name for food like hamburgers, crisps and sweets?'. Hamburgers are often called 'fast food', but junk food can be used for all three (junk = rubbish). Junk food is popular in Britain and some other countries. Do your students have junk food in their country or countries? What type of junk foods are popular? Are they becoming more or less popular? Why?

Key

1 C   2 B   3 B   4 A   5 C

GRAMMAR 2 Page 95 (GR p 219)
Too/Enough

1 Key

Too is used before adjectives to talk about an excess – more than is desirable or required.
Enough is used before nouns or after adjectives to talk about the correct amount or quality.

UNIT 7 *Food for thought*

2 Key

1 haven't been cooked
2 is too much oil on
3 isn't fresh enough
4 costs too much
5 isn't enough cheese
6 haven't got / don't have enough glasses
7 too cold to eat outside
8 too quietly
9 isn't sweet enough
10 too few people in this (NB *aren't enough people in this* is a correct transformation, but not an acceptable answer because it contains six words rather than five. Remind your students that contractions are counted as two words, and that they should check their answers carefully to make sure they use a maximum of five words including the word given.)

READING 2 Page 96
Multiple choice

Pre-activity: Write *Salmonella* and *Listeria* on the board and ask students what they know about these. (Types of bacteria which cause food poisoning.) Ask students to suggest ways of avoiding food poisoning. (eg Handle food carefully, make sure that salad and other raw foods are carefully washed, cook food thoroughly, keep food either very hot or very cold.) Then refer students to the text and get them to answer the multiple-choice questions. Once they have selected their answers, get students to compare with a partner before checking with the whole class.

Key

1 B 2 C 3 D 4 A 5 B

LISTENING 2 Page 97
Instructions

Pre-activity: Either ask students to name their favourite dish and then you select one of these, which will probably include some of the processes listed in the box, **or** ask students how they make an omelette. In each case as they describe each step they will probably require additional vocabulary to help the description. As you provide this write it on the board, dividing it into verbs and nouns. For an omelette the steps might include: beat (the eggs), melt (some butter), pour (the eggs into the pan), fry (the omelette).

1 Refer students to the verbs in the box and ask them to divide the words into the four groups.

Key

Cutting	Mixing	Heating	Other
mince	stir	grill	pour
slice	add	boil	knead
chop	beat	fry	
peel		melt	
carve		roast	
shred		bake	
dice		simmer	
grate			

2 Vary the time spent on this activity depending on how interested your students are in cooking.

3 Ask students to read through the instructions (which are not in the correct order), and decide on the total number of different ingredients mentioned in the recipe (there are seven). If necessary get them to list the ingredients until the correct answer is clear. Ask students which picture matches the recipe (the recipe is for a chocolate cake cut into squares each with a nut on top – picture 5).

Students then listen to the tape and decide on the correct order for the instructions. If they are really keen on cooking they may be able to attempt the ordering before they listen, and then listen to check. After they listen the first time get them to check their answers so far with a partner – this is particularly useful in a listening exercise of this type where if students made one mistake it may lead them to make others.

Key

The correct order is:
1f, 2m, 3c, 4j, 5a, 6h, 7e, 8l, 9g, 10i, 11n, 12d, 13k, 14b

4 If all your students are of the same nationality, you may want to decide together on a suitable national dish which they can describe. The class then work in pairs to complete the writing task. Otherwise encourage students to select a typical dish, and write about it for homework.

GRAMMAR 3 Page 98 (GR p 219)
Conditionals 1

1 Key

1 The tenses used are all either Present simple or Future with *will*.
2 The sentences which have the Present simple in both the *if* clause and the main clause talk about something which has no specific time but is always true in the past, now and in the future – it is a general truth.
The sentences which use *will* in the main clause refer to a specific situation in the future.

56

Food for thought **UNIT 7**

2 Get students to complete this and the following exercise in pairs so that they can discuss their choice of answers.

Key

1 get up	2 eat	3 will stay
4 will phone	5 becomes	6 will become
7 get	8 will get	9 eat
10 melts	11 will melt	12 save

3 Key

1 both forms are possible (always, or tonight)
2 only 'eat' is possible (the speaker is not on holiday at the moment)
3 only 'will' is possible ('tomorrow' is a real future)
4 only 'will' is possible (a real situation, the speaker is waiting for a letter)
5 both forms are possible (always, or the pasta cooking at the moment)
6 only 'will' is possible (a real situation – the pasta cooking at the moment)
7 both forms are possible (always, or the fruit I have the chance to eat now)
8 only 'will' is possible (a real situation – the fruit I have the chance to eat now)
9 both forms are possible (always, or breakfast this morning)
10 both forms are possible (always, or today because the weather is hot)
11 only 'will' is possible (the ice cream in the fridge at the moment)
12 both forms are possible (always, or this year because vegetables are particularly expensive)

4 Refer students to the magazine advertisements and ask where they are from originally. Point out that in this activity the class is organising a meal in a restaurant, and ask which type of conditional sentence is most appropriate: Zero conditional or *will*. They should be able to explain that *will* is suitable because they are talking about a specific event.

Additional vocabulary:
Yeoman of the Guard = guards at the Tower of London (also called 'Beefeaters')
carvery = a self-service buffet with large pieces of roast meat

SPEAKING 2 Page 99
Expressing opinions

Students will now have a good idea of what the different restaurants offer. Tell the class that each student will have extra information which they must use in the discussion. Divide the class into groups of four, A–D. Before they begin this activity refer them to the **Preferences** box and remind them that:

prefer + *-ing* is used to talk about what we prefer in general (*prefer* + *infinitive* is also possible)
would prefer + *infinitive* and *would rather* + *infinitive* are used to talk about what we want to do in a specific situation.
Now tell them to look at the information A, B, C or D. As a follow-up ask students to tell you some of the things that were said during their group discussion (to focus again on the language of preferences), and to give you their group decision on which restaurant was selected and why.

WRITING Page 99
Giving reasons

Students complete the paragraphs individually in class or for homework. Any reasonable answer making use of the information provided is acceptable. Make it clear before they begin writing whether you want students to step outside the roles A-D which they had during the discussion and write only their personal opinions.

LISTENING 3 Page 100
Multiple matching

Play the tape once, get students to compare their answers with a partner, then play the tape again to check.

Key

1 C	2 E	3 D	4 B	5 A

GRAMMAR 4 Page 100 (GR p 219)
If/Unless

1 Refer students to the *if* and *unless* example sentences and ask 'Who does *they* refer to?' (the people working in the restaurant).

Key

Unless + *affirmative* is the same as *if* + *negative*.
Demonstrate this by writing the two example sentences on the board and asking students to exchange *if* and *unless* in each sentence, plus make the other necessary changes:
Unless the owner is Spanish, they *won't* serve traditional Spanish food.
If the owner is Italian, they*'ll* serve traditional Italian food.

2 Key

1 If	2 If	3 Unless	4 If	5 If

UNIT 7 Food for thought

3 Key

1 if we don't
2 unless he studies
3 unless you follow
4 if you haven't got/if you don't have
5 if I don't have
6 unless it

LISTENING 4 Page 100
Listening for specific information

Pre-activity: Before they discuss the vocabulary with a partner, ask students to quickly look through the menu and note anything they are unsure about.

1 Avoid giving detailed explanations of the different foods – just mention the main ingredients to give an idea of what the dish is like. If students are particularly interested, either get them to explain to each other what the different dishes are, or ask them to check the details and to report back in the next lesson.

2 Before students listen to the tape tell them that they will hear a conversation in a restaurant where a couple are ordering a meal. Warn them that the couple discuss the food, ask the waiter about it and might change their minds about what they want. Students have to listen and circle **only** the food chosen, and not all the food mentioned in the conversation.

Key

The food ordered is: orange juice, Highland mineral water, Unlimited salad, Sole with French fries (chips), half a carafe of red wine.

3 Before playing the tape again ask students if they remember what the waiter's questions were when he came to take the order. Elicit corrections where necessary and write all the possibilities on the board. Ask the class to listen and decide which is the correct first question as well as write down the other questions which the waiter asks. Emphasise that they are to listen for the questions when the waiter takes the order, not when the couple first come into the restaurant.

Key

The waiter's questions are:
Are you ready to order now?
Would you like a small mixed salad, or would you rather have an Unlimited Salad?
And for you madam?
Would you like rice or French fries?
Would you like anything else to drink?

Check the answers by getting students to tell you some of their questions or write them on the board.

SPEAKING 3 Page 101
Expressing attitudes and opinions

1 Divide the class into groups of three. Tell them that they will take it in turns to be the waiter and the customers in the restaurant. Remind students before they begin that the waiter should try to use some of the phrases on the board, and establish the type of language which the customers use to indicate their choices (eg I think I'll have ..., Can I have ..., I'd rather have ...).

2 Tell students to look very quickly at the advertisement for Simon's restaurant and ask them what in particular it is advertising (a special discount). Then ask them to read the whole advert and say why the number **12** is significant (the discount is 12% and the minimum number of people is 12). Before students plan their own Mini-menus, ask them these comprehension questions:

What is the name of the special offer? (Mini-menu)
If we all go together can we get a discount? (depends on number of people present)
Can we go tomorrow? (no, you have to book three days in advance)
What must you tell the restaurant when you book? (which dishes you want on the Mini-menu)
How many dishes can you have? (choose from 2 starters, 3 main courses, 2 desserts)
Do we have to go in the evening? (no, for lunch or dinner)

Ask for suggestions about what factors your students need to consider if they are selecting a Mini-menu for the whole class and not just themselves (eg popular/unpopular foods, fish and meat, vegetarians, people on special diets, etc.).
Point out that this is another opportunity for practising the preferences language from earlier in the unit.
Conclude the activity by asking what the most popular dishes were.

GRAMMAR 5 Page 102 (GR p 220)
Future time 2

1 Establish that the people on the tape said these sentences because they were making decisions and that the *will* form is used when we make a decision and speak at the same moment. Point out that *will* is also used when we make promises and offers.

2 Go through the grammatical forms which express each idea, and build up a chart on the board for students to copy:

Pattern	Meaning	Form
I'm going to do (= intention)	already decided	Going to
I'm doing (= arrangement)	already arranged	Present continuous
I'll do	decision now offer now promise now	Will

3 Key

1 is coming (probably arranged)
2 I'll do (offer)
3 is coming (arrangement)
4 am going to look (intention)
5 we'll have (decision)
6 I'll do it (promise)
7 are you leaving (arrangement)
   I'm getting, flying (arrangement)
   is (timetable) leaves, stops, takes (timetable)
   I'll give (offer)
8 I'm giving (arrangement)
9 won't forget (promise)

HELP WITH TALKING ABOUT A PICTURE Page 103

This section is designed to help students develop the skills they will need in the second part of the Speaking test. They will have to compare and contrast two photographs.

Although they are not required to describe each of the photographs in detail, they will need to feel confident about the type of language needed to talk about a photograph, as well as the language of comparisons and contrasts.

Initially, students look at one photograph, in order to concentrate on the language of speculative description in the box at the bottom of the page. Students sometimes have problems in deciding what features of the photograph to focus on and how to develop their ideas. Questions 1–4 will help them.

Question 2 gets students to look at different photographs and then tell each other what they have found. As in the exam, the student who is listening should be prepared to make a comment at the end of his/her partner's turn. Questions 3–5 focus on the language of comparison and contrast that will be useful in the exam and then lead on to an exam-type task which brings together all the skills practised in this section.

For further practice, find more pairs of photos cut from magazines or newspapers, or refer the students to the pictures on page 104.

LISTENING 5 Page 104
Selecting an answer

Introduce the listening text by telling students that they are going to listen to a discussion between an interviewer and the director of a chain of more than 100 roadside restaurants. Give the students a few minutes to read the sentences, then play the tape twice and get students to write T (true) or F (false) next to each sentence.

Key

1 true   2 false   3 false   4 false
5 false   6 true   7 false

READING 3 Page 104
Multiple matching

1 **Pre-activity:** Use the discussion topics to introduce the subject of chocolate. Get pairs of students to report their discussions to the other people in the class.

2 Stress that students should complete this task quickly – they are not expected to read the article in great detail at this stage, but should discuss and justify their answers with a partner before checking with the whole class.

Key

1 225 grams (para 0)
2 sugar addiction (para 1)
3 to let more people understand what true chocolate is really about (para 3) and draw the public's attention to ... (para 4)
4 blind tastings, teach-ins, newsletter information and samples (para 4)
5 the principal ingredient of commercial 'chocolate' is not cocoa ... but sugar (para 4)

3 Key

1 B   2 D   3 A   4 C   5 F

4 Key

A

5 Possible answers

1 Chocoholics are people who claim to be addicted to chocolate.
2 Wrappers are the pieces of paper which are put around chocolate before it is sold.
3 Mayans and Aztecs were ancient civilisations which made chocolate.
4 A newsletter consists of one or more sheets of paper giving information about the activities of a particular group or organisation.
5 Gourmets are people who are experts on good food.
6 Powdered milk is milk which is in dried form.
7 True chocolate is chocolate which has a higher proportion of cocoa solids in it.

UNIT 7 Food for thought

GRAMMAR 6 Page 106 (GR p 220)
Relative clauses

1 Key

The information in the first sentence, *the boy who eats a lot of chocolate*, describes the subject *Ron* and forms a defining relative clause. There is no punctuation around the clause. The information in the second sentence, *who eats a lot of chocolate*, is extra information and is a non-defining relative clause. It has a comma before and after it.

2 Key

1. Chantal Coady is the person who runs Rococo Chocolate in London.
   (defining relative clause)
2. Commercial chocolate, which the British eat in huge quantities, is made with lots of sugar.
   (extra information – a non-defining relative clause)
3. The Chocolate Society, which is being launched next week, aims to inform people about real chocolate.
   (extra information – a non-defining relative clause)
4. Chocolate is a delicacy which has been known to civilisation since the Aztecs.
   (defining relative clause)
5. Rococo, which is in central London, is a shop which does not sell commercial chocolate.
   (extra information – a non-defining relative clause)
6. Some people who eat too much chocolate call themselves chocoholics.
   (defining relative clause)

PRONUNCIATION Page 106
Vowel sounds 2

Read out a few examples and ask students to tell you which column they belong to before getting students to complete their answers in pairs or groups of three.

Key

/eɪ/	/iː/	/ɪ/	/aɪ/	/e/	/ɑː/	/æ/	/ʌ/
state	eat	it	hide	let	are	man	but
plain	each	which	quite	them	dark	can	young
claim	need	give	might	says	can't	gap	much
say	week	thing	guide	any	heart	fat	love
	real				past	lack	

EXAM PRACTICE 7 Page 107

1 Key

1 are	2 from	3 did	4 who
5 to	6 make	7 did	8 some
9 about	10 later	11 out	12 still
13 be	14 but	15 fact	

2 Key

1. enjoy reading
2. weren't hot enough
3. have never eaten
4. is lucky she will
5. did you become
6. avoid frying food
7. would rather go to
8. miss breakfast, I always get
9. not as expensive
10. unless you boil the

4 Key P108 sh bk

1 found	6 lost
2 shopping	7 Assistant
3 breaking	8 filling
4 hidden	9 probably
5 nobody	10 suggestions

UNIT 8

Hi-tech horizons

TOPIC
Technology and Inventions

VOCABULARY FOCUS
Inventions and discoveries
Verbs to describe a process
Word formation – nouns from verbs

LANGUAGE FOCUS
Passive
Agents
Predictions – *Will /Going to*
Expressing opinions
Agreeing and disagreeing: *So/Nor*
Conditionals 2
Pronunciation: /h/

HELP SECTIONS
Help with gapped texts
Help with word formation 2
Help with writing – giving opinions

EXAM FOCUS
Paper 1
Reading for specific information
Gapped text
Multiple matching
Reading for main points
Paper 2
Writing a report
Paper 3
Key word transformations

Paper 4
Matching information
Blank filling
Note-taking
Multiple choice
Short extracts
Paper 5
Talking about photographs
Expressing opinions

EXAM PRACTICE
Discursive article
Multiple-choice cloze
Error correction
Word formation

SPEAKING 1 Page 109
Talking about photographs

Stress to students that when they talk about photographs in the FCE examination they are not expected to know very specific or technical vocabulary. The photographs are a stimulus to conversation, and a general description of the content of the picture is sufficient. Also encourage students to speculate about what they can see – there is no 'right' answer in this part of the exam.

Before students talk about these pictures you may wish to give them a demonstration of what is required by finding two large pictures from magazines or newspapers and talking about them yourself while the class listen. For this purpose, photos which can be linked directly to a discussion theme are better than pictures of famous people or advertisements. You should concentrate on comparing the picures and talk for about a minute. This may include the main action of the photographs as well as the setting and what can be seen in different parts of the pictures. You will probably want to to talk about how the people in the two pictures feel. Remember that the emphasis in the exam is on comparing the pictures rather than simple description. Avoid over-training students in the language of description as this can make them speak mechanically 'parrot fashion' in the exam.

Students talk about and compare their photos with a partner while you circulate, noting particularly good expressions and approaches and also where improvements are possible. Give feedback to the class afterwards. If you want to draw attention to some weaknesses, concentrate on unsuitable approaches to the task (eg describing one photo without attempting to compare it with the second picture), and learnable, generalisable language errors (eg prepositions).

HELP WITH GAPPED TEXTS Page 110

There is a gapped text type of reading task in each version of the FCE Reading test. It is always the third task on the question paper. This type of task requires the student to look at the text very carefully in order to decide where to insert a number of sentences or paragraphs which have been removed from the text. For more information on this type of question, see page vi.

This Help section is designed to prepare students for the gapped text task, increase their awareness of the skills required to complete the task successfully and give some controlled practice. Questions 1 and 2 introduce the topic (CDs and vinyl LPs), and give students a chance to activate some relevant vocabulary before they start to read. Question 3 highlights the type of strategy and decisions which students need to make to complete this type of reading task, question 4 is similar to the exam activity,

UNIT 8 Hi-tech horizons

and the remaining questions exploit the text further and reinforce the the correct approach to this type of task.

3 Key

1. This is not referred to within the sentence. It is necessary to look earlier in the text (perhaps at the previous sentence) to discover what it refers to.
2. Probably before the instructions, since By *following some ...* suggests that the instructions have not yet been given.
3. Something unfortunate or bad which can happen.
4. Something which contrasts with information given in the sentence beginning *But*.
5. LPs.
6. Earlier in the text. Perhaps in the previous sentence.

4 Key

1 B   2 E   3 A   4 G   5 D   6 C   7 I

6 Key

1. making things – manufacture
   correctly – accurately
   read badly – misread
   very small – tiny
   a little bit – slightly
   cannot be played – unplayable
   strangely – mysteriously
   loading again – reloading
   behaves badly – misbehaves
   making a disc – pressing

2. mis – incorrectly or badly
   un – negative
   re – again

3. a   the CD player
   b   the disc / the disc
   c   a CD player
   d   the replacement disc / the fault
   e   a vinyl LP

LISTENING 1 Page 112
The passive

Pre-activity: Ask students – Do you eat pizzas? Where? What is your favourite type? Do you ever make pizzas? How do you do it?
This will elicit some basic vocabulary. If necessary pre-teach *dough* by asking students what the word is for the pizza base before it is cooked (the same word is used in bread-making).
Note that *pizza* can be either countable (plural: *pizzas*) or uncountable in English.

Part One

1. Give students a minute or so to look at the passage before they listen to Part One. For some gaps they can predict the type of answer (eg numbers). Warn students that the listening is quite fast, and they will need to write quickly and be ready to move on to the next answer.

   Key

   1 two million
   2 frozen
   3 chilled
   4 snack
   5 75
   6 nutritious/convenient
   7 convenient/nutritious

2. The passive, formed with part of the verb *to be* and the past participle of the active verb.
   It is used because we do not know (and perhaps are not interested in) who actually makes the pizzas.

3. The completed grid is a useful reference for students. However, it can be confusing to be faced with so many forms at the same time, so get students to fill in the missing information in pairs.

   Key

	Active	**Passive**
Present simple	someone makes the pizza	the pizza is made
Present continuous	someone is making the pizza	the pizza is being made
Present perfect	someone has made the pizza	the pizza has been made
Past simple	someone made the pizza	the pizza was made
Past continuous	someone was making the pizza	the pizza was being made
Past perfect	someone had made the pizza	the pizza had been made
Going to	someone is going to make the pizza	the pizza is going to be made
Will	someone will make the pizza	the pizza will be made
Must	someone must make the pizza	the pizza must be made
Have to	someone has to make the pizza	the pizza has to be made

Part Two

2. Get students to complete the sequencing exercise in pairs and with dictionaries if possible.
   Students now listen to Part Two to check their answers.

Hi-tech horizons UNIT 8

Key

A – mixed	B – rolled	C – stamped
D – cooked	E – coated	F – assembled
G – wrapped	H – frozen	I – delivered

3 Key

1 – dough being mixed
2 – toppings being assembled by hand
3 – pizzas being delivered
4 – bases being cooked

4 Tell students that as they listen they must make brief notes around each of the words in the boxes A–I. They will not have time to write complete sentences during the listening.

Key

the dough is mixed
the dough is rolled
the pizza bases are stamped out
the base is cooked
the pizzas are coated with tomato and cheese
the toppings are assembled by hand
the pizzas are wrapped
then they are frozen
and delivered in freezer lorries to the shops

5 Key

1 is being
2 has to be switched on
3 was caused by
4 will be met
5 are being changed by
6 must be kept at
7 are frozen in
8 are going to be eaten
9 are put in boxes
10 can be bought

SPEAKING 2 Page 114
Expressing and justifying opinions

Pre-activity: Ask a few 'wh' questions formed from the quiz sentences – select the questions depending on the interest of your group.
eg Who invented the telephone? When?
Where was the first McDonald's opened? When?
If students are not absolutely sure of the answers, encourage them to make use of the phrases in the box. Do not accept or reject the answers you are offered, but refer students to the quiz and get them to complete it in pairs or groups of three. Students need to work together on this activity so that they can share their general knowledge – also it's more fun!

Key

1 – e	5 – p	9 – c	13 – h
2 – g	6 – b	10 – m	14 – i
3 – o	7 – f	11 – d	15 – k
4 – a	8 – l	12 – n	16 – j

GRAMMAR 1 Page 115 (GR p 220)
Agents

1.1 Write a passive sentence from the pizza listening on the board as a focus for this discussion:
eg The toppings are assembled by hand.
The passive is used to describe a process, or when we do not know who or what did the action (maybe who did it is not important, or we do not want to say). Ask students how the person who did the action or the thing which caused it is introduced in some passive sentences (using *by*).

1.2 Although the use of the passive indicates that we want to focus on the action, the person or cause can also be important here, and is sometimes included using *by*.
eg The letter was delivered (by the postman).
The letter is more interesting/important than the postman, who may be omitted. This can be contrasted with:
eg The letter was delivered by the policeman.
Here the agent is not omitted because it provides new and surprising information, but we are not saying 'the policeman delivered the letter', which would make the policeman seem more important than the letter.

1.3 Students transform the sentences. The sentences in 1.2 where no agent is shown are more difficult to transform since we have not information about the active object. In sentences a and e a personal object is required, but using either they or he/she suggests that we know the identity of the inventor and the thief. In sentence b, which describes part of a process, the agent is almost impossible to identify – it is a machine. In contrast, sentences c and d are easier to change into the active since the agent/object is known and the new sentences represent only a change of emphasis.

2 Key

Type 1 sentences = **c** and **d**
Type 2 sentences = **a** and **e**
Type 3 sentences = **b**

3 Key

1 A lot of letters have been delivered by the postman this morning. (note that the agent could be omitted)
2 Some money has been stolen from my bag. (agent not identified, therefore omitted)
3 More coffee than tea is being drunk these days. (the agent is unnecessary)

63

UNIT 8 Hi-tech horizons

4 Potatoes were first brought to Europe by Pizzaro in 1554.
5 All videos have to be returned to the shop before 6 p.m. (agent is not specified, therefore omitted)
6 Smoking is not permitted in the cinema. (a general instruction, agent omitted)
7 The water is heated by an electric element in the boiler.
8 Forty five technicians are employed by the company.
9 The Espresso machine was invented in Italy. (agent not known, therefore omitted)
10 Some books have not been returned to the library. (agent not specified, therefore omitted)

4 The choice between active and passive forms can depend on how formal we want to be, or on whether the sentence is spoken or written (eg 3.3, 3.5 and 3.6), as well as emphasis (eg 3.4 and 3.10) and knowledge of the agent (eg 3.2).

SPEAKING 3 Page 115
Expressing attitudes and opinions

1 a If students need prompting, suggest a list of objects to start them off (eg toothbrushes, bicycles, public telephones, postage stamps, newspapers).
  b Again suggest items and ask students to select from your list and add to it (eg pocket computers, video telephones, car fax machines, miniature televisions).

2 Give students a few minutes to discuss these points, then elicit sample answers and write them on the board.

READING 1 Page 116
Reading for specific information

1 Students look through the article quickly and decide which of the trends they discussed are mentioned, and which must be added to the list.

Key

The topics mentioned are – population changes, employment, currency and plastic cards

2 Key

| 1 true | 2 false | 3 true | 4 false | 5 false |
| 6 false | 7 false | 8 true | 9 false | 10 true |

Additional vocabulary:
risky = dangerous and uncertain
currently = at the moment
baby-boom generation = the large number of people born in Western Europe and North America in the 1950s and 60s
implications = results, consequences

ECU = European Currency Unit, the 'hard ECU' is part of a plan to replace European currencies with one single currency
intractable = difficult to change
pretty much = more or less
debit card = plastic card which functions like a cheque – the amount you spend is immediately removed from your bank account
credit rating – system used to decide if individuals can borrow money (eg from a bank)

3 Key

Type 1 = will grow
        will be over 50
        there is a growing trend
Type 2 = is expected to
        most of us can expect to have
        is predicted to fall from
        is likely to
        should be
Type 3 = may have to look
        could routinely be using

SPEAKING 4 Page 117
Expressing opinions

Get students to select topics of interest to them, asking the whole class to discuss one of the topics first, or select one topic and elicit some general areas for discussion of trends within this topic, before students complete the discussion in pairs. Change partners after 3 or 4 topics.

WRITING Page 117
A report

Students can discuss and plan the content of the composition in pairs before they write.

LISTENING 2 Page 117
Blank filling

1 **Pre-activity:** Students will probably guess 'computers' or 'information systems' as the topic of the listening. Remind them that smart cards are mentioned in the 'Trends' reading earlier in the unit and ask: What do you know about smart cards? What are they made of? How big are they? Why are they called smart cards? Do not comment on the answers but say that all this information will be on the tape.

2 Get students to compare their answers with a partner before you check them.

Hi-tech horizons **UNIT 8**

Key

1 France
2 one-third
3 a credit card
4 carrying money
5 buy more/spend more money
6 break down
7 a telephone
8 medical records
9 two cards
10 Scandinavia

GRAMMAR 2 Page 118 (GR p 220)
Will/Going to

1 *Will* is used to talk about predictions, except when there is definite evidence at the time of speaking of what will happen in the near future, then *going to* is used. Note that *going to* or *will* can be used to express complete certainty about events in the near future (eg I am going to be 18 next month).

2 Key

1 will	2 are going to	3 is going to
4 will	5 are going to	6 will
7 am going to	8 will	

READING 2 Page 118
Gapped text

1 Once your students have discussed these topics, elicit some opinions from them about mobile phones and people who use them.

2 Key

1 I 2 G 3 A 4 F 5 C 6 E 7 H 8 B

3 Key

1 Students are allowed to take their mobile phones into class.
2 But they are not allowed to use them in class.
3 If students use phones in class, they will be confiscated.

LISTENING 3 Page 120
Note-taking

Pre-activity: Get students quickly to list the furniture and equipment found in an office.

1 Key

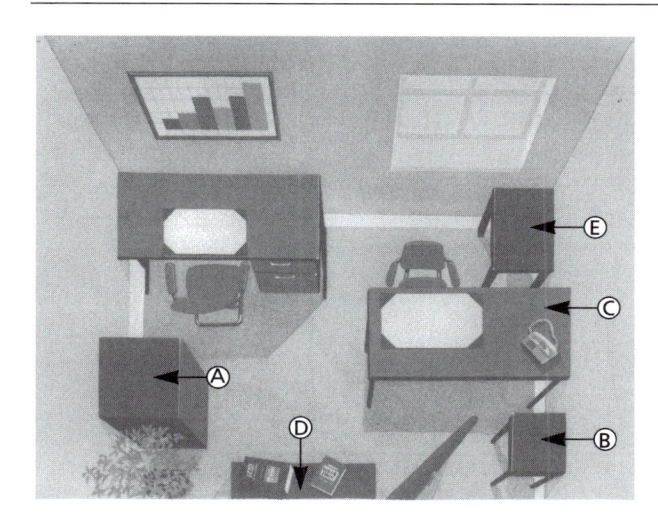

2 When students have read the instructions ask: Who is Michael speaking to? (the boss). What new equipment does he want to buy? (fax and printer). Before you play Part 2 get students to predict which advantages he will mention.

Key

Advantages
(fax) = clearer copies
bigger memory
not so noisy
(printer) = faster
better quality
easy to use
not so noisy

As a follow up, ask: What was decided about buying the new machines? (fax = yes, printer = no, replace the whole system later).

SPEAKING 4 Page 121
Expressing opinions

1 Point out that *So do I* is used for agreement with a positive idea, when this is expressed using *I think* (also *I hope, feel, expect, suppose*).
   eg A: I think we should move the desk.
      B: (agreeing) So do I.

Nor do I is used for agreement with negative ideas expressed using the above verbs.
   eg A: I don't think we should throw away the typewriter.
      B: (agreeing) Nor do I.

2 Before students exchange their opinions in pairs, read out some of these statements and ask for reactions and reasons. Encourage them to use *so/nor do I* or other

65

UNIT 8 Hi-tech horizons

expressions from **1**. If you have time, write the following phrases on pieces of card to make this a pairwork activity.

I think cars should be banned from the centre of cities.
In my opinion all cyclists should wear safety helmets.
Books and newspapers should be printed on recycled paper.
The Olympic Games should always be held in Greece.
I don't think nuclear power is either cheap or harmless.
Everyone should retire at 55.
Factories and offices should have creches for employees' children.
I believe that national borders are unnecessary in the modern world.
Television kills conversation.

GRAMMAR 3 Page 121 (GR p 220)
So/Nor

1 *So* is used with modal verbs to agree with positive statements:
I like pizza. – So do I.
I can swim. – So can she.

Nor is used to agree with negative statements:
I don't like cabbage. – Nor do I.
I haven't done my homework. – Nor has Marion.

So/Nor cannot be used to disagree with statements.

2 Key

1 So do I.	5 Nor can I.	9 Nor should I.
2 Nor do I.	6 So will I.	10 So have I.
3 So would I.	7 So am I.	11 So am I.
4 Nor do I.	8 So would I.	12 Nor have I.

3 Key

a 4	b 5	c 7	d 6	e 9	f 11
g 12	h 1	i 2	j 3	k 8	l 10

HELP WITH WORD FORMATION 2 Page 122

There is a word formation exercise included in the Use of English part of FCE. Exercise 6 in this section is similar to the type of activity found in the examination.

1 **Pre-activity:** Before students look at the book, write the verbs *express, equip, predict* and *discover* on the board and ask students how to transform these into nouns. Then refer students to the complete chart on page 122.

2 Do the first few words with the whole class before students complete the rest of the grid.

Key

	exploration (c)	improvement (b)
organisation (c)	completion (c)	assembly (d)
connection (c)	design	explanation (c)
solution (c)	information (c)	delivery (d)
programme	invention (c)	distribution (c)
encouragement (b)	development (b)	description (c)
employment (b)	production (c)	calculation (c)
replacement (b)	decision (a)	creation (c)
destruction (c)	discussion (a)	

Note that for *programme* and *design* the verb and noun forms are identical.

3 Key

drink (noun/verb)
sweet (adjective)
hand (noun)
manage (verb)
swim (verb/noun)
taste (verb/noun)
up (preposition)
hope (noun)
friend (noun)
modern (adjective)

4 Possible answers

1	er	waiter
2	less	sleeveless
3	able	disposable
4	ing	studying
5	ward	southward
6	ful	cupful
7	ful	tearful
8	en	shorten

5 Key

1 widened	6 eastwards
2 computerisation	7 spoonful
3 Membership	8 retirement
4 production	9 recommendation
5 stressful	10 replacement

6 Key

1 original	6 successful
2 mixture	7 partnership
3 composition	8 handwriting
4 assistants	9 introduction
5 added	10 approval

LISTENING 4 Page 123
Multiple choice

1 If necessary draw the attention of your students to the photo of an electronic organiser on page 123 and get them to tell you what it is and what it is used for. Then ask them to discuss in pairs the uses of electronic organisers in more detail.

2 Give students time to look through the multiple-choice

Hi-tech horizons **UNIT 8**

options and to ask about any vocabulary which they are unsure of before playing the tape once. Get students to check their initial answers with a partner before you play the tape a second time for them to check and confirm their answers.

Key

| 1 B | 2 B | 3 B | 4 B | 5 A | 6 C | 7 A |

PRONUNCIATION Page 124
/h/

1 Key

| 1 A | 2 B | 3 B | 4 A | 5 B | 6 A |
| 7 A | 8 B | 9 B | 10 A |

READING 3 Page 124
Reading for main points

1 Ask students to talk about their own country and how it contributes to and will be affected by global warming and the greenhouse effect.

2.1 Give students one minute to find and identify the numbers in question 1 in the text.

Key

80/½ = In the past 80 years the temperature has increased ½ degree.
2090/30 = By 2090 the temperature in Britain in summer could be 30 degrees.
1988/24 = In 1988 the highest temperature was 24 degrees.
150/24 in the past 150 years carbon dioxide in the atmosphere has increased by 24%.

2.2 Students look quickly again to identify two causes.

Key

The build up of carbon monoxide (from burning fossil fuels), and CFCs (from sprays, foam containers, refrigerators and air conditioning systems).

3 Key

1 important	6 serious
2 increase	7 covered with water
3 not really	8 absence of water
4 strongly believe	9 disturbed
5 getting faster	10 never seen before

Additional vocabulary:
climate of change (title) = (this is a play on words) people are ready to accept change, but it also refers to changes in the weather
informed opinion = the view of experts
rate of increase = speed of the change

arid = too dry to grow anything
food trays = plastic containers used for packing food

4 As you check answers, ask for more information (eg Why is cutting down fewer trees a solution to the problem?)

Key

| 1 c | 2 b | 3 a | 4 b | 5 a | 6 b | 7 b and c |
| 8 c | 9 c | 10 b |

5 Encourage students to complete this in their own words by asking them to make notes first about which points they will include in each paragraph. They should not refer back to the original article until they have completed their own paragraphs.

GRAMMAR 4 Page 126 (GR p 220)
Conditionals 2

1 Get students to discuss the differences in pairs. Elicit from the class that **all** the sentences refer to the future, and **a** sentences express something probably in real future time, while **b** sentences refer to something possible but less likely. Remind students not to use *would/will* in the *if* part of the sentence.

2 Note that the second conditional is also used to talk about things which are hypothetical (eg 'If I were a fish, I would …' Note that in these conditional sentences the past form of *be* is *were*, although it is common in both written and spoken English to use 'If I was …'

Key

In 2 choice depends on climate. For the other sentences (except 5) the choice will depend on individual circumstance and habits. Get students to justify their choices in terms of the probability of the things happening and the proximity to real future time.

3 Key

In 5 only the second conditional is possible – this is a hypothetical or imaginary situation.

HELP WITH WRITING Page 126
Giving opinions

1 Students complete the plan, then check with a partner.

Key

1 Introduction
2 a Scientists do not agree
  b No long-term record of climate change
  c There have been warm and cold periods in history
3 a Climate change could be natural
  b These issues get too much publicity and become fashionable

UNIT 8 Hi-tech horizons

    c Science is about making predictions and theories
4 Conclusion

2 The words and phrases in bold type all given the composition structure and make it easier to read and more effective in conveying its message.

3 Use the topics included in Speaking 5 on page 127 as additional composition titles.

4 Exchanging views will help students to clarify their opinions, and the best way to express these in the composition.
If time allows, get students to complete, say, the second paragraph of the composition in class with a partner who has selected the same topic.

LISTENING 5 Page 127
Short extracts

Note that as in the FCE Listening test, the questions and options A, B and C are recorded on the tape together with each short listening text. In the exam each of the texts is heard twice – the repeat immediately following the first listening. On the tape you will need to rewind at the end of each extract to replicate the format of the exam.

Key

1 B   2 C   3 B   4 B   5 B

SPEAKING 5 Page 127
Expressing and justifying opinions

Before getting students to look at the list of discussion points in the Student's Book, ask for views from the whole class on one or two of the topics. This is a warm-up activity for Reading 4 and is also a useful discussion activity of the type which students might be asked to participate in during the FCE Speaking test. See also the phrases on page 121.

READING 4 Page 128
Multiple matching

Encourage students to use a range of reading skills to complete this task. Rather than reading through all the information before attempting to answer the questions, students should quickly look through the text and find the answers as quickly as possible. To begin, ask the class to find the information on Nelson and get students to explain why the city where he studies has links with his home town (the example). Then get them to find the answers to questions 1 and 2 quickly. Then ask them to complete the task with a partner.

Key

1/2	Eleni/Haider	3	Sabrina
4	Nina	5/6	Marcel/Sabrina
7/8	Juan/Nina	9	Haider
10	Marcel	11	Nina
12/13	Nelson/Eleni	14/15	Sabrina/Nelson

EXAM PRACTICE 8 Page 130

2 Key

1 A 2 A 3 D 4 B 5 A 6 C 7 B 8 B
9 A 10 C 11 B 12 B 13 D 14 B 15 A

3 Key

1 am	2 3	3 they	4 just
5 ✓	6 had	7 ✓	8 as
9 to	10 will	11 not	12 ✓
13 in	14 ourselves	15 ✓	

4 Key

1 communication	6 connection
2 someone	7 reception
3 distance	8 continuous
4 international	9 longest
5 operator	10 underwater

REVISION TEST 4

1 Key

1 C 2 D 3 B 4 D 5 A 6 B 7 A 8 D
9 C 10 B 11 B 12 A 13 B 14 D 15 C

2 Key

1 of	2 whether	3 for	4 as
5 by	6 Another	7 with	8 to
9 of	10 make	11 however	12 it/you
13 on	14 that	15 up	

3 Key

1 is too much salt in
2 would rather go to
3 not early enough
4 if you don't like
5 might be reading
6 will be given
7 is likely to
8 gave it to me for
9 was recommended (to me) by
10 not worth buying a car

4 Key

1 comfortable	2 Visitors	3 darkness
4 construction	5 traditional	6 cheaper
7 lowest	8 heating	9 warmth
10 natural		

REVISION TEST 4

1 Read the text below and decide which word A, B, C or D best fits each space.

Tower of Pizza

Pizza, like most fast food started (**0**) __A__ as a peasant food. It was simple, cheap and filling, and usually very good (**1**) _____ it was made of local (**2**) _____ . And then it came into (**3**) _____ with the USA, and the USA corrupted it. The USA, as we all know, is a land of (**4**) _____ , and so when the food of immigrant peasants was (**5**) _____ to the USA, it got upgraded, or downgraded depending (**6**) _____ your point of (**7**) _____ . In the case of pizza, the simple (**8**) _____ of a thin, crisp dough (**9**) _____ and intensively flavoured tomato puree, cheese, anchovies, etc. was turned into an industrialised production (**10**) _____ . The dough was (**11**) _____ with sugar to make it sweet and injected with fat to make it easy to eat, and then it was (**12**) _____ with almost everything you can imagine – vegetables, meat and even fruit!

So, if ever there was a reason for do-it-yourself cooking, it is to restore the pizza to its (**13**) _____ simplicity. In an ideal world this would (**14**) _____ building your own wood-fired pizza oven, but a (**15**) _____ can be achieved with a gas oven and a food processor in your own kitchen.

0	A off	B away	C on	D back
1	A that	B whereas	C as	D once
2	A materials	B elements	C harvests	D ingredients
3	A compare	B contact	C contrast	D connect
4	A quantity	B enough	C amount	D plenty
5	A transported	B removed	C travelled	D replaced
6	A with	B on	C from	D of
7	A view	B thought	C opinion	D outlook
8	A correspondence	B construction	C composition	D combination
9	A floor	B bottom	C base	D foundation
10	A routine	B process	C course	D practice
11	A joined	B mixed	C added	D united
12	A topped	B headed	C capped	D hidden
13	A occasional	B traditional	C typical	D usual
14	A cause	B make	C need	D mean
15	A heap	B load	C lot	D deal

2 Fill each of the numbered blanks in the following passage. Use only one word in each space.

Updating your Computer

It doesn't matter (**0**) *which* computer you decided to buy, because it was out (**1**) _____ date as soon as it left the shop. The question is really (**2**) _____ or not you want to improve your computer.

Some improvements are good (**3**) _____ your health. Using a mouse or a keyboard for a long time can give you problems, such (**4**) _____ back pain or stiff arms. Some of these problems can be solved (**5**) _____ sitting properly on a good chair at the right height. (**6**) _____ solution could be buying a new mouse; you can buy special mice for left-handed people and for people (**7**) _____ particularly large or very small hands. Other improvements are just for fun. Colour printers are getting cheaper all the time and they add greatly (**8**) _____ the enjoyment that children (**9**) _____ all ages get from the computer. To (**10**) _____ your computer really interesting, (**11**) _____ , you need a modem; a box which allows (**12**) _____ to communicate with other computers on a normal phone line. This means you can read text (**13**) _____ your screen which you did not have to write yourself.

And don't forget (**14**) _____ an up-to-date PC with a modem can also play films and music and even pick (**15**) _____ TV signals. So perhaps you do need the latest model after all ...

REVISION TEST 4

3 Complete the second sentence so that it has a similar meaning to the first sentence. Use the word given and other words to complete each sentence. You must use between two and five words. Do not change the word given.

1. This soup is too salty.
   much
   There _____ this soup.

2. I'd prefer to go to a fast-food restaurant.
   rather
   I _____ a fast-food restaurant.

3. We were too late to get a good table.
   enough
   We were _____ to get a good table.

4. Unless you like live music, don't go to that restaurant.
   if
   Don't go to that restaurant _____ live music.

5. Maybe he's reading his horoscope in the newspaper.
   might
   He _____ his horoscope in the newspaper.

6. Someone at school will give you the recipe for pizza.
   be
   You _____ the recipe for pizza by someone at school.

7. The number of cars will probably increase.
   likely
   The number of cars _____ increase.

8. It was a birthday present from my parents.
   for
   My parents _____ my birthday.

9. A friend recommended the course to me.
   by
   The course _____ a friend.

10. If you don't drive, it's useless to buy a car.
    worth
    It is _____ if you don't drive.

4 Use the word given in capitals at the end of each line to form a word that fits in the space.

Living Below Ground

Jon Jones is a member of a new (**0**) _underground_ society. He   GROUND
believes that living below ground is (**1**) _____, convenient, and a good   COMFORT
way of saving energy and preserving the countryside. (**2**) _____ to   VISIT
his house often imagine Jon living in complete (**3**) _____,   DARK
but in fact plenty of light comes through large windows in the roof.
The biggest problem of the house was the cost of (**4**) _____ . It cost   CONSTRUCT
three times as much as a (**5**) _____ house, but once built it is much   TRADITION
(**6**) _____ to live in thanks to the low cost of maintenance.   CHEAP
The house has the (**7**) _____ domestic energy consumption in the   LOW
country. The central (**8**) _____ system works on solar energy and   HEAT
the absence of outside walls means that the (**9**) _____ is trapped   WARM
inside. This also means that the earth's limited (**10**) _____ resources are not wasted.   NATURE

UNIT 9

Working out

TOPIC	HELP SECTION	Paper 4
Health and fitness	Help with speaking – giving opinions	Short extracts
VOCABULARY FOCUS	**EXAM FOCUS**	Note-taking
Life styles	**Paper 1**	Matching information
Electrical appliances	Multiple matching	Multiple matching
Word formation	Reading for specific information	**Paper 5**
Illness and health	Reading for main points	Talking about photographs
Nouns/verbs from adjectives	Multiple choice	Expressing opinions
LANGUAGE FOCUS	Gapped text	Expressing feelings
Present perfect continuous	**Paper 2**	**EXAM PRACTICE**
Regrets	Writing a report	Open cloze
Conditionals 3	**Paper 3**	Error correction
Pronunciation: Word stress and *th* sounds	Key word transformations	Multiple-choice cloze
	Cloze text	

SPEAKING 1 Page 132
Talking about photographs

Pre-activity: Get students to suggest general headings which might be used to develop comparisons between pictures. For example, what is happening in the pictures, where they were taken, how the people in the pictures feel, why the photos were taken, what your personal view is of what the pictures show, etc. Then get students in pairs to focus on the two sets of pictures on page 132 and to compare them. Afterwards get students to tell you which of the types of comparison they mentioned in their discussion of the photos.

HELP WITH SPEAKING Page 133

For more information on the FCE Speaking test see Introduction page viii.

1 Go through the points listed and ensure students understand these important aspects of the test. Emphasise that students are assessed independently and the performance of one candidate in the pair will not influence the marks of the other. However, it is important for students doing the speaking test to cooperate with each other and discuss the topics they are given in a natural way.

2 Get students to discuss this topic in pairs. Then change the pairs and ask them to talk about it again, or ask two students (from different pairs) to discuss the topic so that the rest of the class can listen to them. Repeat the same procedure for **3**.

READING 1 Page 134
Gapped text

Pre-activity: Write the word **Marathon** on the board and ask the class what they know about this.

1 When students have discussed these questions in pairs, ask them to report back on their answers, especially the experience of anyone who has taken part in a Marathon or a long distance race. (26 miles = 41.84 km)

2 Ask students to complete the exercise by reading the article and the sentences removed from it very carefully. Then get them to compare answers in pairs and justify the answers they have selected by linking aspects of the text with parts of the extracted sentences.

Key

| 1 D | 2 A | 3 E | 4 B | 5 F | 6 G |

3 Key

1 approximately	2 limbs	3 revival
4 notable	5 joyous	6 counterparts
7 vast	8 range	9 rare
10 inadequately		

71

UNIT 9 Working out

4 marathon	imagination	equipment
motivated	throughout	available
approximately	organisers	inadequately
revival	messenger	unbelievably
introduction	specialist	explanation

LISTENING 1 Page 136
Short extracts

Note that each short extract is recorded once only on the tape although students will need to listen twice. After each extract, rewind and play that section again.

Key

1 A   2 B   3 C   4 C   5 A   6 C

READING 2 Page 136
Reading for specific information

Pre-activity: Ask: Do you like sitting in the sun? Why (not)? Is it good for you? Use these questions to elicit a range of views about sunbathing and the dangers of over-exposure to the sun.

1 Discuss these points with the whole class, then ask students to look at the article for just a few seconds and tell you what it is about. (Looking after young children in the sunshine).

2 Before students read the article in detail, ask them to predict in pairs what they expect the answers to the true/false exercise will be. When they have decided on the answers according to the passage, tell the class that there are **5** true answers, and to check once again with this in mind.

Key

1 true	2 false	3 false	4 false
5 true	6 true	7 true	8 true

Additional vocabulary:
to slip on = to put on clothes (especially light clothes which are easy to remove)
sunscreens = chemical creams which protect the skin from sunburn
SPF = Sun Protection Factor (an indication of how effective the sunscreen is)
toddlers = children who have just learned to walk
melanin = a natural chemical in the skin, which helps the skin to tan
pram parasol = a small sun umbrella which is fixed to the pram (= vehicle with wheels to transport a baby)

GRAMMAR 1 Page 137 (GR p 221)
Present perfect continuous

1 Get students to discuss these questions in pairs and then ask for some sample answers (eg She's from Britain, or another cold country. She's on holiday in a hot country, perhaps in the Mediterranean. She's spent too long in the sun. She feels terrible. She's probably not going to enjoy the rest of her holiday).

2 Elicit some examples of what she's been doing this morning and write them on the board. Establish that the form used is present perfect continuous.

Key

1 She's been swimming a number of times. (number of times = several times)
2 She's been wearing a bikini.
3 She's been reading a book.
4 She's been listening to music on a walkman.
5 She's been drinking Coke.
6 She hasn't been sitting under an umbrella.
7 She hasn't been using sunscreen lotion.
8 She's been sleeping in the sun.

3.1 Establish that the sentences talk about activities that began in the past and may or may not be finished, and that it is not important whether they have finished or not – we are interested only in the nature of the activities. The activity has happened more or less continuously, or has been repeated many times during the period mentioned.

3.2 Establish that the sentences are not continuous because in each case the action is finished. These are either activities which don't continue over time, or they were not repeated regularly during the period mentioned. Most of them happened in a moment, for example, or the number of times is specified.

Key

a Waking up happens in a moment.
b Losing happens in a moment.
c Finishing happens in a moment.
d Finishing happens in a moment.
e The number is limited and the action was finished within the time period mentioned.
f Refers to something which has not happened, but which only takes a moment.

4 Key

1 I have written ... is better because the sentence says how many letters have been written. We assume that the letters are finished.
2 I have been writing ... is better because it focuses on the action which has filled most of the time period.
3 I have lost ... is better because the verb *to lose* does not usually occur in the continuous form (when it

has the meaning 'cannot find'). Losing only take a moment.
4 Both forms are possible, with little difference in meaning.
5 ... has been working ... is better because the activity has filled most of the time period.
6 ... has worked ... is better because the action is complete – the visits to each of the five offices are finished and together do not represent one activity that has filled the time period.
7 I have been learning ... is better if the action continues in the present or has only recently finished. You never really finish learning a language!
8 Louise has phoned ... is better, because the number of times is mentioned.

5 Possible answers

1 I've been reading a book in English this week.
2 I've written two letters to friends this week.

6 Key

1 arrived
2 is
3 is
4 have been reading
5 have finished
6 've/have met
7 have told
8 are staying
9 have been
10 are going
11 am/'m
12 am going
13 do not/don't

Tell them short forms are also correct.

VOCABULARY 1 Page 138
Word formation

Key

1 sunset	2 suntan	3 sunglasses
4 sunshine	5 sunroof	6 sunbathing
7 sunflower	8 sunscreen	

LISTENING 2 Page 139
Selecting an answer

Introduce the listening by reminding students of the postcard from notes which they completed earlier in the unit. Explain that Jenny has now returned from her holiday and is telling her friend Sue about what happened. Give students an opportunity to read through the sentences before they listen.

Key

| 1 true | 2 false | 3 false | 4 true |
| 5 false | 6 false | 7 true | |

GRAMMAR 2 Page 139 (GR p 221)
Regrets

1 Key

1 Past perfect
2 Past time
3 Regret about an action or event which happened, or regret that something was not done or did not happen

Check students' understanding of the concepts by asking these questions about the example sentences from the listening:
Did Sue go on holiday with Jenny? (no)
Did Jenny take some books with her? (no)
Did Jenny stay at home? (no)
Was Jenny stupid? (yes)

For each of the above ask:
How does Jenny feel about this? (she regrets it = is sorry about it now)
Why?
Stress that *I wish* and *If only* are interchangeable and that when followed by the Past perfect tense they both express regrets about the past. Another form which has the same function is made with the verb *to regret*. In this case *I regret* is followed by + *-ing*.

2 Key

1 wish I hadn't gone
2 regret not taking that job
3 wishes she had bought
4 wishes he had told
5 only I had booked
6 regret not going
7 they had never got
8 regret not being
9 only I hadn't gone
10 wishes he had told

3 Note that *I wish/If only* are used to talk about events within our control, and about events which we have no control over.
eg I wish I had brought a sunhat.
   If only it hadn't been so hot.

I regret is normally used for events which are within our control. This is a more formal way of expressing these feelings, especially when writing.
eg I regret not working harder for my exams.

UNIT 9 Working out

4 Younger learners might need some help to think of regrets. Suggest that their regrets could be about study, home and family, leisure and sports activities, holidays, etc. Before students tell each other their regrets using *I wish/ if only*, elicit some example sentences from the previous exercise and get students to transform these using the target forms.

LISTENING 3 Page 140
Note-taking

Pre-activity: Write **Aromatherapy** on the board and ask students what it means (the use of natural oils from plants as a medical treatment eg for headaches and stress, or as a tonic). Elicit from students the name of the person who practises aromatherapy, (an aromatherapist) and ask them if they know anything about the job.
Focus students on the article and ask them to answer the three questions as quickly as possible.

Key

1 He died last month.
2 He left it to his local aromatherapist.
3 For this, elicit as many possibilities as your students can think of.

Follow up your students' reading of the article with these checking questions:
Who died? (Mr Grey)
How old was he? (87)
When did he die? (last month)
How much money did he leave? (£1,008,279 – this sum is spoken as 'one million eight thousand two hundred and seventy-nine pounds')
Why were Mr Grey's family shocked? (they did not know that he had so much money)
Why were they enraged (= angry)? (they did not receive any of it)
Introduce the listening by telling students that the newspaper report is not completely accurate, and the family did receive some of Mr Grey's money in his will. Ask: What is a will? (the document people prepare which says what must happen to their money and possessions after they die). Students are going to listen to some people discussing Mr Grey's will on a radio programme and they should complete the missing information.

Key

1 promote aromatherapy
2 Norman Grey
3 pay his debts
4 he owed £50 to Mr Grey
5 Mary
6 sister
7 she measured his furniture
8 £200
9 she refused to look after him

GRAMMAR 3 Page 140 (GR p 221)
Conditionals 3

1 Refer students to the example sentences from the listening text and ask them who each of sentences 1–3 refers to (Norman, Mary and Cecilia). Get them to discuss quickly with a partner the questions A, B and C for each example.

Key

1 a No, he didn't.
  b Because he did not pay back the money he owed Mr Grey.
  c No, he can't – it is too late.
2 a No, she didn't.
  b Because she used to come and measure Mr Grey's furniture.
  c No, she can't.
3 a No, she didn't.
  b Because Mr Grey asked her to look after him but she refused.
  c No, she can't.

4 Elicit the fact that in the *If* clause the past perfect tense is used and in the main clause we use *would* (contracted to **'d**) *have* (sometimes called the perfect conditional). Note that we do not usually find *would* in the *if* clause. The time referred to in each sentence is the past. Point out that the third conditional form is used to talk about events and results in the past which did not happen.

2 Before students read the article in detail ask them to look at it quickly, and answer these questions:
What did June Booker buy? (a frying pan)
Why did she buy it? (it was reduced in a sale)
Why was it an expensive day for her? (she now needs a new kitchen)
Then tell students to read again and answer the question.

Key

She dropped the pan on her foot, and there was a fire in her flat.
Ask: What caused these two accidents? (She was carrying too much shopping, she left the frying pan on the cooker when the phone rang, she threw water on the burning pan.)

3 **Key**

2 i 3 h 4 d 5 b 6 c 7 j
8 k 9 a 10 f 11 g

Note that in sentence 10-f *could* in the *If* clause expresses the idea that this is a possible consequence, but not a certain one. If we are certain, we use *would*.

Working out **UNIT 9**

4 Get students to do this exercise individually and then check their answers in pairs. After the exercise, write on the board some of the complete conditional sentences which students have produced, and ask questions to emphasise again that these sentences talk about the opposite of what actually happened:
eg If it hadn't rained, the picnic wouldn't have been cancelled.
Was the picnic cancelled? Why?

Key

1 wouldn't have been
2 hadn't helped him
3 hadn't been travelling
4 would/could have phoned
5 John had worn a coat
6 he wouldn't have found
7 I wouldn't have known
8 wouldn't have had
9 I had had
10 had worked harder

SPEAKING 2 Page 142
Expressing opinions

To start students off, ask them to think about the kitchen and how electricity can be particularly dangerous there. Elicit some examples (eg If you touched the iron with wet hands, you might get a shock).

1 Key

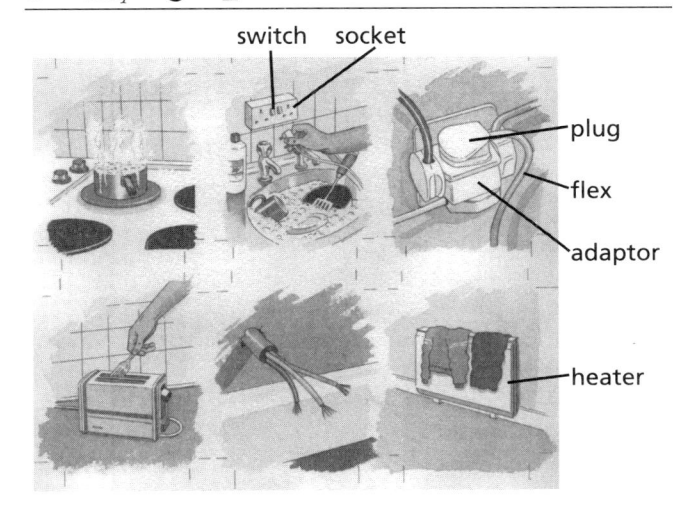

switch   socket
plug
flex
adaptor
heater

2 Get students to describe each of the situations illustrated before they select with a partner the one they think is the most dangerous.

LISTENING 4 Page 142
Matching information

1 The previous activity gives students all the vocabulary they require to answer this question. Introduce the listening by telling the class that they will hear a telephone conversation between two people talking about electrical problems. The first time they listen they only have to decide which problems are discussed.

Key

The problems discussed are: pictures 2, 3 and 5.

2 With a strong class, you can get students in pairs to find the correct multiple choice answers based on the first listening. In any case, give sufficient time for students to read through the questions thoroughly before you play the tape again.

Key

1 A   2 C   3 A   4 B   5 A

SPEAKING 3 Page 143
Expressing opinions and giving advice

1 Ask students if they have ever eaten something bad, and got food poisoning. How did they know? Write – 'stomachache is a symptom of food-poisoning' on the board and ask for other words and expressions with *ache* (eg toothache, backache, headache).

2 If possible, get students to use English-English dictionaries for this activity. Without dictionaries they can probably guess some of the symptoms once they have an idea of the type of illness. These symptoms are typical of a bad cold or 'flu (= influenza), although 'flu' usually includes a fever/high temperature.
For questions 2.1–2.4 get students to discuss in pairs and groups. This is an opportunity for individuals to give personal opinions. After the students' discussion elicit some sample answers.
Ask students if they have ever tried any of these ideas for getting rid of a cold, which they think are worth trying and which they think are just silly.

READING 3 Page 143
Reading for main ideas and specific information

1.1 Pre-activity: Get students to tell you what the article is about and allow them to look at the article for just a few seconds to establish that it describes taking warm and cold showers as a way of avoiding colds. Then ask: What is the technical name for this type of treatment? (hydrotherapy)

1.2 Students will need longer to find and identify these numbers, but emphasise that there will only be time to

75

UNIT 9 Working out

find the numbers, not read the whole article. Set a time limit of two minutes for this.

Key

50 = number of people in the experiment + max age of people
26–40 = (degrees) temperature of the warm showers
18–24 = (degrees) temperature of the cold showers in weeks 1 and 2
12–18 = (degrees) temperature of the cold showers in weeks 3 to 26
35 = total number of colds among the 25 people taking the showers
46 = total number of colds among the 25 people not taking the showers
23 = number of colds during the first 3 months and the second 3 months among the people not taking the showers
100 = the method has been known for 100 years

2 As you check the answers get students to give you supporting information from the article for their answers.

Key

1 true	2 false	3 false	4 true
5 true	6 true	7 false	8 false

Write these discussion points on the board and get students to discuss them in groups:
The article describes the results as 'very exciting', what do you think?
Have you ever tried this method? Did it work?
Will you try it in future? Why (not)?
What do you do to avoid colds or when you start to get a cold? Does it work?

3 Key

1 half-hearted	2 stave off	3 schedule
4 lengthened	5 monitored	6 incidence
7 significant	8 hardening	

4 Key

Adjective	Noun	Verb
long	length	to lengthen
hard	hardness	to harden
wide	width	to widen
deep	depth	to deepen
high	height	to heighten
fresh	freshness	to freshen
large	largeness	to enlarge
strong	strength	to strengthen
weak	weakness	to weaken
soft	softness	to soften
dark	darkness	to darken
bright	brightness	to brighten

Additional vocabulary:
builds up (vb) (para 7) = increases
prophylaxis (9) = method of preventing an illness
naturopaths (n) (10) = people who use natural treatment
euphoria (10) = excitement, happiness
hardiness (10) = power to resist
susceptibility (10) = risk of catching colds
loofah (10) = part of a plant used as a bath sponge or brush
eliminative (adj) (10) = ability to remove unnecessary waste from the body

READING 4 Page 144
Multiple matching

1 Ask students if they know of any allergies or if anyone they know suffers from an allergy. Then get them to discuss the questions in 1 together in small groups.

2 This is an exam-type activity, where students have to insert headings. Point out that it is not necessary to read the complete article and all the headings before starting to make some decisions about which of the headings are impossible/possible/probable.

Key

| 1 I | 2 H | 3 E | 4 F | 5 D | 6 B | 7 C |

WRITING 2 Page 145
Reports

1 Key

1 sniffing
2 sneezing
3 crying
4 inflammation of the lining of the nose (medical name: rhinitis)
5 allergic response to pollen (bright flowers)
6 hereditary problems
7 pollution/desensitisation due to lack of exposue in big cities
8 keep windows/air vents closed
9 go to the seaside
10 buy an air filter+ take advice about drug treatment

SPEAKING 4 Page 145
Expressing feelings

Pre-activity: Briefly elicit some example situations where students were nervous and get them to describe their feelings and reactions. Then refer them to the list on page 145 and ask them to discuss the topic with a partner. After the discussion in 1 and 2 ask some

Working out UNIT 9

students to report back to the class what their partner told them.

3 Key

1 in	2 for	3 to	4 After
5 with	6 not	7 from	8 by
9 got/felt/was		10 that	11 off
12 could	13 to	14 way	15 their

LISTENING 5 Page 146
Multiple matching

Pre-activity: Get students to look at the options A – F before they listen. In pairs get them to predict some of the words and phrases they would expect to hear the speaker using in each case. Ask which of the topics they would expect to be referred to by actors, doctors, or other people; and which are most likely to be in the first person, the second person, or the third person.

Key

1 C 2 E 3 F 4 B 5 A

READING 5 Page 146
Multiple choice

Pre-activity: Get students to focus on the cartoon sketch and to describe what they think is happening. Ask them to look quickly through the article and to find the name of the animal in the picture (a mongoose).

1 Get students to compare with a partner the parts of the article they have selected.

2 Key

A rhino, dog, cat, crocodile, mongoose, cobra
B heel, ankle, teeth, toe, brains, foot
C limped, ran, darting, rushed, shot in, slipped
D nipped, sank (its teeth)

3 Key

1 A 2 C 3 A 4 C 5 C

WRITING 3 Page 148
Reports

1 Give your class a few minutes to consider the topics and to make brief notes for one of the reports. This will help them to confirm that they really do have enough to say on a particular topic.
2 Group students in pairs with someone who has selected the same topic and get them to turn their notes into a plan for the report with their partner.
3 Note that the time limit for writing is mentioned here.

Now that they have done the preparatory work with a partner they can write individual reports either in class (keeping to the time limit), or tell them to time themselves at home. In FCE students have to complete two writing tasks in one hour and thirty minutes.

Point out that in the exam the time limit includes time for selecting, planning and checking as well as actually writing their answers.

PRONUNCIATION Page 148
th sounds

If your students have problems with the different pronunciations of *th* in English, read through the example words in 2-5 and get the students to repeat them individually and in chorus before you allow them to practise independently.

EXAM PRACTICE 9 Page 149

1 Key

1 has	2 from	3 of	4 by
5 same	6 ago	7 Like	8 at
9 about	10 lot	11 in	
12 now/always/often/therefore			
13 given	14 next	15 not	

2 Key

1 it	2 some	3 ✓	4 down
5 is	6 up	7 ✓	8 the
9 he	10 to	11 ✓	12 a
13 of	14 ✓	15 both	

3 Key

1 B	2 D	3 A	4 B
5 A	6 C	7 D	8 A
9 C	10 C	11 A	12 A
13 C	14 B	15 D	

UNIT 10

It's a bargain

TOPIC	HELP SECTION	Paper 4
Shopping and Money	Help with writing a transactional letter	Note-taking
VOCABULARY FOCUS		Short extracts
Shopping	**EXAM FOCUS**	Multiple matching
Words connected with money and trade	**Paper 1**	**Paper 5**
	Multiple choice	Talking about photographs
LANGUAGE FOCUS	Multiple matching	Solving a problem
Obligations	Gapped text	Expressing opinions
Make, let, allow	**Paper 2**	**EXAM PRACTICE**
Wishes	Writing a transactional letter	Multiple choice cloze
Complaints	**Paper 3**	Error correction
Pronunciation: Word linking	Key word transformations	Word formation

SPEAKING 1 Page 151
Talking about photographs

1 **Pre-activity:** Introduce the topic of the unit by asking students to brainstorm in pairs or groups the names for types of shops. Check their lists by asking:
Where can you buy
bread? (a baker's)
meat? (a butcher's)
a hammer? (a hardware store or ironmonger's)
a newspaper? (a newsagent's)
an envelope? (a stationer's)
a packet of aspirin? (a chemist's)
Write these items and names of shops on the board. Point out the use of *'s* to transform the name of the person's job into the type of shop (eg the baker's = the baker's shop). If students suggest reasonable alternatives like supermarket, hyperstore, department store, then add these to the list as places where you can find a lot of different things.

Refer students to picture D, (if department store was not mentioned in the previous activity, get students to identify the type of shop and name a local example).

Tell students to compare the photos, with one student talking firstly about pictures A and B and the other talking about C and D. Give them a couple of minutes to think about their pictures and what they might say about questions **1–5** before asking them to speak. Encourage students to develop their answers and, once they have talked about their own pair of photos, to be prepared to comment on their partner's pictures. Give them a few minutes for discussion and then elicit some example answers.

When students have discussed the photographs with one partner get them to swap and repeat the exercise with another person.

LISTENING 1 Page 151
Short extracts

Warn students that what they will hear are not exact descriptions of the pictures, but people talking about the same general type of shops illustrated. Note that the extracts are very short.
Since there are just three short extracts to listen to here, play the full texts before rewinding the tape. Then get students to decide in pairs on their answers and to justify their answers by recalling key words in the text. Also ask them to tell you what information on the tape appears not to correspond to the pictures they select.

Key

1 D (you don't have to talk to people, and you can try on clothes – so it's probably a department store)
2 B (personal service, trained staff, mentions 'outfits' which indicates clothing, although the picture does not suggest high fashion!)

78

3 C (prices are low, 'we don't have to pay high rents' – this suggests an open market)

SPEAKING 2 Page 152
Expressing and justifying opinions

Ask if anyone has heard of or been to Selfridges in London. If no-one has, describe it to the class as a very large department store in Oxford Street in the centre of London. Explain the activity to the class by adding more context:
- you are staying in London with a friend
- you are returning home in a few days
- you want to buy presents for your hosts and your own family back home
- you need to buy some routine items
- you have a long shopping list
- the shop closes in thirty minutes
- you have to organise the list into departments so you can find the items quickly.

Tell students to either ignore items they do not recognise, or to look them up in a dictionary, if possible. This activity will be much more enjoyable and successful if you get students to work in pairs.

Key

Food Hall	Kitchenware
garlic	saucepan
jam	pepper mill
peanuts	teaspoons
smoked salmon	corkscrew
mushrooms	kettle

Stationery	Toiletries
ink	shampoo
rubber	sponge
ruler	toothpaste
envelopes	bath foam
pencil sharpener	shaving foam

Electrical	Jewellery
plug	earrings
light bulb	necklace
headphones	bracelet
adaptor	brooch
batteries	watch

LISTENING 2 Page 152
Note-taking

Play the tape twice and allow students time between the first and second hearing to compare their answers with a partner.

Key

1	ground	2	Furniture
3	third	4	Hardware
5	two for the price of one	6	lunch
7	top	8	Book
9	first	10	Menswear
11	free tie	12	second

READING 1 Page 153
Multiple choice

1 Get students to discuss this briefly
2 Then ask them to find the answers as quickly as possible.

Key

a 3 types–high-heel(s), evening shoes, pumps (shoes with almost flat heels)
b 150 pairs
c she is a 'high-heel freak' – she loves going out and buying high-heeled shoes
d shoes made by a company called Weitzmann

3 Key

1 A   **2** C   **3** D   **4** C   **5** B

4 Key

1	marble	2	oozes with	3	overspill
4	outrageously	5	maze	6	heads for
7	an outfit	8	flattering	9	stylish
10	reveal				

GRAMMAR 1 Page 154 (GR p 221)
Obligations

Pre-activity: Ask how a supermarket is different from a department store. Tell students to think of four differences, for example regarding what the shops sell, how they are organised, what the shoppers have to do in each place. Elicit some sample answers and accept any reasonable differences which students mention.

1.1 Refer your class to the picture and ask them to identify as many things in the picture as possible, including the things listed in the box.
trolley = the container on wheels which the customers push round the shop
checkout = the area where you pay for the goods.
cashier = the person operating the till
till = the machine which calculates how much you have to pay
carrier bag = a paper or plastic container in which you carry the goods home
aisle = the 'corridors' in the supermarket formed by the lines of shelves

UNIT 10 It's a bargain

1.2 Elicit some opinions and reasons by asking: Do you like going to supermarkets? Why (not)?
Then get students to list some advantages and disadvantages in pairs.

Possible answers:

Advantages
You can choose things quickly
You don't have to talk to people
They are cheap
There is sometimes a big choice of goods

Disadvantages
You sometimes have to wait a long time to pay
You are tempted to buy more than you need
There is no personal service or advice
They are often very crowded

1.3 and **1.4** Elicit some examples by asking: What is the first thing you do when you go into a supermarket? (take a trolley or basket). Get students to make this into a sentence using have to/need to (eg You have to/need to take a trolley). Ask students to think of four other things you must/must not do in this situation, and to write down sentences individually. Then allow students to compare their sentences with a partner. Elicit some examples and write them on the board.
Follow the same procedure with sentences including needn't/don't have to. Stress that these forms are used when there is no obligation – we can decide if we want to do this thing.

2 Pre-activity: Tell students that they will look at an advertising leaflet from a large supermarket. Ask them to look quickly at the leaflet and decide exactly what it is advertising (Multisaver), and briefly to describe the Multisaver system (a discount when you buy a certain quantity/number of a particular product), before they read and answer the questions.

Key

1 don't have to	6 have to
2 don't have to	7 don't have to
3 have to	8 don't have to
4 don't have to	9 have to
5 don't have to	10 have to

3 Key

1 convenient	6 indicated
2 throughout	7 deducted
3 essential	8 spread
4 as well	9 provided
5 single	10 purchased

Additional vocabulary:
transaction = the act of buying or selling something
till screen = the electronic display on the till
dozens = many (one dozen = twelve)
scanning system = the computer which 'reads' the prices from the bar codes on goods

4 Key

1 You need to go = It is necessary for you to go
2 You have to go/**3** You must go = You have no choice but to go
4 You can go = It is possible for you to go if you like
5 You should go = It would be better if you went

In the above exercise *have to* and *must* mean the same thing.

5 Key

1 You don't have to go/**2** You needn't go/**3** You don't need to go = It isn't necessary for you to go
4 You can't go = It isn't possible for you to go
5 You shouldn't go = It would be better not to go
6 You mustn't go = It is forbidden!

Don't have to, don't need to and *needn't* mean the same thing.

6 Point out that each word/expression can be used more than once.

Key

1 have to/need to
2 mustn't
3 must/should
4 can
5 mustn't
6 shouldn't
7 can't
8 don't have to/don't need to/needn't
9 can/should
10 have to/need to
11 can, don't have to/don't need to/needn't
12 mustn't/shouldn't

Discuss why they have chosen each modal verb, and why others are not possible or not appropriate to the context.

LISTENING 3 Page 156
Selecting an answer

Introduce the listening by telling students that they will hear two women talking about a clothes shop called **Fergusons** (write the name on the board). One of the women buys things from this shop regularly, the other woman hardly ever goes there.
Give the class a couple of minutes to read the sentences **1–8** before you play the tape twice. Note than in **1** a *top* is a t-shirt or blouse.

It's a bargain **UNIT 10**

Key

1 true	2 true	3 true	4 false
5 false	6 true	7 true	8 false

GRAMMAR 2 Page 156 (GR p 221)
Make, let, allow

1 Use questions about each sentence to elicit the meaning:
eg What form of payment do they accept? (cash),
Can you pay by other means? (only with a Ferguson's card)
Can you try things on? (no)
Can you pay off the money you owe them? (yes, if you want to)
Establish that *make* means to oblige someone to do something (they have no choice)
let and *allow* mean permit someone to do something (they can do it if they want to)
Point out the form of the three verb phrases:
make + someone do something
let + someone do something
allow + someone to do something

2 Key

1 make	2 allowed	3 made
4 let	5 allowed	6 let
7 let	8 allowed	

3 The discussion topics are designed to appeal to young learners as well as adults. Tell students to discuss some or all of these topics in pairs or groups of three and to use the above forms in their discussions. Elicit some sample opinions after the discussion.

VOCABULARY 1 Page 157
Vocabulary in context

1 **Pre-activity:** Write 'Money' on the board and ask students to work in pairs and make a list of all the words they can think of connected with money (eg bank, wallet, salary, save).
Allow students a short time to discuss this and then elicit some examples as introduction to the gap-fill exercise.

Key

2 discount	3 price	4 deposit
5 instalments	6 afford	7 cost
8 exchange	9 currency	10 buy
11 spending	12 wallet	13 bank
14 cash	15 bill	16 pay
17 sale	18 bargain	19 debt
20 worth		

HELP WITH WRITING Page 157
A transactional letter

For further information on FCE Paper 2 (Writing) see Introduction page vii. Note that a transactional letter means a letter written for a particular purpose. This could be a letter to a friend or a more formal letter, but is not just a routine letter of the sort you might write just to keep in touch with someone you have not seen for some time.

1 Get students to read the advertisement and tell you about the main attractions of the trip, (shopping in Newton Stilton, trip through the Cole valley).
When students have read the advertisement ask:
How many shops are there in Newton Stilton? (133)
What time does the coach leave? (8.30)
How much does the trip cost? (£9.50)
What is the name of the travel company? (Happy coaches Ltd)

2 Students should be able to tell you after just a couple of seconds that the letter is formal and a letter of complaint. Ask for evidence, (the layout, the first sentence).
Ask students to read in detail and complete the paragraph titles working with a partner.

Possible answers:

1 Introduction
2 Leaving time/The journey
3 The shopping complex
4 The return
5 Request for refund

3 The phrases in bold are all typical of a letter of complaint. The expressions in paragraphs **3** and **4** indicate that the complaint is not just about one isolated event, but a whole series of problems.

4 Key

1 According to your leaflet ...
2 ... your leaflet is rather misleading in this respect.
3 You can imagine how disappointed I am ...
4 I feel that your company is directly to blame.
5 I am, therefore, writing to request an immediate refund ...
6 I look forward to receiving your prompt reply.

5 Ask students to tell you what a mail-order company is (a company which sells goods by post).

6 Get students to focus on the note which was received with a package of clothes ordered from a mail order company and which has some extra handwritten details added to it.
Before they write the letter, ask students to tell you what was in the package (2 shirts, long sleeved, black and cherry red colours, extra large size). Then get them to tell you what was ordered (one shirt, short sleeved,

UNIT 10 *It's a bargain*

apple green colour, medium size) and any other reason why they are not very pleased with the Tulip Casual Clothes Co. (the catalogue says delivery in 4 days – had to wait 3 weeks). Ask what the customer is going to do (write a letter explaining the problem, complaining about the service and asking for something else from the catalogue – get students to say what they might select from a clothing catalogue instead of one of these shirts).

SPEAKING 3 Page 160
Expressing opinions

1.1 Elicit one or two examples from students of their experience of making complaints before getting the others to talk about this in pairs.

1.2 Point out to students that in the FCE Speaking test students may be asked to look at a list like this one and make a selection from it or give their own opinions.

2 You may need to help younger students with suggestions about advantages/disadvantages of using credit cards.

READING 2 Page 160
Gapped text

1 Get students to look at the example and to tell you why **1** is the correct answer (*one* refers to *a new suit*, *bought* reflects *buy* in the main text, *for many years* connects to *not something I do very often*). Then get students to read and suggest the answer to number **1** and to justify their choice. Confirm the answer to **1** and then get students to complete the rest of the task.

Key

1 E   2 B   3 D   4 A   5 G   6 C   7 H

2 Key

1 changing   2 assistant   3 unhelpful
4 choice   5 payment   6 Unfortunately
7 embarrassed   8 forgotten   9 buying
10 criminal

LISTENING 4 Page 162
Note-taking

Pre-activity: Introduce the topic before you play the tape by asking: (for younger learners) Have you ever had to complain about something in a shop? (for adults) When was the last time you had to complain about something in a shop? What happened? Were you satisfied with the result?

1 Key

1 A pullover
2 It lost its colour
3 Two other things were damaged
4 – The water was too hot, or there was something wrong with the machine
   – There was something wrong with the pullover
5 His money back / a refund
6 He has not got the receipt
7 Write to the manager
8 The unhelpful shop assistant

The second time you play the tape ask students to check/complete their answers, but also to tell you why the customer cannot talk to the manager immediately (because she's on holiday).

2 Get students to plan the paragraphs of the letter in pairs before they write it in class or for homework.

Possible answers:

1 Introduction
2 The pullover
3 Other things damaged
4 No receipt
5 The shop assistant

3 Remind students to include some of the typical expressions for a letter of complaint in the letter on this page, and to use the same layout.

PRONUNCIATION Page 162
Word linking

3 Key

1 You can't do that
2 He didn't throw it
3 I'm going next year
4 Do you want a small glass or a big glass?
5 I'll look for him outside
6 The problem with this exercise is …
7 He asked the teacher a question
8 She looked through the window
9 I like boiled potatoes
10 He isn't taking the exam

LISTENING 5 Page 162
Note-taking

Pre-activity: Ask students: Do you ever listen to phone-in programmes on the radio? What do you think of them? How could they be improved? If necessary, explain that a phone-in is where listeners can call and talk to the programme presenter live on the radio (or TV).

Tell the class that they are going to hear part of a phone-

It's a bargain **UNIT 10**

in programme where there is a prize for the best contribution. The topic of the programme is *wishes* (what people would really like to do), and the person who phones with the most interesting wish will win a prize. Point out that when they listen students must note the name, wish and reason for the wish – there will only be time to make very short notes (two or three words maximum), not complete sentences.

NB Ask students to note their answers on a separate piece of paper – so that they have plenty of space to write.

1 Key

	Name	**Wish**	**Reason**
1st caller	Jenny	ski	for skiing holiday
2nd caller	Pam	be rich	for Cancer Research (a charity)
3rd caller	Rob	play international football	always wanted to
4th caller	Rachel	dinner with presenter	her birthday (72)

2 In addition to listening a second time to check and complete answers, ask students to make a note of what prize is offered (tickets for a Folk Concert). Afterwards, ask students to decide who gets the prize.

GRAMMAR 3 Page 162 (GR p 221)
Wishes

You will need the listening cassette for the second part of this section.

1 Note that the form *I wish + I (did)* is used to talk about things we cannot do but we want to do. It does not refer to the past, but to the present and future. In some situations the form *I wish I were rich* is preferred to *I wish I was rich*, although in modern spoken English the latter is much more common.

2 Make it clear that the questions they are to ask themselves are those in the examples in **1**.
This is the complete list of sentences using *I wish*:
I wish I could do it now
I wish I could just get on the skis
I wish you luck
I wish I was really rich
I wish I had so much money I never had to worry
I wish I was an England international
I wish I could play for England
I wish you'd take me out to dinner
I wish I was!

There are altogether five types of *wish* sentences in the passage. Elicit the structures from the class and write them on the board. Then ask students to read out sentences from their lists, saying which type they are, until all the possible sentences have been mentioned.
Sentence types:
I wish + I (was/had)
I wish + I (could)
I wish + I (had asked)
I wish + you (luck)
I wish + you'd (take me out)

3 Key

| 1 d | 2 – | 3 b | 4 e | 5 a | 6 f |
| 7 – | 8 h | 9 g | 10 c | | |

4 Sentences **2** and **7** cannot be matched because they are real rather than hypothetical wishes.
Sentence 10 expresses a past regret (indicated by the use of *I wish* + Past perfect), see Unit 9, page 139.

6 Get students to complete this individually, but elicit an example of each type of sentence from the class before they begin.

7 If possible, allow students to move round the room and tell lots of other people their wishes, emphasise that the object is to find another person with the same wish. If moving around is difficult to organise, then get students to do the same thing in groups of 4 or 6.

8 Key
1 wish you could come
2 wish he wouldn't keep
3 wishes she could
4 you luck
5 wish I had
6 wishes he saw his grandchildren
7 wish he would accept
8 wish I were/was (more)
9 wish it would stop
10 was/were bigger

LISTENING 6 Page 164
Multiple matching

1 Pre-activity: Establish that students know what a vending machine is and elicit one or two examples before the class go on to discuss these points in pairs.

2 For these linked short extracts, as in this section of the FCE Listening test, play all five speakers once without pausing, and then play them all a second time, ie do not rewind the tape between one speaker and the next.

Key

| 1 C | 2 E | 3 F | 4 A | 5 B |

83

UNIT 10 It's a bargain

READING 4 Page 164
Multiple matching

Pre-activity: Go through the list of places which prompt the questions **1 – 15** and make sure that students are focused on the type of information they need to identify. Point out that they do not need to read every word in the extracts about the places to buy Christmas presents in order to complete the task. Then get them to find places where they can buy jewellery, as quickly as possible – get half the class to start reading through quickly from the beginning (Extract A) and the other half to start reading from the end (Extract I). Once they've found the references for jewellery, get them to read the rest of the items and apply the same technique to finding the references. They should then find a partner from the other half of the class and check their answers, going back to check on any discrepancies.
Point out that in the exam where more than one answer is required (eg **1**, **2** and **3**), the order in which they identify the answers is not important.

Key

1/2/3: D/G/I	4/5/6: G/H/J	7 A
8 H	9/10/11: C/H/I	12 F
13/14/15: D/E/G		

EXAM PRACTICE 10 Page 166

1 Key

| 1 C | 2 B | 3 A | 4 B | 5 B | 6 D | 7 D | 8 A |
| 9 D | 10 B | 11 A | 12 C | 13 D | 14 A | 15 A | |

2 Key

1 ✓	2 the	3 by	4 it
5 big	6 up	7 these	8 ✓
9 at	10 a	11 ✓	12 far
13 ✓	14 too	15 do	

3 Key

1 swapping	2 dependent	3 agreement
4 exchange	5 introduction	6 officially
7 became	8 anything	9 acceptable
10 reality		

REVISION TEST 5

1 Key

1 one	2 when	3 Like
4 just/only	5 but	6 way
7 had/needed	8 by	9 because/as
10 were	11 less	12 with
13 over	14 its/their	15 in

2 Key

1 only I had not / hadn't been
2 regret not taking
3 would not have / wouldn't have been
4 do not / don't let you
5 wish I could play
6 wish Marcus would stop
7 do not /don't have to
8 have been to the opera
9 get very bored
10 is going to be

3 Key

1 more	2 of	3 have	4 ✓
5 the	6 been	7 ✓	8 which
9 much	10 to	11 what	12 ✓
13 so	14 ✓	15 it	

4 Key

1 popularity
2 imperfect
3 production
4 successful
5 throughout
6 exhibition
7 specialise
8 recently
9 playground
10 improvements

REVISION TEST 5

1 Fill each of the numbered blanks in the following passage. Use only one word in each space.

The Blackout

It was the biggest electrical power failure (0) __*in*__ US history. It only lasted one night, but everyone in New York had a story worth telling in the morning.

My role was a modest (1) _____ , I was at home watching television after school (2) _____ the picture disappeared into a grey dot. (3) _____ everyone else, I became slowly aware and increasingly amazed that it was not (4) _____ the apartment, the building, even the neighbourhood that was without electricity, (5) _____ the whole city. Worst affected were people on their (6) _____ home from work. People were trapped in subway trains and (7) _____ to be guided out of the tunnels (8) _____ guards with torches. Some people wouldn't leave the trains (9) _____ they didn't want to walk home through strange neighbourhoods, so they spent the night where they (10) _____ guarded by police. Other people were even (11) _____ comfortable, like those who spent the night stuck in lifts.

The emergency wards of the hospitals were crowded (12) _____ people who had tripped (13) _____ something in the dark. Fortunately, the telephone system worked throughout the crisis because the phone company used (14) _____ own generators, and so people (15) _____ difficulty could get help.

2 Complete the second sentence so that it has a similar meaning to the first sentence. Use the word given and other words to complete each sentence. You must use between two and five words. Do not change the word given.

1 I wish I hadn't been so angry.
 only
 If _____ so angry.

2 I wish I'd taken a few books with me.
 regret
 I _____ a few books with me.

3 The match was postponed because it was snowing.
 not
 If it hadn't been snowing the match _____ postponed.

4 You are not allowed to try things on in that shop.
 let
 They _____ try things on in that shop.

5 I cannot play the guitar, which is a pity.
 wish
 I _____ the guitar.

6 Marcus keeps laughing at me, which is not nice.
 stop
 I _____ laughing at me.

7 It's not necessary to pay by credit card.
 have
 You _____ pay by credit card.

8 This is my third visit to the opera.
 been
 I _____ twice before.

9 It's very boring waiting for buses.
 get
 I _____ waiting for buses.

10 They are going to make the swimming pool deeper next year.
 be
 The swimming pool _____ deepened next year.

REVISION TEST 5

3 Read this article and look carefully at each line. Some of the lines are correct and some have a word which should not be there. If a line is correct put a tick (✓). If the line has a word which should not be there, write down the word. There are two example lines at the beginning.

Dreams of Football

I dream about playing with football. I dream about it often and	**0**	*with*
it's usually the same dream. I spent most of my childhood	**00**	✓
playing football. I was never more happier than when I was	**1**	....
kicking a ball. I spent hours just kicking of a ball against a wall.	**2**	....
Then I have got a job and I just stopped playing. Years	**3**	....
went by. I reached 30. Someone told me that if you played	**4**	....
after 30 you ran a high the risk of getting a serious knee	**5**	....
injury. It seemed a good excuse for not been playing. Then I	**6**	....
reached 35; it struck me that time was running out. I'd heard	**7**	....
professionals talking about their legs which giving them trouble	**8**	....
in their mid thirties. For all I knew, it was already too much late.	**9**	....
So when someone suggested to playing football after work, I	**10**	....
thought "Why not?". It didn't go well. I was not as fit as I what	**11**	....
used to be and after 40 minutes, I twisted my ankle and had	**12**	....
so to go in goal for the rest of the game. A week later, I played	**13**	....
again. It got worse. With my first kick of the ball, I pulled a	**14**	....
muscle in my leg and couldn't play it again for three weeks.	**15**	....

Then I decided to give it one last chance before retiring for ever. It went like a dream. I felt my old skills returning and I scored a goal.

4 Use the word given in capitals at the end of each line to form a word that fits in the space.

Factory Shopping

Factory shopping – where the producer sells (**0**) *directly* to the	DIRECT
public – has grown greatly in (**1**) _____ in recent years. Some	POPULAR
of the goods on sale are (**2**) _____ , although often only the	PERFECT
packing is damaged, others result from excess (**3**) _____ at	PRODUCE
the factory.	
Ferguson's Woollen Mills have a highly (**4**) _____ chain of	SUCCESS
factory shops (**5**) _____ Britain. Several shops offer a factory	THROUGH
tour and an (**6**) _____ on cloth making and the history of the	EXHIBIT
Scottish tartan which they (**7**) _____ in. At their Glasgow	SPECIAL
factory they have (**8**) _____ opened a restaurant and	RECENT
enlarged the car park. There is also a children's (**9**) _____	GROUND
and work is continuing on (**10**) _____ to the shopping area	IMPROVE
which will increase the floor space by 60%.	

UNIT 11

Our World

| **TOPIC**
The environment

VOCABULARY FOCUS
Prepositions
Parts of a car

LANGUAGE FOCUS
Reported speech
Impersonal passive
Reporting verbs
It's time
Complaints
Pronunciation: Shifting stress and word stress | **EXAM FOCUS**
Paper 1
Reading for specific information
Multiple choice
Paper 2
Writing a discursive composition
Writing a report
Paper 3
Open cloze
Key word transformations
Paper 4
Short extracts
Note-taking
Multiple matching | Multiple choice
Paper 5
Talking about photographs
Expressing opinions

EXAM PRACTICE
Multiple choice cloze
Key word transformations
Word formation |

SPEAKING 1 Page 168
Talking about photographs

Point out that questions **1–3** are all things which students might talk about in the FCE speaking test. It will certainly be useful if they can include some of the information covered by question **1** during the initial opportunity which they have to talk about photographs. Stress that knowledge of very specific vocabulary is **not** required and students should try to paraphrase when they want to describe something for which they do not have the exact word. For example, they are not expected to know *smog mask*, but if they talk about *a thing which covers the mouth and nose and stops you breathing dangerous or unpleasant chemicals*, this would be a very acceptable description.

This phase will usually allow students about a minute to talk about their pictures uninterrupted. Point out that questions like those in **3** extend the discussion away from the photograph and onto a theme, the intention being to make the conversation more spontaneous and natural. Students should be prepared to volunteer such comments and not wait to be asked.

LISTENING 1 Page 168
Short extracts

Play the short extract twice and ask your students to decide on the answer and be prepared to justify it from what they hear.

Key

C (The extract includes: *people avoided my gaze, I felt ridiculous, I felt vaguely sick, I can't see them catching on.*)

SPEAKING 2 Page 168
Expressing and justifying opinions

As a link with the previous activity, ask students if they think that wearing a smog mask would make them feel ridiculous and uncomfortable. Ask what solutions your students can suggest in the case of very bad air pollution. Then introduce the list of solutions and get students to discuss the advantages and disadvantages in pairs or groups of three. Give them about five minutes for this discussion, then ask them to decide together which are the two best ideas and the two least effective. Elicit some sample opinions and try to establish whether there is a class consensus on the topic.

READING 1 Page 169
Multiple choice

Pre-activity: Tell students that they are going to read the article which accompanies the photo of a woman wearing a smog mask at the beginning of the unit. Tell them to look at questions **1.1** and **1.3** and to predict with a partner what the article might say about these things.

UNIT 11 Our World

Give students a couple of minutes to talk about this, then elicit some sample opinions before you get students to read the whole article and check their predictions.

1 Key

1 filter toxic gases out of the air we breathe
2 they are a frequent accessory for cyclists
3 pedestrians, traffic wardens (= officials with power to control traffic: eg illegal parking), messengers, transport police
4 that London could become as polluted as Los Angeles or Athens within 15 years
5 police officers, traffic wardens
6 men with beards, people who wear glasses or someone with a big nose
7 Friends of the Earth air pollution experts say wearing of masks is not a long-term solution
8 car usage has to be curbed

2 Key

1 toxic	2 alarming	3 cocktail
4 lung	5 prone to	6 (first) priority
7 (a perfect) seal	8 curbed	

3 Key

1 C   2 C   3 D

VOCABULARY 1 Page 170
Prepositions

Key

1 in	2 to	3 from	4 for	5 of
6 in	7 to	8 in	9 at	10 of
11 to/by	12 in	13 on/off	14 on	15 of

WRITING 1 Page 170
Discursive writing

Point out to students that making notes on the main points to be mentioned in an answer will improve the internal organisation of their written work and also help them to be sure before they begin to write that they have selected a topic which they can write enough about. If you think it would be a useful exercise for your group, get them to discuss the contents of, and to plan, all three tasks before they select one to write.

GRAMMAR 1 Page 170 (GR p 222)
Reported speech: Statements

1 Go through the verb forms used very quickly with the whole class, and then get students to identify the verb forms used in pairs.

Key

Alice:	Present simple
Andrew:	Present perfect continuous, Present perfect
Norman:	Past continuous
Jane:	Past continuous, Past simple
Alan:	'going to', Present simple
Liz:	Present continuous
Sally:	Present perfect

When you have established which verb forms are used, either get students to build up a chart on the board which shows the changes to each form in reported speech (see below), or with a strong group move straight on to rewriting the statements in pairs. Before you begin do the first statement (Alice's) with the whole class so that you are sure that they have a clear idea of what is required.

Tense Changes

Direct Speech	Reported Speech
Present simple	Past simple
Present continuous	Past continuous
Present perfect	Past perfect
Present perfect continuous	Past perfect continuous
'am/is/are going to'	'was/were going to'
Past simple	Past perfect
Past continuous	Past perfect continuous

2 Key

Alice said that she supported Friends of the Earth and other environmental movements.
Andrew said that he had been living in Athens for ten years and he had noticed the pollution getting worse.
Norman said that he had been living in London during the famous smogs of the nineteen-fifties.
Jane said that she had been visiting/was visiting Los Angeles the previous year/the year before and had been very surprised by levels of atmospheric pollution there.
Alan said that he was going to buy a car that used unleaded petrol the next time.
Liz said that she was organising a campaign in favour of banning cars from her city centre / the centre of her city.
Sally said that she had always supported the idea of using public transport instead of private cars.

3 Before students complete this exercise individually go through the sentences and get them to indicate the tense changes which are necessary, (eg 1 Past simple/Past perfect – Present simple/Past simple).
Ask students to compare their answers with a partner's and justify any differences.

Our World **UNIT 11**

Key

1 Andrew said, 'There are going to be further restrictions on traffic in Athens.'
2 Norman said, 'London is much cleaner than it was in 1960.'
3 Jane said, 'Underground railways are being built in California.'
4 Alan said, 'I've been trying to use my car less.'
5 Liz said, 'I've been using the bus every day for ten years.'
6 Sally said, 'I never use my car unless it's really necessary.'

LISTENING 2 Page 171
Note-taking

1 Introduce **Part One** of the listening by giving some additional background to the situation. Tell students that they will hear part of a radio programme where people are giving their views on the best way to reduce pollution. In the first part two people give their opinions.

Key

| 1 Lidia | 2 Les | 3 Lidia | 4 Les |

1.1 Write the verbs: can, may, must, will on the board and elicit from students that in reported speech they become
can – could
may – might
must – had to
will – would

1.2 Get students to discuss before they listen again what they remember about the opinions expressed by Lidia and Les. Accept all suggestions offered and make a list on the board under separate headings for the two people. When students listen the second time they should identify which points were mentioned and put any additional ones on the list.

1.3 Ask students to write sentences in reported speech using the notes which they made in the previous exercise.

2 Introduce **Part Two** of the listening by explaining that the presenter of the programme now gives a summary to the next caller of what has been said by Lidia and Les. He uses reported speech and students can check the sentences which they wrote in the previous activity with his summary.

Possible answers

Lidia said that she thought more people who could drive had to use public transport instead.
Les said that people would not stop using their cars until there were improvements in public transport.

Students' sentences will probably be slightly different. Tell the class to listen particularly for the verb forms, and note any differences for discussion afterwards.

3 Tell students that in **Part Three** they will hear two other people phoning the programme and giving their opinions.

Key

| 1 Gordon | 2 Gordon/Mary | 3 Gordon |
| 4 Mary | 5 Mary | |

3.1 In reported speech these modal verbs do not change.
3.2 Stress that students should only make notes (including the verb used) when listening for the second time.
3.3 From their notes, students should be able to write sentences like these:

Possible answers

Gordon said that we should make special routes for cyclists.
Mary said that she would like to ban cyclists from main roads, and that cyclists ought to be made to take a test.

GRAMMAR 2 Page 172 (GR p 222)
Reported speech: Time changes

2 Before students look at the book, write the words and expressions numbered **1–10** on the board and get students to give your their reported speech equivalents. The matching exercise can then be done as reinforcement, for homework if necessary.

Key

| 1 c | 2 j | 3 g | 4 h | 5 a | 6 d |
| 7 e | 8 i | 9 f | 10 b | | |

LISTENING 3 Page 172
Selecting an answer

1 Get students to discuss these points in pairs or groups of three as an introduction to the listening topic.

Possible answers

recycling = changing waste material into something which can be used again. Materials that are recycled vary a lot from country to country. If you are teaching a multi-national group get them to compare approaches to recycling in various countries.
Advantages: re-using waste material, saving energy, getting money from waste. Disadvantages: requires individual effort as well as a lot of organisation; can be expensive.

UNIT 11 Our World

2 Students label the car, using dictionaries if necessary.

Key

1 – headlights	2 – bonnet
3 – windscreen wiper	4 – dashboard
5 – windscreen	6 – rear-view mirror
7 – aerial	8 – sunroof
9 – boot	10 – number plate
11 – bumper	

3 Ask students what they think the following listening will be about (recycling cars). Tell them to look at the true/false sentences **1–9** and with a partner to predict what the correct answers will be. Give them a few minutes to discuss this and to make notes about their predictions. As they listen, students should check their predictions carefully.

Key

1 true	2 true	3 false	4 true
5 false	6 false	7 true	8 false
9 true			

GRAMMAR 3 Page 173
Reported questions

You will need the listening cassette for this section.

1 Play the recording from Listening 3 again after students have read the instruction. Warn students that they will have to write quite quickly, but point out that answers to Nick's questions are quite long, so there should be time to write the questions down.

Key

Are there other parts that can be recycled?
Are we talking about bumpers and things like that?
Are the particles used to make new bumpers?
Why isn't the car 100% recyclable?
Will we get more money back on our old cars?

2 With a strong class ask them to attempt the transformations into reported questions without any further introduction. Otherwise, take the first of the above questions, write it on the board and elicit the reported question from the group.

Key

1 Nick asked Jenny if/whether there were any other parts that could be recycled.
2 Nick asked Jenny if/whether they were talking about bumpers and things like that.
3 Nick asked Jenny if/whether the particles were used to make new bumpers.
4 Nick asked Jenny why the car wasn't 100% recyclable.
5 Nick asked Jenny if/whether people would get more money back on their old cars.

Note that sentence **4** is different because it is an information (or **open**) question rather than a yes/no (or **closed**) question.

3 Key

1 asked Frances what time
2 if she was coming
3 if she could borrow his (NOT: to lend him – key word must be used)
4 he knew what was
5 whether he had finished his
6 'Will/Would/Can you feed my cat
7 Will/Would/Can you get me
8 What time will the meeting
9 Could I have another knife, (NOT: could you give me another knife – five words only allowed)
10 Have you got

4 Key

1 *If/whether* is used to report yes/no questions.
2 An infinitive is used to report requests or commands.
3 A question word is used to report information questions (when a question word is used in the original sentence).

In exercise **3** above:
1 can be understood as an information question or as a request (Tim asked Frances to tell him the time).
3 can be understood as a yes/no question, or as a request (Jill asked Sam to lend her his pen).
4 can be understood as a yes/no question, or as an information question (Pam asked James what was on at the cinema), or as a request (Pam asked James to tell her what was on at the cinema).

Further practice: Show pictures of two famous people and ask students to write down an imaginary conversation between them.
Students then exchange their sentences/dialogues and transform them into reported speech, which is handed back to the original author for checking.

READING 2 Page 174
Grammar in context

1 Cover these introductory questions in a brief class discussion. Input vocabulary as required (eg the rain forests are being cut down, they are being burned).
2 This exercise is to teach vocabulary before students begin to read. If students recognise a few of the words, they can probably make a good guess about the meaning of the others by a process of elimination. Encourage students to check their guesses in a dictionary.

Key

1 b   2 d   3 a   4 e   5 f   6 c

3 Give students a time limit of five minutes or longer for this exercise – depending on the level of your group and whether you want to make this a dictionary exercise.

Key

a flooding, drought, dams
b chemist, DIY (Do It Yourself) stores
c cancer, AIDS, heart disease
d doors, window frames, toilet seats
e logging, mining, construction industry
f shot, poisoned, infected with disease

4 Key

The passive forms are:
rainforests *are cleared and burned...*
tonnes of carbon dioxide *are released* ...
One in four purchases from your chemists *is derived* ...
before they *are lost* for ever ...
people in the rainforests *have been shot, poisoned* and *infected* ...

Elicit that in each case the passive form is used because the writer wants to emphasise the action rather than the person or people responsible, or that person or people are not known.

5 Focus students on the part of the leaflet entitled 'What Friends of the Earth has done'. Before students begin this exercise point out that the subject of the new sentences will not be Friends of the Earth but the things achieved.

Possible sentences

The British Government and even timber trade organisations have been forced to acknowledge how short-sighted the devastation is.
Major international companies have been persuaded to stop industrial activities that harm the rainforests.
Consumer pressure has been mobilised and imports of tropical timber into the UK have been reduced by nearly a third.

SPEAKING 3 Page 175
Expressing and justifying opinions

Pre-activity: Set the scene by asking students to think about an advertising campaign for Friends of the Earth and what images they think are particularly suitable or unsuitable. Use some pictures from magazine advertisements for various products to stimulate ideas. Then ask students what things mentioned in the article on page 174 could be used in a poster campaign.

1 Refer students to the photographs and ask them to compare the pictures, working in pairs.
Get students to discuss the effectiveness of each of the pictures as a Friends of the Earth advertisement. (With a multi-national group encourage discussion of why different pictures might be more or less appropriate to different countries.)
Ensure that students have made fairly detailed notes about the good and bad points before they complete the task – to write 120-180 words telling Friends of the Earth why they chose a particular photograph for a poster.

WRITING 1 Page 176
Reports

This final writing exercise can be done in class with students working in pairs, or for homework. They should write their report on a separate piece of paper rather than in the Student's Book.

GRAMMAR 4 Page 176 (GR p 222)
Impersonal passive

1 Remind students that the passive form was used in the Friends of the Earth leaflet earlier in this unit because the focus was on the action or because the person/people responsible were unknown. Focus on the example of impersonal passive and ask for suggestions about the use of this form.

2 Refer students to the sentences in the box and questions **1 – 3**. Focus on the first sentence: *His wife is believed to be from the USA.* Ask: Why don't we say, 'His wife is from the USA'? (Because we are not sure. Perhaps we have been told by someone but there is some doubt about whether the information is true.) Go through the other example sentences eliciting similar information.
If necessary, tell students that these phrases are useful if we want to suggest that something may not be true without actually saying 'I don't really believe this'. It also avoids the need to give the name of the person who supplied the information. They are especially useful to journalists who want to protect their sources of information, or who report what is only rumour. Point out that these expressions are quite formal and are used with only a limited number of verbs, eg verbs of perception as in these examples.

3 Key

1 is said to have
2 is thought to be
3 says that Graham is
4 believe that the world is
5 understand that Britt is

Further practice: Write the names of some famous people on the board (TV/film stars, singers, etc.) who have been in the news recently. Ask students what gossip (= interesting 'private' information) they have heard

UNIT 11 *Our World*

about these people. Get students to write their own sentences about the famous people, using the target forms in the box. Students then compare sentences with a partner.

LISTENING 4 Page 176
Multiple choice

1 Give students a few minutes to discuss these questions, then ask them to report back to the rest of the class. Do not comment on the answers, but encourage a range of possibilities.

2 Give students time to read through the multiple-choice questions and deal with any queries before you play the tape twice.

Key

1 B   2 B   3 B   4 C

3 Key

1 thought/believed	2 from	3 have
4 that	5 hit/struck	6 the
7 by	8 led	9 still/currently/now
10 which	11 made	12 under
13 it	14 as	15 few

READING 3 Page 178
Gapped text

1 Go through the list of disasters in the box and check that students understand what they are by asking students to describe the effects and consequences of each event.

2 Key

1 E   2 A   3 G   4 C   5 F   6 B   7 H

3 someone who studies volcanoes = vulcanologist
for a short time = temporarily
financially ruined = bankrupt
for the reason that = on the grounds that
made angry = maddened
very heavy rain = torrential rains
lived through a difficult period = survived

4 eruption   threatened   civilisation
opposite   revolution   organise
Scandinavian   intended   atmosphere
ambitious   aristocratic collapsed
government   Indonesia   Eskimo
exceptionally

LISTENING 5 Page 179
Short extracts

Pre-activity: This listening exercise consists of eight very short conversations. In each case students have to decide which reporting verb is most appropriate. Before listening, go through the reporting verbs, listing them on the board and eliciting how each one is used:

warn = tell someone about a danger or problem
advise = tell someone the best thing to do or the best way to do something
persuade = convince someone to do what you tell them
invite = to ask someone if they would like to do something
encourage = try to convince someone to do something
remind = tell someone not to forget / to remember something
recommend = advise (see above)
tell = say to someone
offer = say that you will do something for another person, or give something to another person
admit = say that you have done something wrong
deny = say that something is not true
apologise = say you are sorry about something you did or said
promise = guarantee to do something
refuse = say that you will not do what someone has asked you to do

The first time you play the tape, pause after each dialogue to allow students to focus on the next group of reporting verbs. Pause again the second time and allow students to compare their answers.

1 Key

1 A   2 A   3 A   4 C   5 B   6 B   7 B   8 B

2 This focuses on the most commonly confused reporting verbs from the listening exercise.

Key

See **Pre-activity** above.

3 Key

Type A	Type B	Type C
warned	offered	admitted
advised	promised	denied
persuaded	refused	
invited		
encouraged		
reminded		
told		

Note that *apologised for* + *ing*, *persuaded* + pronoun + *that* and *recommended* + noun are different forms.

Our World **UNIT 11**

READING 4 Page 180
Multiple choice

Pre-activity: Ask students to decribe some fast-food restaurants which they know of and ask them if they like them or not. Are they usually clean and tidy? Then get them to discuss the points in **1** with a partner.

2 Key

1. wrapped in paper (line **2**), on plastic plates (**10**), cardboard plates (**10**), in chip cones (**16**)
2. The Netherlands/Holland (Dutch, line **21**)
3. powdered potato, wheat flour, vegetable oil and salt (line **26**)
4. Belfast (line **29**)
5. It needs to be bigger (lines **50 – 53**)

3 Key

1 D 2 C 3 C 4 C

4 Key

1 cuisine (line 1)	8 portions (18/25)
2 discarded (5)	9 consumed (19)
3 conventional (9)	10 litter (20, 22)
4 dumped (10)	11 impervious (27)
5 launched (13)	12 prerequisite (39)
6 edible (16)	13 re-examine (50)
7 biodegradable (16)	14 adapted (53)

5 Key

international	estimated	successfully
associated	containers	exhibitions
environmental	conventional	reception
pollution	manufacturers	appetite
packaging	approximately	expected

LISTENING 6 Page 181
Selecting an answer

Pre-activity: Before students look at the book, tell them that they will hear someone talking about how a college can become more 'environmentally friendly'. Ask students what topics they think will be discussed (eg recycling paper). Elicit a list of topics, then refer students to exercise **1** in the Student's Book. Point out that students must listen and tick the boxes to indicate the things which the speaker proposes (not necessarily all the things which are mentioned).

1 Key

Students tick:
recycling waste paper
using paper bags instead of plastic
changing cleaning materials
providing more vegetarian menus

2 Check the responses to the previous exercise before you play the tape again. Then ask students to compare answers with a partner. When checking this exercise do not be too precise about exactly which words are underlined – any answer is acceptable if it indicates that students understood the difference between the written version and Tanya's original speech.

Key

The differences are:
- she did not say that handouts were rubbish.
- she did not say that most handouts got thrown away.
- she did not say that paper was wasted because secretaries did not type on both sides of the paper.
- she did not suggest that secretaries type on the back of old worksheets.
- she did not say that the cafeteria should serve only vegetarian meals.
- she did not say that students should wash up the plastic plates and cups.

WRITING 2 Page 181
Letters

1 Ask students to correct the mistakes in the article by deciding what Tanya actually said.

2 Discuss the content of the letter with your class and establish that it will probably be semi-formal and will include a complaint about the inaccurate article.

2.1 Tell students to use the underlined (incorrect) parts of the article to help them plan the letter.
The plan might include:
1. Introduction – the complaint
2. Handouts
3. The college office
4. Vegetarian menus
5. Plastic cups
6. Conclusion

2.2 By comparing plans with a partner, students have an opportunity to check that they have included all the important points.

2.3 Get students to write in pairs in class or individually for homework.
Draw attention to the instruction about using reported speech and tell students to refer to the Grammar Reference Section (page 222) before they start to write.

Sample Answer

Dear Editor,
I am writing to complain about your article reporting a recent speech which Tanya Butler gave at a meeting of the Ecology Society.
Firstly, she did not say that handouts were rubbish or got thrown away. She said that handouts were given out each day, that they were often printed on one side

UNIT 11 Our World

and she was sure that teachers could coordinate the photocopying better.

Secondly, she did not say that paper was being wasted in the office. She said that it was high time all paper was separated from other rubbish and then recycled. Thirdly, she certainly did not say that only vegetarian meals should be served in the cafeteria. She said that there was only one vegetarian dish on the menu, and there were many students who would like a choice. Finally, Tanya did not say that students should wash up plastic plates and cups. What she said was that these were not recyclable and that it was time we used china cups and plates, which could be re-used.

I hope you will print this letter and correct all the mistakes in your article.

Yours faithfully

GRAMMAR 5 Page 182 (GR p 222)
It's time

1 Key

1 The sentences refer to the present.
2 The main parts of the sentences include the Past simple tense (this hypothetical use is called the subjunctive).

2 *It's (high) time we went* is much stronger than *It's time to go*. Play the tape again and ask students to write down four examples of *It's (high) time ....* Point out that while they listen students should only make notes, so that they can reconstruct sentences afterwards.

Possible answers

It's high time we became a lot more ecology conscious.
It's time this college woke up to the fact that a lot of resources are being wasted.
It's high time all the waste paper from the college was recycled.
It's time we went back to proper china cups and plates.
It's time we made a big effort.
It's high time a range of vegetarian meals was on offer.
It's time we had a balance of meat and vegetarian dishes on offer.

3 Key

1 (high) time this room was
2 (high) time the college was
3 I had something
4 high time I left
5 (high) time I had
6 time James had his hair (five words)
7 high time Rosemary went

Further practice: Ask students to write more sentences about their own lives, or about their school or work using these target forms.

READING 5 Page 182
Reading for main points and specific information

Pre-activity: Get students to focus on the two photographs and ask them which image they prefer and why. Then get them to discuss the points in **1**.

2 Key

1 an anti-fur group
2 Carol McKenna = the Lynx Campaign Director
   Yasmin Le Bon = a model
   Mike Allen = someone from the Fur Education Council (a pro-fur group)
   Rifat Ozbek = fashion designer
3 **5000** = the number of fur coats collect by Lynx
   2 = it is two years since Lynx declared an 'amnesty' for people to give them fur coats to be destroyed
   6 = 6 out of 10 fur retailers have closed
   millions = number of beautiful wild animals killed each year for fur

3 Key

1 mark	2 hand over	3 sanctuary
4 celebrities	5 retail outlets	6 profitable
7 drop-off	8 self-conscious	

4 Key

1 because of the Lynx campaign (and people's shock and horror)
2 warm winters (and the success Lynx had in intimidating women)
3 a drop-off in demand

SPEAKING 4 Page 184
Expressing opinions

Encourage students to discuss these topics in pairs or groups. If your students are very interested in this area, ask them to select one topic for a composition. Get them to discuss the advantages/disadvantages and/or give their opinion, whichever is appropriate.

LISTENING 7 Page 184
Multiple matching

Pre-activity: Check before playing the tape that students understand the situation which they will hear comments on. Also that students understand the names A–F of the possible speakers – you may need to explain: council officer = a local government official, senior citizen = a retired person, developer = a person or company which builds new projects.

Key

1 C   2 B   3 E   4 F   5 A

94

PRONUNCIATION Page 184
Shifting stress

1 and 2 Key

con**trol**	verb
per**mit**	verb
object	noun
transfer	noun
exports	noun
pre**sent**	verb

3 and 4 Key

con**trols**	noun
permit	noun
ob**ject**	verb
trans**fer**	verb
ex**ports**	verb
presents	noun

5 Key

It's a new world **record**.
I'd like to **record** that song.
I'd like to **contrast** the two photos.
There's quite a **contrast** between them.
I'd like to **protest** about this problem.
I'd like to make a formal **protest**.
There's been an **increase** in crime.
Crime has **increased** in recent years.
The police **suspect** him of burgling the house.
The police have arrested a **suspect**.

3 Key

1	hidden	2	probably
3	terrorists	4	explosions
5	bought	6	regularly
7	unpacking	8	lost
9	unzipping	10	discovered

EXAM PRACTICE 11 Page 185

1 Key

1 B	2 D	3 A	4 A	5 C	6 B	7 D	8 A
9 B	10 D	11 B	12 B	13 A	14 B	15 B	

2 Key

1 such nice weather
2 in spite of having
3 wish you had come
4 regret not finishing
5 he would not have felt
6 was caused by
7 advised Lorna to go to
8 reminded the children
9 warned/told me not to touch
10 he had been to a

UNIT 12
Finishing touches

TOPIC	EXAM FOCUS	Short extracts
Relationships/biographies	**Paper 1**	Listening for specific information
VOCABULARY FOCUS	Multiple matching	Blank filling
Word formation	Reading for specific information	**Paper 5**
Alone and *lonely*	Multiple choice	Giving personal information
Pets	**Paper 2**	Expressing opinions
Biographies	Writing a transactional letter	Talking about photographs
Relationships	Writing an article	**EXAM PRACTICE**
LANGUAGE FOCUS	**Paper 3**	Multiple choice cloze
Review of tenses	Word formation	Key word transformations
Question tags	Error correction	Word formation
Future in the past	Open cloze	Open cloze
Pronunciation: Contractions	**Paper 4**	
Uses of *do*	Note-taking	
	Multiple matching	

LISTENING 1 Page 187
Note-taking

1 Quickly go through the headings which students will use to make brief notes. Then play the tape once and get students to compare answers in pairs before going on to play the tape a second time. It may be easier for students to copy the grid onto another piece of paper, rather than making their notes in the Student's Book.

Key

	Paul	Catherine
Place of birth:	London	Leeds *(a city in Yorkshire, Northern England)*
Place of residence:	Scotland	Leeds
Occupation:	student	student
Hobby/Favourite subject:	travelling	Art, Design & Technology
Ambition:	work in 3rd world country	work as designer
Current project:	French/Spanish at evening classes	learning to drive
Intention:	take up 3rd language next year	take test as soon as possible

2 If necessary play the tape a third time for students to identify the tenses used to talk about each piece of information.

Key

Paul:
past simple: When I was two years old ...
present continuous: I'm studying engineering
present perfect continuous: I've been studying French and Spanish
present perfect simple: I've lived in Scotland for as long as I can remember
verb + infinitive: my parents went to live in Scotland; I hope to get a job as ...; I intend to take up a third language
past passive: I was born in London
present simple: My main hobby is travelling

Catherine:
past simple: When I was four ...; My parents moved house, then I came back to Leeds
present continuous: I'm attending a secondary school in Leeds
present perfect continuous: I've been taking driving lessons for two months
present perfect simple: I've always lived in Yorkshire
verb + infinitive: I went to live with my grandmother ...; I hope to get a job as ...; I intend to take my test as soon as possible

past passive: I was born in Leeds
present simple: My favourite subjects are Art, Design and Technology

3 Get students to think briefly about the answers they would give to these questions and which verb form they should use. Ask them to complete the third column.

SPEAKING 1 Page 187
Giving personal information

1 Elicit an example of the types of answers expected from one or two students with the whole class listening. Also draw attention to the range of tenses used. Then ask students to practise in pairs.

2 After a few minutes get them to swap pairs and repeat the activity with another partner or partners.

3 Get students to write the paragraph about themselves. Emphasise that they should use the notes they made earlier and a range of tenses, as appropriate to the information they are giving. Once the class has completed the paragraph, ask them to swap their work with that of another student and make corrections/suggestions for improvements. Read out some selected examples to the rest of the class.

READING 1 Page 188
Multiple matching

Pre-activity: Write three or four different star signs on the board and ask students what these are and to add to them – until you have all twelve of them, or at least until all the star signs of the people in the class are listed. If you think your students are likely to be interested in horoscopes, get them to tell you the symbol which is associated with each of the signs you have written on the board:

Aries	ram
Taurus	bull
Gemini	twins
Cancer	crab
Leo	lion
Virgo	a virgin
Libra	scales
Scorpio	scorpion
Sagittarius	archer
Capricorn	goat
Aquarius	water
Pisces	fish

1 Ask students in pairs or small groups to compare their knowledge of and opinions on horoscopes with a partner. In addition, ask students to tell their partners what qualities are typically associated with their own star sign.

2 Remind students that there is a reading task similar to this one in the FCE exam. Emphasise that it is not necessary or desirable for students to read all of the horoscopes in detail before they begin to answer the questions 1–16. As an introduction, draw students' attention to the two examples and ask them to find and underline the relevant information:
Virgo   *You can gain financially*
Aries   *you're in a lucky streak financially*

Before students do the task, go through the items which they have to identify and focus on the key words included in each statement (ie spend time and money, meeting someone, delay…making a decision, keep physically active, feel nervous at first, etc.). This will help students when they complete the exercise.
Give students five to ten minutes to complete as much of the exercise as possible, then ask them to compare answers in pairs or groups of three and complete the task.

Key

1/2	Aries/Sagittarius	3/4	Scorpio/Pisces
5	Gemini	6	Sagittarius
7	Gemini	8	Virgo
9	Capricorn	10/11	Leo/Libra
12/13	Taurus/Cancer	14	Leo
15	Aquarius	16	Libra

Note that where more than one answer is required (eg 1/2 or 10/11) the order in which the answers are recorded is not important.

3 Students should be able to complete most of this grid without referring to the text.

Key

VERB	NOUN	NOUN	ADJECTIVE
warn	warning	tension	tense
advise	advice	threat	threatening
encourage	encouragement	confidence	confident
promise	promise	excitement	exciting
enjoy	enjoyment	popularity	popular
recognise	recognition	romance	romantic
attract	attraction	fortune	fortunate
persuade	persuasion	caution	cautious
arrange	arrangement	hesitation	hesitant
improve	improvement	enthusiasm	enthusiastic
respond	response	irritation	irritable
satisfy	satisfaction	aggression	aggressive

UNIT 12 Finishing touches

LISTENING 2 Page 190
Short extracts

Give students time to look through the questions and respond to any queries about them before playing the tape. Point out that in the FCE Listening exam students will hear the question and the three alternative answers on the tape exactly as they are printed on the question paper, then the short extract heard twice, one immediately after the other. The instructions and questions are not repeated. On this tape you need to rewind the tape immediately after each short extract in order to play it again.

Key

1 B 2 C 3 C 4 A

GRAMMAR 1 Page 190
Question tags

1 **Pre-activity:** With Student's Books closed, write on the board the four example sentences from the previous task, but leave a blank for the question tags.
eg You've booked a single, _____ ?
Ask students to complete the blanks and to tell you the name for this form (question tags).

2 Refer students to page 190 of the book, question 2 and get them to discuss these in pairs or groups. Elicit a summary of the rules for forming question tags from the whole class.

Key

2.1 Form
A question tag is a short interrogative phrase added to a statement.
It's cold,   isn't it?
statement   tag
Negative tags are added to positive statements and positive tags to negative statements: *It's not cold, is it?* The question tag repeats the auxiliary verb or modal auxiliary verb from the statement, and the subject pronoun. If there is no auxiliary verb in the statement, *do* is used: *You like oranges, don't you?*
Note that there are some exceptions:
Imperatives have a question tag formed with *will/shall*: *Open the window, will you?*
A question tag formed with *to be* in the first person becomes: *I'm late, aren't I?* (but *'I'm not late, am I?'*)

2.2 Use
When we want to make questions we may use them to help the conversation: *It's a lovely day, isn't it?*
When we think the information in the statement is correct, but we are not completely certain, we can use them to check: *Your birthday's in July, isn't it?*

Question tags are used:
- with a rising intonation as genuine questions
- with falling intonation as conversational gambits, to help social interaction. In this case we do not need to answer – these are not real questions.

3 Key

1 a aren't you?
  b isn't it?
  c hasn't she?
  d didn't you?
  e doesn't he?
  f can't you?
  g will you?
  h shall we? (note that will we? is not possible)
  i haven't you?
  j do you?
  k have you?
  l won't you?

2 Practise some of the examples with rising and falling intonation with the whole class before asking students to work in pairs, reading out exercise **1**. If the intonation is falling (conversation gambits) tell them to nod their heads, look interested and say things like *Umm* to show their agreement. If the intonation is rising – a request to check information – they should either confirm the information or correct it. Note that some of the sentences from the exercise can only have falling intonation: **b** is talking about the weather, **g** and **h** are a reminder and a suggestion – none of these will usually have rising intonation.

4 Tell students to think about a variety of topics (eg age, family, home, habits and routines, likes and dislikes, hobbies, places visited etc.). Demonstrate what is required by thinking of some statements yourself about various students in the class, some of which you know to be true, and some of which you think might be true. Read them to the class and get the students concerned to respond appropriately using the language in the box. Then get the class to practise in pairs.

SPEAKING 2 Page 191
Expressing opinions

Pre-activity: With books closed, get students to name animals which they have as pets and suggest other animals which people have as pets. Make a list on the board, then refer students to page 191 and check the names of the animals in the picture: cat, rat, budgerigar, dog, rabbit, snake, frog (or toad)

1 Get students to discuss these points in pairs or groups. Then ask some students to report back to the rest of the class on what they decided about both discussion points.

98

Finishing touches **UNIT 12**

In particular, ask your students what they think about keeping a snake as a pet – its advantages and disadvantages.

2 Key

1 for	2 would	3 ✓	4 in
5 when	6 if	7 are	8 ✓
9 ✓	10 goes	11 ✓	12 any
13 much	14 where	15 ✓	

READING 2 Page 192
Multiple choice

1 Get students to suggest answers to **1 – 3** by quickly reading through the text. Note that in **11** students should simply identify what they know about these people who are mentioned in the story.

Key

1. Anna: a woman at the centre of the story – visited at her home by Maria
   Richard: a close friend of, or the partner of Anna
   Kate: a friend of Anna's
   Maria: a woman who likes cats
   Griselda: Anna's mother's cat
   Melusina: one of Maria's cats, which has died

2. Anna: was driving too fast and killed the cat – she is anxious, and later relieved when Maria left
   Richard: feels that Anna should not give in to Maria's demands
   Kate: doesn't see Maria as a very serious problem
   Maria: wants Anna to compensate her for the death of the cat

3. Get students to speculate about a range of things which might happen next. Return to this once students have completed the remaining reading tasks and ask them to vote on what they think the most likely outcome is – it seems to be something unpleasant for Anna, possibly involving Griselda (her mother's cat).

2 Key

1 D   2 A   3 C   4 C   5 C   6 A   7 C

Point out that question **2** asks about difficult vocabulary. There will often be a question of this type in the FCE Reading test. As in this exercise, the line reference will always be given for the relevant word, and it will be possible to guess the meaning of the word from the context.

In question **7** students are asked to decide what 'it' refers to. Point out that students may need to look backwards or forwards in the text to find the answer. This again is a typical FCE question, and the line reference will be given.

LISTENING 3 Page 194
Note-taking

Pre-activity: Before you play the tape, focus on the picture on the same page and ask : 'Who is this?' If your students recognise Mozart as a young boy, then ask: 'What do you know about Mozart's life?' it is not important if they know very little. This is only to stimulate interest and introduce the topic of the listening. If they do not recognise Mozart, tell students to listen and identify the person in the picture as well as complete the biographical notes. Before they listen, ask: 'How old do you think the person in the picture is?'
Play the tape twice.

Key

1 was born	2 pianist	3 Vienna
4 operas	5 court composer	6 died

GRAMMAR 2 Page 194
Future in the past

1 Key

The time referred to is the past. The tense used is called future in the past.
Refer students to the time line and elicit example sentences using the target expressions (including past perfect and future in the past) and the information which students noted down in their answers to the previous listening exercises.

2 Get students to look at the picture and read the biographical information before you ask: 'When was this picture taken?' (in 1938), and 'How old is he in the picture?' (about 27).
Elicit sentences from your class about each stage of Reagan's career using the past perfect tense for events before the photograph was taken (eg He had been born in Tampico, Illinois, USA. He had been educated at Ureka College, Illinois), and the future in the past tense forms for events which happened after the photograph was taken (eg He was to go to Hollywood in 1937. He was going to make his first film in 1937. He went on to make over 50 films between 1937 – 1962).
Get students in pairs to write the script for the quiz show presenter with either Reagan or Albert Einstein as the subject. For homework ask students to find out some biographical details of a famous person(perhaps from a magazine or newspaper article), and to draw a sketch of that person in the early part of their life or career (this is important if students are to use the future in the past forms) – emphasise that not only is artistic ability not necessary, in fact the more difficult it is to recognise the person the better. Students then write the quiz show presenter's script for this person's life. In the next lesson get some students to show their pictures and read

UNIT 12 Finishing touches

their descriptions while the rest of the class guess the identity.

LISTENING 4 Page 196
Note-taking

Pre-activity: Write the word 'wax' on the board and ask students where it comes from (eg from bees, although there are lots of other sources), and what it is used for (eg candles, polishing furniture, making models of people). Then get them to discuss in pairs what they know about Madam Tussaud's Waxworks in London. Note that Madam Tussaud's is among London's most popular tourist attractions and if any of your students have been to London as tourists, they will probably have visited Madam Tussaud's.

Part 1 Blank filling

Get students to read through the notes and ask them to suggest the type of answer which might go in each space before you play this part of the tape twice.

Key

1 housekeeper
2 model wax
3 art teacher
4 The doctor
5 heads of (dead) aristocrats
6 a supporter
7 went to England
8 waxworks museum
9 permanent exhibition
10 1850

Part 2 Multiple matching

Key

1 E   2 A   3 C   4 F   5 B

READING 3 Page 197
Reading for specific information

Pre-activity: To stimulate interest and introduce the topic, select one of the events in **1.1** yourself and tell the class about it. Think about what you want to say beforehand and try to include plenty of detail in your account.

1 Once students have had an opportunity to discuss these points in pairs, ask a few of your students to report back to the rest of the class.

2 Key

1 A   2 C   3 B   4 C   5 C   6 C

READING 4 Page 198
Multiple matching

Pre-activity: Before referring students to the list of qualities of a friend, ask the class as a whole to describe some qualities of a good friend. Then ask students to focus on the list in **1** and to discuss them in pairs.

2 Before students read, point out that they should look carefully through the list of headings **A – I**, so that they can start to form views on the right answers immediately they start to look at the article. It is not necessary to read the entire article before starting to come to decisions about which heading might fit with each part. They may have to complete the whole article before they can be quite sure of the correct sequence of answers, but they should be able to eliminate/select some of the answers as they read

Key

1 E   2 H   3 A   4 D   5 B   6 C   7 F

3 Key

1 so *such.*	2 of	3 in	4 it
5 ✓	6 one	7 this	8 some
9 yourself	10 ✓	11 with	12 ✓
13 as	14 be	15 ✓	

WRITING 1 Page 200
A transactional letter

Before students start to plan their writing, check through the additional handwritten information provided to ensure they have understood it and understood the need to ensure that the points in these notes are addressed in their letter.
Remind students that as far as possible they should avoid repeating complete phrases from the input text (ie the advertisement and the notes) in their answer. For example, they should not write: *I want to come to your school because it is situated in beautiful countryside, close to the ancient city of Cotsford where all ......*, etc, etc. This is a technique which will create a very poor impression on the examiner who assesses their work.

SPEAKING 3 Page 201
Talking about photographs

Take this opportunity to remind students of the format of the FCE Speaking test (see Introduction page viii), and what type of activity they will be required to complete with their partner in each part of the test.

Finishing touches **UNIT 12**

LISTENING 5 Page 202
Blank filling

Before students listen, ask them to read through the notes carefully and to suggest where possible the type of answer, or a possible answer which might fit into each gap. Tell students that in the FCE Listening test, incorrect spelling (especially of names) is not penalised as long as the answer is recognisable, ie it is much better if students spell correctly in the Listening test, but they will not suffer if they make the occasional slip. Then play the tape twice.

Key

1 marriage/weddings
2 the Manchester branch
3 friendships
4 a bar or disco
5 a client
6 have arguments
7 to resign/leave
8 don't say anything
9 work suffered
10 don't concentrate

GRAMMAR 3 Page 202
Uses of do

1 and 2

Elicit from the class the use of forms of *do* in each of these sentences from the listening text. If necessary, play the tape once more and ask students to focus on these forms.

Key

1 part of the question form
2 part of the negative form
3 replacement for a previously mentioned phrase (realise that a relationship at work gets in the way of doing the job properly)
4 emphasis/contradiction of what has been said earlier
5 part of the negative form, given emphasis by not contracting this to *don't*

3 Tapescript and Key

Interviewer:
Apparently over half of office romances end up with the sound of wedding bells. So, if you met your current partner at work, you could be well on your way towards marriage. It's all come out in a romantic survey today put together by the Recruitment Consultants Company and the manager of their Manchester branch is Lorna Telford and she's here with me to explain it. Lorna, good morning to you.
Lorna:
Good morning, John.

Interviewer:
So, how **does (question form)** it happen, romance in the work environment, is it love at first sight?
Lorna:
No, I mean, in our office in Manchester three out of the five people met their partners through work, and they all stress it was friendship first and then it turned into something different, but it depends on age and personal circumstances, of course.
Interviewer:
It seems almost like a pair of shoes, **doesn't (negative form)** it, in that you wear them in and then you become comfortable in the relationship. Whereas if you meet people in a bar or disco, then it's all a bit more difficult.
Lorna:
You're very right there. I mean the time we spend at work has a strong link with the relationships we build at work compared to those we build with people we meet in public places and situations like that. You **do (emphasis)** get used to somebody and you get to know their ways and then, suddenly, love takes over and your feelings are so intensified, one would imagine, that it changes the whole thing.
Interviewer:
I must ask, **do (question form)** you have personal experience of this?
Lorna:
Yes, but it was through work, rather than at work. My husband was actually a client of mine but we'll say no more about that ...
Interviewer:
But, of course, it can be a problem, I would have thought, as well, because couples have an argument and you're still in the same environment eight hours a day – Oh I can see problems there ...
Lorna:
You **do (emphasis)** find that. From the survey, although not many people were asked to leave their jobs, more females than males **did (emphasis)** decide to resign and I think it's because it became intolerable to be in the same environment – not only if a relationship had broken down, but can you imagine being with your partner 24 hours a day? I mean, no thanks! *(ironic)*
Interviewer:
What else **did (question form)** the survey show up then?
Lorna:
One very important point was that managers **didn't (negative form)** seem to be at all bothered, according to those having relationships, but we found that, in fact, managers **do (emphasis/contradiction)** mind and they **do not (negative/emphasis)** like relationships at work, regardless of the fact that nothing's ever said about it, they **don't (negative)** like it and so it can have a negative effect on your career. Another interesting fact that it **did (emphasis)** show up was that according to

the individuals who were carrying on a relationship, their work **didn't (negative)** suffer. However, when their colleagues were asked, they felt that yes, work **did (emphasis)** suffer. So, there's a misconception there of how well you're doing at work and how others see you.
Interviewer:
So, presumably the other people will think that the relationship is going to get in the way of work?
Lorna:
Exactly, and it seems it **does (emphasis)** get in the way of people's ability to actually **do (replaces a verb** like *complete)* the job properly. The people having the relationship **don't (negative)** realise this, but those who are observing **do (replacing a longer phrase)**.
Interviewer:
Well, if you're in love, you're happy, everything is great, **doesn't (negative question)** that make you work better?
Lorna:
I think you feel like that , but with all due respect, what actually happens is that you're not really concentrating on your work, and it is noticed.
Interviewer:
What about secret relationships? Does your survey touch on those at all?
Lorna:
It **does, (replaces a longer phrase)** yes. What we found was that people ...

4 Key

1 My brother studies English but my sister **doesn't** .
2 I don't like classical music, but my parents **do**.
3 I didn't go to Olga's party, but Joanne **did**.
4 Lorna met her partner through her work, but John **didn't** .
5 Most people don't like filling in questionnaires, but Roy **does**.

5 Key

1 People **do** think that the relationship affects their work.
2 What we found was that people **do** try to keep these relationships secret.
3 Rosie **does** find it difficult to make friends at parties.
4 You may think your mother didn't notice, but she **did**.
5 Pete! How nice to see you. **Do** come and have a cup of coffee.

WRITING 2 Page 203
An article

Get students to select, think about and plan their article individually, then put them into pairs or groups of three with other students who have selected the same topic. Ask them to compare ideas and to make suggestions about other things which they might include in their answers. Then get students to complete their writing in about 35 minutes. Note that in the exam students have one hour and thirty minutes to complete two answers, but this includes the time necessary to select, plan and check their final answer. Hence the shorter time limit suggested here.

PRONUNCIATION Page 203
Contractions

Remind students of some of the phrases using forms of *do* which they looked at in Grammar 3 and which were contracted or uncontracted.
Make sure that you read and get the class to repeat the examples individually or chorally before asking them to practise in pairs.

LISTENING 6 Page 204
Multiple matching

Pre-activity: Go through the list of options A – F and ask students to think of life as one of a family of very famous singers. For each topic elicit what types of problems might occur and why. This will help students to focus on the options when they come to listen to the tape.

Key

1 D 2 B 3 A 4 E 5 F

READING 5 Page 204
Multiple matching

1.1 Key

Alone – suggests being on your own without other people around you, and is generally used as a neutral word.
Lonely – means being very unhappy because there are no other people around you (or at least you feel this – it is possible to be lonely when you are in a crowd of people if you do not know anyone).

2 Get students to focus on the topic, the instructions and in particular the example. Then ask students to decide in pairs which extract fits into space **1** and to justify their decision. (The key to **1** is **G**, as it describes a long journey from his home in the country and the text continues: *Most of his classmates make similar journeys every day.*) Then get students individually to complete the rest of the task before they compare and justify answers.

Key

1 G 2 A 3 F 4 D 5 B 6 H 7 E

EXAM PRACTICE Page 206

1 Key

| 1 C | 2 A | 3 B | 4 D | 5 A | 6 C | 7 A | 8 C |
| 9 A | 10 D | 11 B | 12 A | 13 A | 14 C | 15 A |

2 Key

1. been collecting stamps for
2. does this wallet belong
3. a two-year translation
4. write as clearly as
5. her injured ankle/having injured her ankle
6. blame me if the
7. his father for
8. had had enough lessons
9. was so long
10. have been taught how

3 Key

1 unsurprising	2 anger	3 pretence
4 dramatic	5 caught	6 endless
7 understanding	8 arguments	9 outcome
10 unreasonable		

4 Key

1 like	2 after	3 family	4 up
5 never/rarely	6 for	7 many	8 in
9 another	10 without	11 took	12 get
13 so	14 has	15 an	

SAMPLE ANSWER SHEETS Pages 209–210

Answer sheets are used by students to record answers for FCE papers 1, 3 and 4. Sometimes the students complete a small box to indicate their answer (eg in Paper 1, Reading) and this is directly read by a computer. Sometimes students write their answers (eg Paper 3 Use of English, Part 2) and their answer is checked by a marker in Cambridge before the marks for correct answers are recorded by a computer.

Note that students must use pencil only on the answer sheet. If they want to change an answer they should use an eraser to cancel out the original.

The example answer sheets in the book are approximately half full size. Students will find that in the real exam they have plenty of space to write their answers. Give students plenty of practice in marking answers on the answer sheets and suggest to students the best way of transferring their answers.

In Papers 1 and 3 students can, if they want to, mark their answers on the question paper and then copy them on to the answer sheet. If they choose to do this they should transfer answers at the end of each Part, rather than at the end of the exam. They should leave time to check that they have transferred correct answers to the correct part of the answer sheet, and they should remember that no additional time is allowed at the end of the exam for transferring answers.

In Paper 4, Listening, students have exactly five minutes to transfer their answers once all the listening texts have finished. They should not attempt to complete the answer sheet while they are listening, or at the end of each individual Part, but should simply record their answers on the question paper until told (on the tape) to transfer them to the answer sheet. Transfer must be completed within the five minutes allowed (this period is recorded on the tape).

REVISION TEST 6

1 Key

| 1 C | 2 A | 3 D | 4 A | 5 D | 6 B | 7 A | 8 C |
| 9 B | 10 D | 11 B | 12 A | 13 B | 14 D | 15 C |

2 Key

1. If she would buy/get him
2. Have you got many friends
3. is said to be
4. reminded Lisa to bring
5. apologised for forgetting

3 Key

1 much	2 of	3 ✓	4 for
5 ✓	6 if	7 times	8 to
9 ✓	10 they	11 where	12 ✓
13 need	14 despite	15 ✓	

4 Key

1 powerful	2 interesting	3 scientists
4 network	5 necessarily	6 intelligence
7 unfolded	8 movement	9 information
10 personality		

REVISION TEST 6

1 Read the text below and decide which word A, B, C or D best fits each space.

Sing-a-long-a-fax

In the 1920s, a popular (0) __A__ for many families was standing around the piano singing a song. This (1)_____ that sales of sheet music were very large. A five-million copy (2)_____ was not uncommon and publishers put (3)_____ up to ten songs a day. Salesmen travelled the country singing them to (4)_____ customers in the days before recorded music, radio and TV were (5)_____ and people's appreciation of music became more passive.

Today, however (6)_____ music for pleasure is staging a dramatic comeback. It is (7)_____ that five million people in Britain are currently playing an instrument for pleasure. And, strangely, it is (8)_____ mainly to the technology which put it out of (9)_____ in the first place. You no (10)_____ have to visit a music shop to buy sheet music, you just key a few numbers into a fax machine, and a copy of (11)_____ from Bach's Prelude to Elton John's Crocodile Rock is yours to play.

It has taken two years to (12)_____ the project which (13)_____ anyone with access to a fax machine to (14)_____ a song from a list of two thousand classical and popular pieces and have a perfectly printed copy (15)_____ a few seconds.

0	A pastime	B leisure	C relaxation	D retirement
1	A led	B represented	C meant	D indicated
2	A hit	B strike	C gain	D mark
3	A away	B on	C off	D out
4	A likely	B awaited	C believed	D probably
5	A announced	B advanced	C founded	D introduced
6	A giving	B making	C doing	D getting
7	A estimated	B counted	C invented	D valued
8	A regards	B account	C thanks	D according
9	A taste	B fashion	C style	D manner
10	A sooner	B further	C better	D longer
11	A whatever	B anything	C somewhere	D everything
12	A develop	B grow	C broaden	D result
13	A lets	B allows	C makes	D leaves
14	A switch	B pay	C point	D select
15	A through	B by	C within	D around

2 Complete the second sentence so that it has a similar meaning to the first sentence. Use the word given and other words to complete each sentence. You must use between two and five words. Do not change the word given.

1 'Would you get me a newspaper while you're out, please?' said Lorna to John.
if
John asked Lorna _____ a newspaper while she was out.

2 Dan asked Mary if she had many friends.
got
Dan said, _____, Mary?'

3 Everyone says that New York is very exciting.
be
New York _____ very exciting.

4 'Don't forget to bring some cakes to the party, Lisa' said David.
reminded
David _____ some cakes to the party.

5 'I'm sorry I forgot your birthday' Ellie said to me.
apologised
Ellie _____ my birthday.

3 Read this article and look carefully at each line. Some of the lines are correct and some have a word which should not be there. If a line is correct put a tick (/). If the line has a word which should not be there, write down the word. There are two example lines at the beginning.

Desktop publishing

The basic idea behind desktop publishing is that all it the	**0**	*it*
equipment necessary to produce booklets, handouts and so	**00**	✓
on, can fit on top of a desk. Basically, it is a very much complex	**1**	....
computer system.		
First the operator types the text of into the computer, then	**2**	....
she can try out different sizes of text and sizes of type. It is also	**3**	....
possible for to alter the margins around the text, the width of	**4**	....
the lines, the spaces between them, and so on. She will be	**5**	....
able to see on the screen what if the finished pages will look	**6**	....
like. If there are too many times words on a page, she can	**7**	....
to try changing the type size or margins, or just cut the text.	**8**	....
The desktop publisher acts as editor and designer. She can	**9**	....
also be the illustrator. Most desktop publishing systems they	**10**	....
have a scanner, where pictures where from any source can	**11**	....
be transferred to the screen.		
Desktop publishing can be used by authors who want to	**12**	....
produce a small number of their own books without need going	**13**	....
to a publisher. Despite it is widely used for companies for their	**14**	....
brochures, newsletters and information booklets for their	**15**	....
customers or clients.		

4 Use the word given in capitals at the end of each line to form a word that fits in the space.

Brain power

The brain is one of the (**0**) *largest* organs of the human body,	LARGE
and certainly the most complicated and (**1**) _____. It is also	POWER
one of the most (**2**) ____ . It has been studies by philosophers	INTEREST
and (**3**) _____ since ancient Greek times.	SCIENCE
The human brain is a vast communications (**4**) _____, but	NET
big brains are not (**5**) _____ better. Whales have larger brains	NECESSARY
than humans but do not have the same level of (**6**) _____.	INTELLIGENT
We have lots of 'folded' grey matter, or thinking area, which if (**7**) ___,	FOLD
would cover an area the size of a pillowcase.	
This grey matter controls all conscious (**8**) _____ and enables us	MOVE
to think, remember and dream. It receives all the (**9**) ____ picked	INFORM
up by the ears, eyes and other senses. It also gives us (**10**) _____	PERSON
and emotions, making us outgoing or shy, razor-sharp or absent-minded.	

Listening scripts

Unit 1 Listening 1

The police are looking for a woman who held up a post office in Liverpool yesterday. The woman, who is described as being tall, in her late thirties with short brown curly hair and blue eyes, spoke with a London accent.
Cashier Anne Jones, who was today under sedation at her home in the city, said that the woman had seemed like an ordinary customer, asking for three first class stamps before suddenly pulling out a gun. The woman walked into the Post Office in Littleton Road at two o'clock yesterday afternoon and forced the cashier to hand over ten thousand pounds at gunpoint. No customers were in the post office at the time, but eyewitnesses who saw her running away along Station Road afterwards described her as wearing a short grey woollen overcoat over a skirt and carrying a brown leather shoulder bag and an umbrella. She was wearing high-heeled shoes. The police are asking anyone who may have seen the woman in Littleton Road to come forward.

Unit 1 Listening 2

Peter: I have with me today our old friend, Rosie Lawsdon, who's been doing some research into faces, isn't that right, Rosie?
Rosie: Well, yeah, I've been reading a new book all about the character traits associated with various shapes of face and the various features, you know, eyes, nose, ears, that sort of thing.....
Peter: You mean like whether your ears stick out and all that?
Rosie: Yeah. But people take this very seriously, Peter.
Peter: OK, then so shall I. Tell us more.
Rosie: Well, basically, the shape of the face tells you a lot. If you've got a round face, like me, this is associated with lazy people and a home-loving attitude. Not that I'm like that. Anyway, a square-shaped face indicates, on the other hand, someone practical, and reliable.
Peter: Like me?
Rosie: Well, no. Your face is more, kind of rectangular, which is said to be for lucky people, good leaders and those who are successful in life. Is that you, Peter?
Peter: Yes, that sounds great. But I wasn't lucky with my ears. Look, they stick out a mile.
Rosie: Um, you've got large ears which again is a sign of a lively and enthusiastic person, but I'm afraid sticking-out ears generally mean someone who is bossy and selfish, quite difficult to get on with actually.
Peter: Oh no, that's not true, Rosie, I'm ever so friendly.
Rosie: Maybe that's because you've got big eyes, which is a sign of friendliness, and thick eyebrows which is again often found in good leaders, people who are strong and independent.
Peter: I must say this is all most flattering, Rosie, do tell me more.
Rosie: Let me see, sticking with you for a while, you have, of course got a big mouth....
Peter: Now, careful Rosie, be careful what you're saying....
Rosie: Large, I mean, in the sense of full lips and a wide smile. This denotes someone sociable, warm, charming and popular.
Peter: You know, I'm beginning to like my face.
Rosie: and, of course, you've got a large full nose which is always a sign of someone easy-going, artistic.....
Peter: Oh, yes. That's me exactly....
Rosie: ....and of course, vain.
Peter: Vain? Rosie!
Rosie: Yes, vanity always goes with a large nose, big mouth and thick, bushy eyebrows, didn't you know?
Peter: OK Rosie, that's enough about me. What about people with long, thin noses? I bet they're pretty horrid, aren't they?

Unit 1 Pronunciation
Word Stress

1 Look at the words in the box. How many syllables are there in each word?
Here is an example: so/cia/ble

2 Listen to the words. Which syllable is stressed in each word?

so ciable	thoughtful	adven turous
realistic	creative	enthusiastic
helpful	unemotional	imaginative
independent	understanding	idealistic
reserved	analytical	lazy
religious	lucky	fair
communicative	indecisive	

Unit 1 Listening 3

Speaker: Good morning, my name's Mike Matthews and I shall be in charge of the party during the whole trip to Scotland. I've asked you all to come along to this briefing today to give you some advice about what to take with you on the trip, how best to equip yourselves, what will be provided, and so on and so forth.
Now, I know you've all looked at the programme, so if I go through my list of points first, then I'll take any questions. Please ask about anything you're unsure of, OK?
Right. Firstly, luggage – we're travelling to Scotland on the overnight sleeper train and then getting around by coach. Although we won't have to carry anything very far, we will be staying in a different hostel each night and so we have to transfer all the luggage from the coach to the hostel every time. So please bring a rucksack, or something easy to carry. Now, that's one large piece of luggage per person only, please.
Then you must bring a small waterproof bag, a small rucksack is good for this, to carry onto the coach and on the walks. We'll have to carry a packed lunch and study materials with us each day. Now, don't forget: put your name and address inside and outside each piece of luggage in case it gets lost – this is important.
Next thing, coats. You must bring a full-length waterproof coat – an anorak or something with a hood is best. Now, although it's spring, the weather can be quite cold and wet in the Highlands and so you need plenty of pairs of socks in case you get wet feet, and a couple of good thick pullovers in case it gets very cold. Gloves are essential for the walking trips and skiing gloves are best. Footwear. We're not going mountain climbing as such, but we'll be crossing some rough country and you must have strong walking boots. If possible, bring old comfortable ones because we're going on some long walks. If you have to buy new boots, go for a good long walk before we leave in case they rub or hurt your feet. So this is another good reason to bring lots of pairs of thick socks. Oh, and don't forget to bring some casual shoes to change into in the evening in case your boots get wet and dirty. You don't want to be eating dinner and relaxing in your smelly old boots if you've had them on all day, do you?
Now, we'll have a first-aid kit on the coach, but in case you have an accident while out walking, bring a small first aid-kit – some plasters, a bandage, that sort of thing to keep in a pocket of your small rucksack. Put in some glucose tablets, chocolate, that sort of thing, just in case you get lost or exhausted on any of the walks.
Right, and that's about all on my list – has anyone got any questions?

Unit 1 Writing 1
Exercise 3

Student 1: The thing that I don't like about school uniform is that you have to wear it. I mean, they are always such horrible colours and styles and you don't get any choice – even if the things don't suit you.
Student 2: Well, one good thing is that if you see kids in uniform you know which school they come from, whether they are in school or not. So if they're being naughty, for example, they can be identified.
Student 3: I like the uniform, it's really nice to see everyone looking smart and wearing the same things. In my sister's school they don't have a proper uniform and the kids look really scruffy – especially in photos and on trips and that sort of thing.
Student 4: One good thing is that it makes everyone look the same and so the rich kids look the same as the poor kids and everyone's equal. It means you can be proud of your school, you have a common identity.
Student 5: I think that's stupid. You can always tell the kids with poor parents, whether they're in uniform or not, because they wear old worn-out uniforms that don't fit them properly. It just makes it more expensive for their parents having to buy the stuff, that's all.

Unit 2 Listening 1

Carole: First of all, I'd like to thank you very much for inviting me here today. It's strange being back in this room. It seems like a lifetime since I left, my life has changed so much. Anyway, I think you've prepared some questions, so why don't we start with them? I'm not very good at giving speeches, so who'd like to start?
Student 1: How did you get your present job?
Carole: I saw an advert in the paper and wrote off for an application form. They wanted someone with languages – I've got Spanish and French at A-level and I can understand Italian.
Student 1: Were the subjects you studied at school useful in your work?
Carole: Oh, Yes. I never really liked school much and I didn't work very hard, but I enjoyed my A-level subjects, and I liked the teachers in the sixth form, so yes, the languages have been useful in my job and the other subjects, of course. I've got A-level geography.
Student 2: Did you apply for many different jobs?
Carole: Oh yes. All different kinds of things, too. I really wanted to be a translator or an interpreter, but I didn't want to go to university. I wanted to get out to work as soon as possible. But I get to do some translating now, of course.
Student 2: Did you have to have an interview?
Carole: Yes, and they made me speak in French and Spanish, as well.
Student 3: How much training did they give you when you started?
Carole: Very little! I spent two months at head office in London, learning about the company. But in this job it's experience that counts. It was my first season in Italy that really taught me about the job.
Student 3: So, what have you got out of the job?
Carole: I've had lots of experience of dealing with people – usually they come to me when there are problems, not when they're happy. And then I've learned how to sort out those problems, often using my languages – you know, it's um dealing with the local people, too, not just the customers. I've had the chance to develop my interpersonal skills and my language skills and of course it's wonderful living in another country.
Student 4: What hours do you work?
Carole: Oh, it's very hard work. I sometimes feel I work twenty-four hours a day. I've sometimes received phone calls in the middle of the night, if there's a crisis, or something. There are no fixed hours.
Student 4: What's the worst crisis you've had to deal with?
Carole: The worst was explaining to 200 holidaymakers that their flight home had been delayed for forty-eight hours because of a strike, and that their hotel rooms had already been occupied by new arrivals.
Student 4: What did you do?
Carole: They had to sleep in the airport, and I had to deal with all the complaints. Those are the sort of problems we have to be ready for – you know, strikes, delays, overbooking, people getting ill – it's all part of the job – you have to try and keep smiling.
Student 1: And what about the salary? Is it, is it worth it?
Carole: The money isn't so good at the beginning, but for someone of my age it's about average. And, of course, there are lots of advantages, like the weather and cheap holidays.

Unit 2 Pronunciation

Past tense endings
There are three ways of pronouncing the regular past tense ending e-d.
Listen to the examples.
enjoyed   enjoyed
wanted   wanted
liked   liked

1 Add the words you hear to the correct column.
printed /ɪd/   described /d/   worked /t/
helped /t/   answered /d/   dressed /t/
robbed /d/   asked /t/   waited /ɪd/
lived /d/   decided /ɪd/   included /ɪd/

4 Now listen to the words in the box.
arrived /d/   sounded /ɪd/   educated /ɪd/
needed /ɪd/   disappointed /ɪd/   passed /t/
listened /d/   trained /d/   tried /d/
washed /t/   packed /t/   turned /d/
helped /t/   discussed /t/   skilled /d/

Unit 2 Listening 2

Interviewer: Good morning, can I help you?
Lucy: Yes, I'm looking for a job. I'd like something for a short period – a few months.
Int: I see, are you a student?
Lucy: Yes.
Int: So you're looking for something for the vacation, just for the holidays?
Lucy: Yes, that's it.
Int: Well, if you'd like to have a seat, I'll just get a form. Right, now, first of all I'll just ask you a few questions so that we know something about you and then we'll look at vacancies which are available. First of all, what's your name please?
Lucy: Lucy Bennett.
Int: Can you spell Bennett for me please?
Lucy: Yes, it's B-E double N-E double T.
Int: B-E double N-E double T, right. And your address?
Lucy: It's 15 Conway Street, Cambridge.
Int: Right. Now, I just need to ask you about the sort of work you've done in the past and things you've studied. First of all, what are you studying?
Lucy: Well, erm, I'm studying Italian, I'm at the University.
Int: Good, we get demand sometimes for people who can speak foreign languages, you know. Now, can you cook or have you ever worked in a restaurant?
Lucy: Well, no. I've never done that sort of work, but I'm quite a good cook.
Int: How about sports, play any games?
Lucy: No, not really, I haven't got time.
Int: Do you drive, Lucy?
Lucy: Yes.
Inter: You've got a full driving licence … and can you type?
Lucy: um, not very well, but I've got a word processor. And I did do a course a couple of years ago.
Int: OK, that seems to complete the skills part … what sort of work experience have you had so far? Have you done any jobs?
Lucy: Yes, I worked in a department store one holiday and another time …
Int: What short of thing did you do in the department store?
Lucy: I was just a shop assistant …
Int: What, taking the money and … .
Lucy: Well, no I wasn't taking the money actually, I wasn't allowed to work on the till, but I did everything else in the shop. And another time I worked for the Post Office sorting letters … when I was at school I worked in a cake shop at weekends, oh, yes, I had a job in a bar, playing the piano in the evening.
Int: Playing the piano, right. Now, have you ever done any work with children?
Lucy: No, but I like children and I'd like to try working with them.
Int: Right. You want a job for the summer ….
Lucy: Three or four months if possible …
Int: Have you got any idea of what other sort of work you want to do?
Lucy: Well, I don't think I'd like office work very much. Maybe I'd like working as a waitress.
Int: Yes … Are you looking for a full time job or …?
Lucy: Oh, well full-time for preference but I'm pretty flexible about hours and well, obviously I want to earn as much as I can.
Int: Right. I've got some cards here with some information about jobs, so let's have a look at those and see which ones might be of interest …

Unit 2 Listening 3

….and now it's time for jobwatch, your chance to hear about the jobs on offer in town this week.
And first of all, we have a request for a mature, enthusiastic person with good phone manner and accurate typing skills. Now this person is being sought by a media company in need of someone to answer the phone and help with all aspects of the business. The hours are 9.30 till 5.30 Monday to Friday and there is a starting salary of £8000 a year. Phone Tony on 388965 if you're interested. (pause)
Next, a sewing machinist is required by a new clothing company. Experience of doing alterations is essential and the person must be friendly and must enjoy working with other people. The salary is between £3.50 and £4.00 per hour, but full-time work may not always be available with the actual hours worked varying from week to week. The number to ring is 450092 if you fit the bill, that's 450092. (pause)
A courier company is seeking an owner/rider to do despatch work in the city centre. Now any size machine will do, but experience is preferred and you must have a clean driving licence. The hours are 8.00 am to 6.00 pm weekdays and for that you get £200 per week plus petrol. Phone Dave on 223189 for further details. (pause)
Articulate, well-spoken people of any age are needed to work as interviewers. You'll join a team carrying out ad hoc market research assignments. You must be smart and well-educated, but no experience is necessary. The salary is £5.00 per hour with working hours varying according to the project. Now the person to ring for this one is Sandra on 447605. That's 447605 and ask for Sandra. (pause)
Finally, an office junior with good typing skills and computer literacy is needed to work for a mechanical servicing company, doing all the normal junior duties including computer input. Normal office hours Monday to Friday for a starting salary of £8000 per annum. Call Debbie now on 721436. Debbie is waiting for your call.

Unit 2 Listening 4

F: That was the last one. Can we go through their application forms again and try to make a decision?
M: Sure, let's do it now while we remember. OK, they've all got the basic qualifications we asked for in the advert.
F: Except Pattie, remember. She hasn't got her driving licence, yet. She said she's doing the test next week.
M: Right. Now, first we interviewed Terry. What did you think of him?
F: He's certainly experienced at organising conferences, we want someone with good experience, don't we?
M: Oh yes, but it's not the only important thing, is it?
F: No, no, of course not, but I liked him. I think he's got a good personality, don't you? – He'd be good with people.
M: Yes and that's essential in this work, as we know well.
F: It certainly is.
M: I must say though, I was a bit concerned about his appearance. He was rather untidy and his shoes were dirty. Did you notice?
F: Yes, and first impressions count a lot in this job. Yes, we want someone smart and certainly Terry isn't as smart as Jack or Pattie.
M: And this is the interview. What would he be like in the job?
F: Um, and he hasn't got the computer graphics experience we want.
M: That's just what I was thinking.
F: Pattie's got much more experience of computers than him.
M: Yes, let's talk about Pattie. She's got graphics experience, which would be very useful in the team.
F: That's right, we need someone who knows about that side of things.
M: Yes, but she doesn't have as much experience of organising conferences as Terry, very little experience, in fact, which worries me a bit.
F: I know what you mean, but I felt she was a calm, sensible sort of person – I can imagine her in a crisis. I think she seemed more able to cope than the other two.
M: Yes, her answers were very sensible, and she looked right for the job – very smartly dressed. She was much smarter than Terry. But there is the problem of her driving test.
F: Yes, the driving licence is essential, and she is very young, of course.
M: Well, how about the third one: Jack?
F: Now he's older, and he's got lots of experience. He's certainly got more experience of organising conferences than the other two.
M: Yes, that's true.
F: And I thought he seemed very enthusiastic about the job.
M: Um, there is that bad reference from his last company though.
F: Yes, yes, it sounds as if they had a lot of problems with him. We don't want anyone unreliable working for us, do we? It's a risk, and he seemed very nervous. I wonder how he would react under stress?
M: Yes, in the circumstances I think we should wait until Pattie does her driving test before we make any offers, don't you?
F: OK.

Unit 3 Listening 1
Part 1

Mother: Hello?
Sharon: Hi Mum, I've found a flat!
Mother: Oh, that's marvellous news dear.
Sharon: Yes, I'm so excited. I'm moving in next week.
Mother: Good. Well, what's it like then?
Sharon: Well, it's on the fifth floor of a block of flats. It's an old building – there's a funny old-fashioned lift, and you go into the flat and straight ahead there's the living room. It's got two windows on one side and a little balcony on the other. It's really nice.
Mother: It sounds ideal. What are the other rooms like?
Sharon: As you go in the front door the bedroom's on the right and then the bathroom's next to it. The bathroom's very small, actually, and it hasn't got a bath, just a shower, which is a pity.
Mother: Never mind, love. What about the kitchen?
Sharon: Oh, that's at the end of the living room; you have to walk through the living room to get to it. It's tiny. Just room for one person to stand up, but I don't cook much, so it doesn't matter. And there's a cooker, but I'll have to buy a fridge.
Mother: It sounds perfect. Is it expensive?
Sharon: The rent's OK, I can manage that each month. I think. The problem is that I've got to pay a big deposit, in case anything gets damaged. Now, I was wondering whether you and Dad might …

Unit 3 Listening 1
Part 2

Mother: Is there anything which needs doing in the flat? Maybe your father and I could help you …?
Sharon: I've got to do some cleaning. The bathroom needs cleaning thoroughly and all the windows need washing, but I can do that sort of thing myself.
Mother: Does the lock need changing, maybe?
Sharon: I'm having a new lock fitted on the front door actually. A friend offered to do that for me as soon as I moved in.
Mother: What about decorating, does anything need repainting?
Sharon: Yes, the kitchen walls need repainting, but I'll do that myself one weekend, it's such a small room.
Mother: Well, maybe we could help.
Sharon: You can only get one person in there at a time, unfortunately.

Listening scripts

Mother: Oh, yes. I was forgetting.
Sharon: But I think the light switches need replacing. They're all old and cracked.
Mother: Oh, get an electrician to do that because it could be dangerous to try yourself.
Sharon: Yes, I'll have it done professionally, I'll have all the switches replaced with new ones.
Mother: Well, it doesn't sound as if you need us …
Sharon: Well, the central heating's making funny noises, I think it needs servicing. And that's something I can't do myself.
Mother: Oh, yes. You must have that done before it gets cold.
Sharon: And I've got a towel rail that needs putting up in the bathroom.
Mother: Maybe we could do that for you …
Sharon: Thanks, that would be a big help.

Unit 3 Listening 2

Ray: 439262
Margaret: Hi, how are you?
Ray: Margaret! Well, this is a surprise. I haven't heard from you for ages.
Margaret: I've been very busy at work, what with one thing and another. I don't think we've talked since Christmas, have we?
Ray: No, so what have you got to tell me?
Margaret: I've moved house.
Ray: Really?
Margaret: Yes, that's why I'm ringing; to tell you my address and phone number.
Ray: So, where are you now?
Margaret: I've moved to Valentine Road.
Ray: Valentine Road? That's near here, that's wonderful. We'll have no excuse for not seeing each other now.
Margaret: It's number 15 Valentine Road on the corner of East Street, near the newsagent's. Do you know it?
Ray: Yes, but that's a big house, Margaret, if I'm thinking of the right one.
Margaret: Yes, it's a big four-bedroomed detached house.
Ray: Isn't it a bit big for you?
Margaret: Well, it's not only for me.
Ray: What do you mean?
Margaret: Well, you see, I'm married.
Ray: MARRIED!!??
Margaret: Yes, this is my husband's house. I've been married for two weeks and that's when I moved in.
Ray: But hang on. I don't want to be rude, but who are you married to?
Margaret: My husband's name is Peter. You don't know him. He's only lived here for three months.
Ray: But you didn't say anything about this when I saw you at Christmas.
Margaret: Well, no. I've only known Peter since New Year's Eve. We met at a party.
Ray: But that's incredible!
Margaret: You don't sound pleased, Ray. Aren't you going to congratulate me?
Ray: Sorry, yes. Congratulations.

Unit 3 Listening 3
Part 1

Interviewer: And first on the line we have Mrs Romsey, who lives in north-east London. Good morning Mrs Romsey.
Mrs Romsey: Good morning, yes, I'd like to ask for some advice about weddings. My daughter's getting married later in the year and I'd like to know, should I make the guest list, the people to invite, or should my daughter?
Interviewer: Well, usually the bride's parents can choose the guests, because they pay for the wedding.
Mrs Romsey: Yes, but ought I to ask for suggestions?
Interviewer: Yes, you should ask the bridegroom's parents for suggestions.
Mrs Romsey: And is it all right if I give them a maximum number?
Interviewer: Oh yes, yes, usually this depends on the size of the church or how much you want to spend on the reception, but you should invite members of your family and the bridegroom's family in equal proportion.
Mrs Romsey: But what should I do about my daughter's friends? Are they counted as family, or not?
Interviewer: Um, you could ask your daughter and her boyfriend to give you a list of the friends they would like to invite. So then you have three groups of guests: your family, the other family and the couple's friends.
Mrs Romsey: I see, thank you. One thing, can I decide how many friends they should invite?
Interviewer: Oh, yes. If you're paying.
Mrs Romsey: Thank you.

Unit 3 Listening 3
Part 2

Interviewer: And the next caller on the line is Mr Smith from Upton. Good morning Mr Smith.
Mr Smith: Good morning. Um, I'm getting married in the spring and I want to know if it is a good idea to make a list of the presents we would like, or not? (pause)
Interviewer: Um, it can certainly avoid your getting the same present from two different people! Yes, it's OK, and many guests will welcome it. Remember that you should include some less-expensive items on the list and that you can't force people to cooperate with it. Some people have their own ideas or may want the gift to be a surprise, and that's up to them.

Unit 3 Listening 3
Part 3

Interviewer: Next on the line we have Mr Humphries from South London. Good morning.
Mr Humphries: Morning. I'm Australian, so I don't know what the form is in Britain. If I go to a wedding, do I take the present with me, or do I send it on by post, or what? (pause)
Interviewer: Well, traditionally the present should be sent to arrive at the bride's home before the wedding takes place. But very often these days guests take their presents to the reception, especially where it's held in a private house.

Unit 3 Listening 3
Part 4

Interviewer: Finally, our last call is from Mr Hill from Coventry. Good morning.
Mr Hill: Oh, hello, um, I've got a problem. Last August my son decided to get engaged and we had a big party and lots of people bought presents. A few weeks ago the engagement was called off – he's, he's changed his mind – and we were wondering whether we should return the presents, or not. (pause)
Interviewer: Yes, strictly speaking engagement presents should be returned if the wedding is called off. But it depends, if there was a party which everyone enjoyed, or maybe if the gifts were not large expensive items, then it would probably be more embarrassing to return them now, than just to forget the whole matter, especially if it was some time ago. But if your son gets engaged again, I don't think he can expect to receive any more presents.

Unit 3 Pronunciation
Vowel sounds

2 Now listen and check your answers.

/ɜː/ - girl, first, heard, work
/ʊ/ - good, could, should, cook, would
/ɒ/ - got, lock, off, block
/uː/ - room, groom, move, choose
/aʊ/ - how, found, house, now
/ɔː/ - more, floor, sure, bought, door
/əʊ/ - know, don't, own, phone, only

Unit 3 Help with multiple choice questions

3 Well, some people say that the only advantage of working in an office is that the environment is clean, warm and generally pleasant. But compared to people who work for themselves the office worker has the added comfort of regular hours, a regular salary and all the equipment needed for the job. Office work can be tedious, however, and many a clerk or typist has longed to make a complete break with routine. Few, however, have been brave enough to take the risk of giving up the security of a nine to five job for the hard work and long hours involved in setting up their own small business. For many people, the ideal solution is working from home, which combines the comforts of office work with some of the freedoms that office workers dream of, like the chance to organise your own working hours. But how easy is it to find work that can be done where you like, when you like? Sue Murray investigates …

Unit 3 Listening 4

You will hear people talking in five different situations. Choose the best answer A, B or C for each question 1-5.

One: You will hear an employee talking to a customer. Where are they?
A At the dentist's
B At the dressmaker's
C At the hairdresser's

Lucy: Hallo there, Mrs McDonald. How are you?
Mrs M: Hello Lucy, yes I'm fine thank you.
Lucy: Good. What's it to be today then?
Mrs M: Well, I'd like it cut - but not too much. You know, the same style, but a bit shorter.
Lucy: Um, you don't want to have it coloured at all, err……., have a slight wave put in it?
Mrs M: Oh no - not this time, Lucy, thanks.
Lucy: OK. Let's get it washed then, shall we?
Mrs M: yes, OK…..

Two: You will hear a man talking to someone who is going to do some work at his house.
What are they discussing?
A Electrical work
B Decorating work
C Carpentry work

M1: Mr Bates?
Bates: Yes.
M1: I've come about the kitchen.
Bates: Oh good. Yes, come in…it's through here.
M1: Now, what seems to be the problem?
Bates: Look, it's all peeling off the wall!
M1: Oh, yes. That's because someone's painted over the paper instead of stripping it down….it lifts after a while.
Bates: What can you do?
M1: Well, the best thing would be to have it all taken off and start again.
Bates: Oh, dear….How much will that cost?

Three: You will hear someone making enquiries at a garage. How does the customer feel?
A Disappointed
B Suspicious
C Angry

M2: Morning.
M1: Yes, I'd like to have some work done on my car.
M2: Yes, what sort of work would that be, sir.
M1: I'd like to have a sun-roof fitted, if possible.
M2: That's no problem, we could do that in a couple of days.
M1: Here? You mean at this garage?
M2: Yes, it's a quick job, a sun roof.
M1: Really? Um…..I rather thought it would have to be sent away.
M2: No, one of the lads could do that by Thursday for you….one hundred and fifty pounds it would be.
M1: But, will it really be….well, never mind, I'll have to think about it. Thank you.
M2: Suit yourself, gov.

Four: You will hear two people talking about a wedding. Who is the woman you hear talking?
A The bride
B The bride's mother
C The bride's grandmother

M: And what about the dress – are you making it yourself?
F: No, unfortunately, I'd have loved to but we're having it made at Banley's in the High Street.
M: Wow, that'll cost you a bit, I bet.
F: Well, it's only once in a lifetime for Maria and it's what she wants.
M: Yes, you're right, I suppose.
F: But we're not having the cake made – no, I insisted on doing that myself.
M: Really?
F: Yes, I did it for her mother's wedding, and I'll do it for her - of course, I did the dress as well on that occasion.
M: Oh, really, Peggy, you are wonderful.

Five: You hear someone talking to a new employee. Where is she working?
A In a shop
B In a restaurant
C In someone's house

M: It's your first day, isn't it?
F: Yeah, that's right.
M: OK, well there's quite a bit needs doing before we open.
F: Right, OK.
M: Yes, we have to have all the tables laid before the first customer comes in.
F: Right.
M: And then we have to make sure all the cruets are full.
F: Cruets?
M: You know, for salt and pepper and all that.
F: Oh, right. Yeah.
M: And your shelf needs organizing.
F: Shelf?
M: Yes, you've each got a shelf in the kitchen for your order book, spare cutlery, napkins and everything.
F: Right, I'll get started, then.

Unit 4 Listening 1

Woman: Hello, I want to report a break-in at my house.
Policeman: Yes, madam. Just a moment. Could I have your name, please?
Woman: It's Anna Webb, W-E-double B.
Police: And the address where the break-in happened?
Woman: It's 52 George Street.
Police: George Street? Just round the corner from here?
Woman: Yes, but it doesn't seem to put off the burglars, does it?
Police: When did the break-in occur?
Woman: I got home and found the door open. They got in while I was out shopping. As I was walking along the road to my house I noticed that the front door was open. My neighbour was cleaning her windows, so before I went in I called to her and we went into the house together. It must have happened sometime this afternoon, because I was home at lunchtime and I went out at about two o'clock.
Police: So it was sometime this afternoon, the, err, 17th of June, isn't it?
Woman: There's a terrible mess and of course they took some money and other things.
Police: How much money was taken, madam?
Woman: Well, not money, exactly – I never leave money in the house. I had some travellers' cheques in dollars. I'm going on holiday next week and I picked up the travellers' cheques this morning.
Police: How much were they worth?
Woman: There was $250 in travellers' cheques, and the name of the bank is, er …, the First National Bank. I'll have to phone the bank and tell them, won't I? And get some replacements, of course.
Police: Yes, tell the bank as soon as possible. Just in case someone tries to cash them. Was anything else taken?
Woman: Well, that's it. I think my passport's gone too. Oh dear, that means going to the passport office to get a new one, and I'm supposed to be flying to San Francisco on Monday evening.
Police: Travellers' cheques and passport, tut. Have you got any details of the passport?
Woman: Yes, it's one of the new types, you know, with a red cover. Not the old blue type, and I've got the number written down somewhere here … At least that should make it a bit easier to get a replacement. It's D 531087.
Police: Right, got that. Anything else?
Woman: Everything's in a terrible mess, but I think there's a gold watch missing. It's quite old, it was my grandmother's, and I don't wear it very often.
Police: Do you know how much it's worth?
Women: It's insured for £125, but it's the sentimental value that counts when this sort of thing happens, isn't it?
Police: Yes, I know what you mean. I'm afraid it is. You said there was some damage?
Woman: There are things all over the place. I suppose there isn't much missing. I've been quite lucky. And the lock's been broken. That's how they got in. I'll have to get someone to come and fix it.
Police: Right, if you just wait a moment, I'll give you a copy of the report for your insurance claim.
Woman: Oh, thanks.

Unit 4 Listening 2

Interviewer: Good morning. This is Openline, and on today's programme we have Alan Best, who is a security expert and former London policeman.
Alan: Hello.
I: He's here to answer your questions about crime prevention. And our first call today is from Mr Marsh.
Mr Marsh: Hello. Mine isn't a question really, but I wanted to phone you to warn people. You see, someone stole some things from my house last month – a clock and some jewellery – and the thing is, I was at home all the time. I mean, I was in the next room. I didn't know I'd been burgled until I went into the other room and found things all over the floor.
I: He must have been a very brave thief, Alan?
Alan: He *or* she, of course. I'm afraid this happens a lot. You know you think when you're at home, your property's safe. In fact a lot of burglaries are like that. I think, Mr Marsh, your door can't have been locked.
Mr Marsh: That's right.
Alan: OK. Now when you're at home keep the door locked, not just closed. You must have been watching television or listening to music, Mr Marsh, is that right?
Mr Marsh: Yes, I was watching the telly.
Alan: So of course you didn't hear anything.
I: And what about windows?
Alan: Yes, windows too. You can get window locks for ground floor windows. They're cheap and easy to use. I recommend them. Remember that thieves can get in even through very small windows.
I: Thank you Mr Marsh. Our next caller's Lesley Ward. Go ahead Lesley.
Lesley: Hello, I wanted to warn people, as well. I was on holiday in Paris, and I went to have dinner at a restaurant and I put my bag on the floor by the table and when it was time to pay the bill my bag had disappeared, with my credit cards and ticket home in it!
Alan: Oh dear. This happens in lots of places where there are tourists, especially big cities. Do you know who took it?
Lesley: Oh, I don't know, it could have been the people at the next table, I suppose. But it was quite an expensive restaurant, and they didn't look like thieves. Ooh, it might have been one of the waiters, but it seems very unlikely, doesn't it?
Alan: That's the problem: thieves come in all shapes and sizes, I'm afraid. Now firstly, never put your bag on the floor – that's asking for trouble. Then, don't trust strangers, especially when you're on holiday – thieves seem to like tourists.
I: And this sort of thing can really spoil your holiday for you, can't it?
Alan: Absolutely. The other thing, of course, is don't carry all your documents and money in one bag – that's just making it easy for the thief, isn't it?

Unit 4 Pronunciation
Compound nouns

passport   guide book   hairdresser
penknife   first aid kit   vacuum cleaner
newspaper   shoplifter   walkman
suitcase   light switch   travellers' cheques

Unit 4 Listening 3

Interviewer: When Neil Wilson first turned to crime, what he did wasn't a crime – he was a computer hacker. Having left school without many qualifications, his hobby of logging on to computer databases by telephone from the safety of his bedroom became more than a hobby as he got deeper and deeper into forbidden territory. He'd become an electronic terrorist, spending hours at his keyboard breaking into supposedly secure computer systems – not to do damage but just for a bit of fun, for the thrill of beating the computer managers and their increasingly strong defences . He could have done damage but he says he didn't. It was just a game. He paid his own huge telephone bills and his parents were happy that he wasn't getting into trouble on the streets. When a new law was introduced, he was the first person to be arrested. He was found guilty and spent eight months in a top-security prison. Now he's doing a degree in artificial intelligence and works with computers full time. There are many hackers like Neil Wilson. There's even a special unit at Scotland Yard to catch them. I spoke to Inspector James at Scotland Yard.
Insp. James: It's a very long and difficult process trying to detect who's committed crimes such as these because, of course, they're committed mostly, quite often, from a bedroom, or sometimes from an office in a big organisation. But you have to follow a chain back, and the chain can go through different telephone exchanges and the different connections made through computer networks. So, it's very much old-fashioned detective work; Sherlock Holmes would have appreciated it. Of course, the people who commit the crimes tend to live in a very strange world, at times. Neil was a good example of that; once he was in the actual computer system, he'd leave messages for the systems manager. He'd leave quite a few messages. Some of them would sort of be, in the early stages, were in the nature of jokes like: "I'm here again", "You can't stop me", "Don't mess with the best" – you wouldn't take them seriously, really. His messages, however, after he became convinced that he was locked out for good, turned to rude and then nasty, and his targets, not that he possibly knew this, but his targets were often young staff, many of them women working night shifts, who very much felt threatened by the nature of his language and his constant ability to pop up under a new disguise.
Interviewer: I asked Neil why he did it.
Neil Wilson: I'd just think to myself, when the staff comes in the morning they're going to go "Oh no, he's got in yet again". I thought their attitude would be that I was just a little irritating hacker – I mean they had all that experience and I figured that if I was being a real pain, they could easily, sort of, flick me off the system. I was only this one nineteen-year-old little hacker and I'd wind them up something chronic, but I didn't mean any harm, it was a game.

Unit 5 Listening 1

2 You will hear five different people talking about a new type of night club, where people play board games. For questions 1–5, choose the phrase A–H which best summarises what each person is talking about.

1 This is a game I used to play when I was about six. I had one in my room and it's the first time I've played for about twenty years. It's just a basic shoot 'em up, like they used to have. It's a bit like Space Invaders

Listening Scripts

played on a table. The aim is to get the little ball in the middle of the table, shoot some metal bullets out of your little gun, the aim is to get it into the goal. It's like playing football, or playing Space Invaders. It's for all those little boys out there who like playing with guns, I think, or at this club for those of us who haven't really grown up.

2 It's set up like a restaurant, so people come in and they show you to a table, hand you a menu, and you choose whatever you like. There's several sections: There's a starter for two, which is set out in that way, so, you know, there's nothing worse than wanting to play a game for five when there's only two of you. Then there's the standards, like Monopoly, things you've probably got at home anyway, and a big word section with, like, Scrabble, and that sort of thing. Then they've got lots of quiz games and then everything that's left piled into that section at the end. So, they come back and take your order, or if you want to reserve a game for later, for when other people have finished with it or whenever, and so you can play whatever you want all night long.

3 You can often go out in the evening and not speak to anyone, or be in a noisy disco and not really get down and have a good chat. Games are a good opportunity for that, they're very social, very interactive and, you know, they bring out the best in people, sometimes the worst! The idea is to attract people who want to end their evening less energetically than in a typical night club. Although there's no dancing, the bar is open until two a.m. and there's more than enough to attract people.

4 There are more than 60 board games to choose from. Some of them rare, which the owners have hunted down from second-hand sales, junk shops and manufacturers. It's really nice when you go and pick up that classic seventies game that you can't get anymore, you know, they're priceless, antique pieces really. They've also got games which you can't get in the shops yet, and some which are popular but so expensive to get hold of that there's not many about. It's better than going out and spending twenty pounds on a game and finding out you don't like it. Here you can try it out for five minutes, and if you don't like it, try another game.

5 If you spend the early hours of the morning, you know, playing Mindtrap or Totally Dingbats, the lack of a more traditional night club atmosphere doesn't mean not having a really good night out, but although it's not smoky, and well, there's lots of things to choose from and you can meet people, I'd say it's good for midweek, but not for Saturday night, possibly, because it would be better if it was , you know, quite sleazy and dark and more atmospheric. You get to sit with a group of friends, have fun. We're really having a good time here, it's excellent, it's great, but I think there should be music, maybe a jukebox or something.

Unit 5 Listening 2

Interviewer: I have with me in the studio today John Osgoodby, who is a prominent sports historian. John, welcome.
John: Thanks Ian.
I: Tell us John, if we look at the big spectator sports like cricket, football and tennis, how far back do they go?
J: Well, many sports and games are as old as the human race itself. The ancient Egyptians were playing bat and ball games over 5000 years ago, as can be seen from carvings on tombs and other places. Our modern ball games probably arrived in Europe from North Africa around the eleventh century, and spread to England through Spain and France.
I: So, what type of games were there?
J: Well, there were games in which balls were kicked or carried, these were the ancestors of modern football and rugby, and others where balls were hit with sticks and clubs, as in cricket, baseball and hockey. The invention of rackets came much later in about the sixteenth century and from then on we start seeing games like tennis and squash developing.
I: So most of our sports developed out of these old games?
J: Yes, what happened was that each town or district used to have its own version of the same game, and people used to work out the rules over the years – and so kept changing them. That's why British and American sports are so different. The early colonists took over versions of football and cricket which were changed over time into American football and baseball.
I: So when did people start playing the modern versions of these sports?
J: Well, in the form in which we know them, most can be dated back to the nineteenth century. But what was happening then was that the games that people had played for centuries were organised formally for the first time. So rules were decided upon and written down where before they had been vague or different in different parts of the country. National leagues or championships could then be formed and the development of public transport meant that it was no longer just one village against another, for example, but a local team regularly meeting others from quite a wide area.
I: But the basic games themselves had been around for a long time before all this?
J: Yes, but in the nineteenth century, especially in schools and colleges, people began to set down rules which everyone had to follow and decide things like what players should wear and what equipment they should use, the size of the pitch or court and all that sort of thing. The industrial revolution meant that standardized equipment could be mass produced for a range of games that developed out of the traditional sports. So we get rugby football, American football and soccer all developing out of the old English football game at about the same time, but in quite different ways. At about the same time tennis, squash and badminton appear, based on the old racket sports but using different equipment, courts and rules.
I: And of course new sports are developing all the time.
J: Yes, yes, some are the result of new technology, like windsurfing or skateboarding, whilst others, like American football, which is now becoming so popular in Europe, are just variations on the old English football game that people have been playing for centuries.
I: John, thank you.

Unit 5 Listening 3

Alice: Have you ever tried skiing?
Barry: Yes, but I'm not very enthusiastic about it really.
A: Why's that? I think it's great.
B: Well, that's what lots of people say, but my experience is very different.
A: What do you mean? Did you break a leg or something? I can't think of anything better. You're outside in the fresh air, it's good healthy exercise and you're usually in beautiful places. I really love the mountains.
B: OK, agreed. Being in the mountains is very nice. But I really don't understand why people want to ski.
A: What happened when you tried skiing?
B: Well, I used to live in a place in Italy, near the border with Austria. And when I first went there people said, 'You must come skiing', But I had to wait until there was enough snow. You can't learn at the top of the mountain, you know.
A: But you went with them eventually?
B: Well, not as soon as it snowed because I couldn't find any other beginners to learn with, everyone was an expert already and I'd never tried it before. I felt a bit silly being the only beginner. Apart from the fact that lessons are so expensive.
A: But you found someone in the end?
B: Yes, and we agreed to go off skiing with a group of friends who had been skiing together for years. They'd already had lots of practice.
A: So you went for a week?
B: No, no. A weekend. They used to leave on Saturday morning and then stay in a hotel that night. That was a shock. You see this group used to go skiing together nearly every weekend and got up incredibly early on Saturday morning. Now I like a good long sleep usually so I wasn't very happy to start with.
A: Well, you have to start early because the days are too short otherwise.
B: OK, but not at five in the morning! Then we arrived and I had to hire skis and ski boots and ski sticks and things – none of it cheap.
A: Oh yes, skiing isn't a cheap hobby.
B: It certainly isn't. Well, I booked a skiing lesson, but these skiing friends used to go to Austria and the instructor only spoke German. Now, I don't understand a word of German. It was a complete waste of money. He tried, poor man, but I just kept falling over and after a bit we had to stop. It wasn't his fault.
A: Didn't your friends try to help out?
B: Oh yes. But remember they used to go skiing every week, so they were good at it. Well, after the lesson someone said, 'Just follow me' and we went up a ski lift thing to the top of the mountain.
A: So you did do some proper skiing on your first day?
B: I remember we had to wait ages because there were so many people about. Then when we got to the top she said, 'Just do exactly what I do. It's easy'. And she disappeared down the mountain. Oh yes, it's easy when you can already do it! I tried to follow her but I kept falling over so I stopped and took off my skis.
A: What happened then? Did someone come and help you?
B: No, they didn't. I had to walk down the mountain, it took ages and I was freezing cold when I got to the bottom and back to the hotel. I'd never felt so miserable in my life.

Unit 5 Pronunciation
Intonation

1 Listen to a phrase read by two different people. How is the phrase different.
   1 although it was raining. ↘
   2 although it was raining... ↗

2 Listen to the phrases 1–10 and decide if the intonation is falling or rising.
   1 despite the weather ↘
   2 although he had a map ↗
   3 after drinking our coffee ↗
   4 before leaving the bar ↘
   5 after finishing our sandwiches ↗
   6 a few years ago ↗
   7 after a moment's silence ↗
   8 after about an hour ↘
   9 to make matters worse ↘
   10 before it closed at five p.m. ↗

Unit 5 Listening 4

Passage One
There's a lot of complaints nowadays about how sport has become commercialised, but if you go back two or three hundred years, sport was already very commercialised, depending what you mean by commercialised, of course. It wasn't commercialised in the sense that people had to pay to watch, but it was commercialised in the sense that you had professional players, and in the sense that pubs often put on sporting events in the hope of selling more beer, for example.

Passage Two
Presenter: Now, John, over to you. Which sport uses a piece of equipment called a crosse?
John: Oh dear. I don't know. It can't be lacrosse, that's too obvious....ummm.... how about croquet?
Presenter: No, sorry, I'll offer that one to Sue for a bonus. Sue?
Sue: Lacrosse?
Presenter: Lacrosse it is. Rather gave that one away John, eh? So that's put Sue back in the lead with 22 points to John's 21!

Passage Three
Now, I don't actually like getting gestures of affection from strange women. No, I don't truly. I mean, yesterday, I was in a supermarket, I won't name it, and ... and I slipped on a grape by the vegetable counter which had been carelessly dropped on the floor by some other shopper, and fell right over. Now the woman in charge, the manager, rushed over and said, ' Are you all right

darling?' and I said, 'I'm not a darling, I'm a customer.' I don't like all this over familiarity, it's unneccesary, isn't it?

Passage Four
Well, what you have to do, you have to cut up a piece of thin card, a breakfast cereal packet or something like that, and what you have to do is cut some fishy shapes out of the card like this … Then you get one piece of string per player and attach a small magnet to the end of the string like so … You can then try to catch the fish, the one with the most fish at the end being the winner.

Passage Five
The 12.37 express to London is running approximately 28 minutes late. We apologise to passengers for the late running of the London service. (pause) The 13.00 express to Manchester and Liverpool, is now approaching platform 5, calling at Stafford and Crewe. Buffet and trolley service will be available. First class accommodation is located in the first three carriages. That's platform 5 for the 13.00 express service to Manchester and Liverpool.

Passage Six
Written and directed by Arabella herself, this is far removed from the black and white epics of her earlier shows. It relies heavily on colour imagery, dance and fair helpings of her well-known humour. All the hits and album favourites are here performed against a background of a glorious jazz-age city which has a kind of dream-like realism with simple images of intense beauty. Fans will flock to buy this whilst others are guaranteed 91 minutes of the strangest rock entertainment ever.

Unit 6 Listening 1

Thank you for calling the International Airways information line providing updated information on International Airways flights and passenger services. Firstly, we are pleased to announce our new Superior class cabin on flights to Athens. Superior class offers all the comforts of Business Class at just a few pounds above the Economy fare. There's a lot of extra leg room in Superior Class, so you'll be able to stretch out and enjoy a choice of hot food on the menu and our specially-trained cabin staff on hand to help you choose. And with priority check-in at London airport, you'll avoid all the queues and have time for a drink in the designated Superior Class lounge. I'm sure you'll agree that Superior Class represents a few extra pounds well spent. And you'll arrive feeling ready to make the most of your holiday from day one.
Secondly, we have some important information for transatlantic passengers. From October the first, there'll be a new daily International Airways flight direct from London to Atlanta, offering great connections to all other US destinations. This will replace the present weekend only service with additional flights on weekdays from London to Atlanta beginning on October the first.
Lastly, a reminder to all our passengers of our frequent flyers scheme. If you fly with us more than three times in any one year, we'll invite you to join our Frequent Flyers Club, with a free flight bag on your sixth flight and special discounts on our in-flight shopping catalogue. Then you'll be able to fill your free bag with tasteful gifts. You save all round by flying regularly with International Airways.
So thank you for calling the International Airways information line. We look forward to welcoming you on board one of our flights very soon.

Unit 6 Pronunciation
Consonants

1 Listen and decide which word, A, or B, is being said.

1 flight	6 west	11 train	16 joke
2 fryer	7 leaf	12 fright	17 off
3 flee	8 view	13 road	18 ice
4 vet	9 price	14 back	19 lose
5 fan	10 yet	15 sock	20 rate

2 Now listen to all the words and repeat.

1 fright	flight	11 train	drain
2 fryer	flier	12 fright	fried
3 free	flee	13 wrote	road
4 wet	vet	14 pack	back
5 fan	van	15 sock	shock
6 west	vest	16 joke	yolk
7 leaf	leave	17 off	of
8 few	view	18 ice	eyes
9 price	prize	19 loose	lose
10 jet	yet	20 rate	laid

Unit 6 Listening 2 *man difficult*

Travel Agent: Can I help you sir?
Customer: Yes, er, I've booked a holiday and I wanted to know if the price includes travel insurance?
T.A.: Oh, yes. Certainly, where is it you're going to?
C: Spain. To, er, Madrid.
T.A.: Which company?
C: I can't remember, er, oh, I think it's that brochure over there. The one with the blue cover.
T.A.: This one?
C: Yes, I think so.
T.A.: Ah, now, let's see. Madrid, er, (flicking). Ah, yes. Is this the holiday you've booked? The Hotel Bristol?
C: Yes, that's the one.
T.A.: Right, no, no, there's no insurance cover included with that holiday. But we can arrange insurance separately if you would like to.
C: How much will that be, then?
T.A.: Have you booked for the seven night trip, or fourteen?
C: Oh, er, let me see … yes, a fortnight I think it was. Yes, yes, that's it.
T.A.: Right, up to seventeen nights in Europe. That will be twelve pounds thirty.
C: Now, what does that include, what am I covered for?
T.A.: Well, it's the medical expenses you want really, isn't it? That's the important thing, I always think. Now, for medical cover this policy gives you up to a million pounds.
C: A million pounds! That sounds a lot of money to me!
T.A.: Well, yes. You see it can be very expensive if you have an accident or you're ill abroad. And it includes an air-ambulance to bring you home if necessary.
C: Yeah, well that sounds O.K. But what about if I'm ill and I can't go?
T.A.: Well, you generally get something back from the holiday company if you let them know that you're ill, it depends. But there's always some sort of cancellation charge and this insurance would pay the cancellation charges up to one thousand five hundred pounds.
C: That sounds really good. But this friend of mine, he didn't wake up in time on the morning of his holiday and he missed the plane, he got to the airport an hour late! And then they made him pay extra to go on another flight!
T.A.: Ah, well, our insurance wouldn't cover you for that sort of thing, but it would cover you if you couldn't get to the airport because of a strike or something like that.
C: What you mean if the bus didn't turn up – that sort of thing?
T.A.: That's right, something beyond your control.
C: And what's that? One thousand pounds?
T.A.: No, that's only two hundred pounds. But you do get one thousand five hundred pounds if your plane is delayed so much that it's not worth going.
C: What, you mean for days?
T.A.: Oh, yes. it happens sometimes. And you get sixty pounds for every twelve hours you wait, going or coming back. And one thousand five hundred pounds if you decide to give up and go home after twelve hours, because the holiday company wouldn't give you any money back unless THEY cancelled the trip.
C: Sixty pounds doesn't sound much if you are abroad and you have to find a hotel for the night.
T.A.: Oh, well for the return journey, there's up to two hundred pounds for additional accommodation and travel expenses because of strikes and things.
C: That sounds like the sort of thing I was looking for. But isn't there anything about things getting stolen or lost?
T.A.: Oh, yes yes. It will pay up to a thousand pounds for lost or stolen baggage and even two hundred pounds for lost money if you get your wallet stolen.
C: Fine, I'll take it then.
T.A.: Well, if you'd just like to fill in this form ….

Unit 6 Listening 3

Dave: Hallo, 394621?
Joanne: Hi, it's Joanne.
D: Oh, hello. What's the problem? We're expecting you any moment.
J: It's OK, I'm coming. It's just that I've come out without my map. Could you give me directions from the station?
D: Sure, no problem. Hang on, let me see now. Which station are you at?
J: Walthamstow Station.
D: Well, there's more than one, I'm afraid. We're closest to Blackhorse Road Station.
J: Oh, no, I'm at Walthamstow Central.
D: That's alright. You can walk from there. Just a minute, let me get my map … here we are. Right, do you want to write this down?
J: Yes, I've got a pen, I'll put it in my diary. OK, ready.
D: Right. Come out of the station and you'll see a place where all the buses turn round.
J: Yes, that's where I'm phoning from.
D: Good. Turn right as you come out of the station and go up a little hill and you'll soon come to a main road at the top.
J: Oh, yeah, I can see the main road.
D: That's called Hoe Street. H-O-E. Turn left along Hoe Street and walk as far as the High Street, that's the next crossroads. Turn left into the High Street. There's lots of shops down there and the library on your left. Keep walking down High Street as far as Erskine Road, that's E-R-S-K-I-N-E. Erskine.
J: Is that a crossroads?
D: No, not really. Erskine Road will be on your right, it's the third turning on the right off the High Street.
J: OK. Then what?
D: Walk along Erskine Road and then take the fourth turning on the left.
J: The fourth?
D: Yeah, that's called Elmsdale Road.
J: OK. Is it much further?
D: No, go down Elmsdale Road and at the bottom you come to Palmerston Road. Go across Palmerston Road into Northcote Road, which is opposite.
J: Opposite what?
D: Opposite Elmsdale Road.
J: OK. I see. So I don't turn into Palmerston Road?
D: No you just cross it.
J: OK.
D: And then, as soon as you're in Northcote Road turn right immediately into Warner Road.
J: Warner Road. Isn't that where you live?
D: That's it. You'll find my house on the left, OK?
J: Right, well I just hope I can follow this! You should see me in a few minutes. If you don't, you'll know it's not my fault. OK? Thanks, see you.
D: Bye.

Unit 6 Listening 4

Dave: 2317246?
Gianna: Hi Dave, it's Gianna.
D: Hi, how are you?
G: We're fine, thanks. Look, we've managed to get a flight.
D: Great! When are you arriving? I'll come and meet you at the airport.
G: Well, thanks for the offer but there's a bit of a problem there, Dave, you see we arrive at different airports. I arrive at Stansted and Angelo arrives at Heathrow Airport, on the same day, Thursday.
D: But how come?
G: It's a long story. I'll tell you when I see you. Basically, the travel agent got it all wrong. Anyway, we need to know how to get from the airports to your place.
D: Yeah, sure. But can't I come and meet you?
G: No, I think it's better if you stay at home, in case one of us is delayed, or something.

Listening scripts

D: OK. Well, look, give me your flight numbers and I'll see what I can do.
G: OK. I'm flying from Florence airport to Stansted airport in London. Is that a new one?
D: Well, it's been open a few years. But I didn't know there was an airport in Florence.
G: Well, it's only small, you know. Anyway, my flight number is UK 927 and it arrives at Stansted at 15.20.
D: That's UK 927 at 15.20, OK, I've got that.
G: And Angelo arrives at Heathrow airport at 16.40 on a flight from Pisa, the number is flight BA 603.
D: BA 603 at 16.40 … from Pisa. So you're not even leaving from the same airport?
G: That's right, Dave. It's very complicated.
D: Well, look, I'll find the best way for you to get here by public transport, OK?
G: Oh, thanks a lot Dave. You can fax me the information at my father's office if you want to. Have you got the number?
D: Can you give it to me again anyway?
G: OK, it's 01039, that's the code for Italy …
D: 01039 …
G: Then 2 89 34 617.
D: OK, I'll get on to that straight away, and send you the information.

Unit 7 Listening 1

Interviewer: Good morning, Dr Cooper.
Dr Cooper: Morning.
Interviewer: Now, you're something of a campaigner for the British diet, aren't you?
Dr Cooper: Yeah. Well, I feel very strongly that much of the problem in this country comes from a lack of understanding of what constitutes a healthy diet. We are too ready to be influenced by food advertising and we don't listen enough to doctors and dieticians. People eat the processed food which they see on the TV and in magazines. Now, this is often less healthy and more expensive than other simpler foods which people always used to eat.
I: And what does the food industry say in reply to your criticisms?
Dr C: Well, they say there's no such thing as bad food, only bad diets. The processed or junk foods as they're known, are not bad in themselves, it depends on how much you eat of them and whether you eat other things. If your diet is varied enough, then there's no problem.
I: And do some people eat too much junk food and things out of packets and tins?
Dr C: More than some! Recent research in Glasgow has shown that an estimated one in five men never eats vegetables of any kind and one third of the population never consciously eats fruit.
I: And is that such a bad thing?
Dr C: Well, yes. It means they're eating too much heavily refined and processed food which contains large amounts of fats, sugar and salt and not enough fibre or important vitamins or minerals. This is a direct cause of many major illnesses, especially heart disease.
I: So, what should we do?
Dr C: Well, eat more natural foods and try to be less influenced by food advertising. That's my advice. Eat junk foods if you like them, but be careful not to eat too much sugar, salt or fat. And make sure you eat enough fresh food as well, so you have a balanced diet.
I: Dr Cooper, thank you.

Unit 7 Listening 2

OK, well, this is really a North American speciality and it's really rich and tasty, and great if like me you like sweet things. First you melt some butter and pour it into a bowl, then add the sugar and stir them together. Now you add the eggs, and you have to beat the eggs into this mixture one at a time. If you add them all at once, you get lumps which are difficult to get rid of. Then you stir the flour and the cocoa into this mixture, and put in some nuts. My American friend, who gave me the recipe, says you have to use pecan nuts, but if you don't have any pecans, the other sort will be quite all right. Then you pour the mixture into a square container and cook it in the oven for about forty minutes. After forty minutes, take it out of the oven and leave it to get cool. It smells fantastic but don't eat it yet!
Now comes the best bit, you get a bar of chocolate and break it into pieces, put the pieces into a bowl and melt the chocolate over some warm water – it shouldn't boil. If you boil chocolate, you spoil the taste. When the chocolate's melted, beat in one egg and some sugar, not too much because it's already very rich.
Then spread this all over the top. Cut it into pieces and decorate each piece with a nut. Then, if you're like me, you'll sit down and eat the lot!

Unit 7 Listening 3

Hello, and thank you for calling Restaurant Line. We have chosen some of the best new restaurants which have opened in London this year. The prices given here are for an average meal for two people including dessert and coffee but not including drinks and service charges. We begin with Gulliver's Cafe, at 138 Ross Road. This is a restaurant in a modern setting with a modern menu which concentrates on fashionable Californian-style food. The restaurant has been open for the best part of a year and is always very popular, so we recommend that you book a table. A meal for two will cost around £30 at lunch time and £45 in the evening. By the way, they do not accept credit cards. The number to ring is 0181 436722.
Next we have The Garden Room Restaurant at 34 Stockwell Street, which offers exciting modern versions of traditional English cooking in an unusual courtyard setting in the heart of clubland in London's theatre district. It's a perfect place to begin or end a night on the town. A meal for two will cost about £40 and they are closed all day Sunday and on Monday evening. The phone number for The Garden Room is 0181 711477.
The Cenci at 2 Bradwell Street, is another new restaurant which has established a reputation for good value and interesting food. The emphasis here is on Italian and Greek cuisine and the chef-proprietor David Cenci is always looking out for new ways to serve traditional dishes. In fine weather, The Cenci has tables laid out on a riverside terrace where a meal for two will cost from £35 to £50 and where you'll have one of the best views in town. The Cenci is closed on Saturday lunch time and Sunday evenings and the number is 0171 482230.
For the really adventurous, there's always Petals in Canterbury Square, here the combination of foods is truly original, as is the penthouse setting. Be ready to come across small fruits like raspberries and blackberries in a pasta sauce based on mushrooms and asparagus. And all dishes are decorated with yellow and orange edible flowers. The menu is not extensive and you have to put your faith in the chef's judgement. Needless to say, it's not cheap at £50, but it's certainly a very special experience. Petals accepts bookings on 0171 555448, but note that their largest table only seats six people.
Finally, why not try fish and chips? There's a revival of this traditional fast food at Walley's Fish Bar in Romsey Road. There you'll find a good range of fried and grilled fish, including favourites like rock salmon, plaice and skate as well as a good range of shellfish and some meat pies. The quality is excellent as is the service in an authentic nineteen-fifties atmosphere. And it'll only set you back about £20. There's no need to book, but take away meals can be ordered on 0181 786420.

Unit 7 Listening 4

Waiter: Good evening, sir, madam. A table for two, was it?
Man: Yes, that's right.
Waiter: Would you like a table in the garden, or inside?
Man: What do you think, it's not so warm this evening, is it?
Woman: Oh, let's sit outside. It's a lovely evening. That table in the corner will do.
Waiter: Fine. Now, would you like a drink while you're looking at the menu? A glass of wine, perhaps?
Woman: Yes, I'll have an orange juice, please.
Man: Nothing for me. No, can I have some mineral water?
Waiter: Certainly, sir. We have Malvern water, which is sparkling, or Highland water, which is still.
Man: Still, yes.
Waiter: OK, a Highland mineral water and an orange juice. Thank you, here's the menu.
Man: Thanks … that sparkling water always gives me terrible indigestion. So, what shall we have?
Woman: Mmm, do you want a starter?
Man: Well, what is there? Let's see. Oh, Fried Mushrooms sound nice. No, no, they come with garlic sauce. Garlic gives me …
Woman: … terrible indigestion, I know.
Man: The other things aren't very interesting, really, are they? Let's go on to the main course, shall we?
Woman: OK.
Waiter: There we are, your drinks. Are you ready to order now?
Man: Well, errm … Yes, I think so. What would you recommend?
Waiter: Well, the Chicken Kiev is today's speciality. That's breast of chicken, fried, stuffed with garlic and butter and served with French fries.
Man: No, I can't … erm. No, I think I'll just have a salad.
Waiter: Would you like a small mixed salad, or would you rather have an Unlimited Salad from our Salad Bar? Then you can eat as much as you want.
Man: Oh, that sounds interesting. Yes I'll have the Unlimited Salad. Maybe I'll have a dessert later.
Waiter: And for you madam?
Woman: I'll have the Sole, please.
Waiter: Would you like rice or French fries?
Woman: Um, I'll have chips, please.
Waiter: Right, Sole and French fries. Would you like anything else to drink?
Woman: Shall we have some wine?
Man: Yes, red or white?
Woman: Is the house white dry or sweet?
Waiter: It's medium dry, madam.
Woman: Oh, no, I'd rather have red in that case. Half a carafe.
Waiter: Half a carafe. Thank you.

Unit 7 Listening 5

Interviewer: Your company has built more than 100 roadside restaurants around Britain, and apart from minor exterior differences, they're all identical. They have the same tables, cutlery, crockery, carpets, curtains, lights, even the same menu. It's their sameness that offers value for money – but why does the interior have to be so boring?
Director: I don't think it's boring any more than I think my own dining room's boring. I've had the same carpet, curtains and cutlery since I moved house two years ago – and I haven't got bored with that yet, and I haven't got bored with the restaurants either. I think it's just people's expectations – that they think they'll find something different when they eat away from home, and if you are a regular traveller, then I can see that you might think it could do with a change. But by the time you reach that stage, hopefully you'll find it has been changed.
I: So how much difference would it make to the price of a meal if you used different decorating materials, if you used different pictures on the wall, if you had different menus?
D: As far as pictures on the wall are concerned, not that much difference, which is why the pictures on the wall are all different, so that every restaurant you go into you'll find a different series of pictures, and the pictures are very often chosen locally. I think the estimate of the benefit we get by buying the same things are that it would make a difference of between 20 and 25 percent of the cost of fitting out an individual restaurant, and that obviously would have to be reflected in the price.
I: You offer a very good and a very high standard at a very reasonable cost. But of course it is one standard, isn't it? At the the same time as being the minimum standard it's also the maximum standard because no individual restaurant manager is ever allowed to introduce anything they might want to do. You could

never have a variation of any kind at any of your restaurants, could you?
D: You can have a variation in terms of customer service and the way in which people talk to customers, perhaps, or the way in which they greet them. You could improve on that if you were a good manager, that's probably where you could concentrate your efforts. The problem we would have if we allowed managers to organise something special, I mean you could have a manager who'd say "Sunday morning, I'm going to organise the Sunday papers with breakfast for my customers".
I: That would be nice!
D: Which would be very nice, and then the next Sunday you eat in a restaurant and that manager hasn't had that idea, he's maybe thought of something different and you'd be disappointed, because you'd be looking forward to your newspaper with your breakfast and you wouldn't get it. So there's always a negative to whatever the positive might be.
I: So, I can't look forward to any pleasant surprises in your restaurants in the future?
D: No I suppose not. It's a tried and tested formula that works very well at the moment.

Unit 7 Pronunciation
Vowel Sounds 2

eɪ state, plain, claim, say
iː eat, each, need, week, real
ɪ it, which, give, thing
aɪ hide, quite, might, guide
e let, them, says, any
ɑː are, dark, can't, heart, past
æ man, can, gap, fat, lack
ʌ but, young, much, love

Unit 8 Listening 1 *Part 1*

Interviewer: Pizza has become one of the most popular foods in Britain in recent years and you can buy it in various forms. You can go and sit down in a pizzeria, find a take away or even have it delivered to your door. The most popular type of pizza, however, is the one you buy in the supermarket, probably frozen or picked up from the cold cabinet with a choice of toppings. Well, I'm here at Britain's largest pizza factory, near Oxford, and with me is Peter Eriksson the marketing manager. So, how many pizzas are made here, Peter?
Peter: Well, we make about two million pizzas each week – most of which are immediately frozen down to a temperature of minus 25 degrees, and the rest are chilled in refrigerators ready for immediate distribution to shops.
I: And what type of pizzas are most popular?
P: Well, the real boom has been in snack-sized pizza rather than the larger ones. The snack-size account for about 75% of all the pizzas bought in shops in Britain, whether frozen or chilled.
I: And why are they so popular?
P: Well, they're seen as a very convenient snack which is also nutritious, especially for children. It's a useful thing to have in the freezer for lunches or unexpected guests, that sort of thing.

Unit 8 Listening 1 *Part 2*

I: And how are the pizzas actually made?
P: Well, first the dough is mixed in large containers …
I: That's the bread base of the pizza, is it?
P: That's right. It's a kind of bread dough, in fact. We have four production lines operating at the same time and so when the dough is ready, it's rolled out into large sheets which are fed onto the conveyer belts. The pizza bases are then stamped out of this continuous sheet of dough before being conveyed through ovens on the conveyer belt. The ovens are kept at a constant temperature and the belts move at a constant speed, and so the base is cooked for just the right amount of time.
I: And then …?
P: And then the pizzas are automatically coated with tomato sauce and grated cheese.
I: What? Do they stay on the belt?
P: They stay on the belt and after coming out of the oven they are conveyed through the tomato spraying area and then on through the grated cheese.
I: Is the cheese sprayed on?
P: No. No, no, it er …, it sort of falls, like heavy rain … and the pizzas are coated with cheese as it sticks to the tomato.
I: And what about the other toppings? The ham, mushrooms or whatever?
P: Yes, yes. Well, once the tomato and cheese are in place the toppings are assembled by hand.
I: By hand?
P: Yes, yes, because they are assembled artistically – to make them look attractive – that's where you have more than one item. If it's only mushrooms, for example, it can be done mechanically. But most of the larger pizzas are done by hand, in fact.
I: And when they're frozen.
P: Well, first they're wrapped in plastic and the larger ones are put in boxes. All of that is done automatically.
I: And then they're frozen?
P: Yes, then they're frozen or chilled in batches of twelve and delivered in freezer lorries to the shops.

Unit 8 Listening 2

Interviewer: First of all on this afternoon's programme, are you ready for the smart card? Like me you've probably got several cards in your wallet – a credit card, bank card, telephone cards – and you probably think they're pretty clever things. But have you heard about smart cards? They're already very popular in France where people can use them for lots of things from bank transactions to paying for satellite television channels. This afternoon we have Mick Dunbar, a smart card expert. Mick, what is the difference between ordinary magnetic cards and the new smart cards?
Mick Dunbar: Well, Sue, all the cards we have at the moment have a brown magnetic strip on the back and that strip holds a small amount of information to identify the card and you.(uh,huh). The smart card contains within it a micro-computer and if you look here I've got a smart card with the back cut open and you can see the micro chip inside. It's about one third of the thickness of the card.
I: And the card is just the same size as all those credit cards I carry about at the moment.
M.D.: Yes, just the same size. Now, obviously they have many uses – especially when you need to carry money safely.
I: How do you carry money on a card?
M.D.: For example, if you're a member of a sports club, you can go to the club, pay some money and that figure is registered electronically on your card.
I: Right.
M.D.: Now, every time you go to the club, use a tennis court, buy something from the club shop or have a drink in the bar, you give in your card and the money is deducted from the total – you don't need to carry cash.
I: Does that mean that people tend to buy more things using one of these cards?
M.D.: Well, yes. That's certainly one reason why they're popular with club owners.
I: And how about the club members? How do they feel about it?
M.D.: Some people say they don't want to load the card with money in advance – spend the money in advance if you like, and sometimes the machines which read the cards can be a bit slow or break down, which is a bit irritating if you just want to buy a coca cola.
I: But you can just buy a coca cola with it?
M.D.: Oh yes.
I: Do you need a fancy computer to read the card?
M.D.: No, no, just a computer about the size of a small telephone, with a keyboard and a screen, that's all, and these units are getting more reliable all the time.
I: Does the card have any other uses?
M.D.: Oh, yes. Smart cards can be used to store medical information. At the moment doctors or dentists and hospitals might have computers but these computers don't usually talk to each other. Now, if you can carry your own medical records around with you on a smart card, the information the doctor sees or the hospital sees will always be up to date.
I: You can get information from the hospital?
MD: No. The hospital gets information about you from the card.
I: Ah, but is the information confidential?
M.D.: This is very important, of course. The advantage of the smart card is that your card can hold information about who can see it. So, your doctor or dentist have their own cards which they use to tell the machine which reads the cards that they are allowed to see your card. So, yes it's completely confidential.
I: Ah, so you need two cards to access the information?
M.D.: That's right.
I: Do you think Smart Cards could well become pretty essential in the future?
MD: Yes. I think everyone will have them in ten years from now. From tests which have been carried out in Scandinavia, we can see that they're going to be very popular there, so I think people will use them here too.
I: So, it's not going to be long before we start seeing them regularly in Britain?
M.D.: That's right, like phone cards and credit cards they'll become part of everyday life.

Unit 8 Listening 3 *Part 1*

Ruth: What have you got there, Michael?
Michael: It's a plan of this room. I'm trying to work out how we can rearrange things so that's it's a bit more comfortable for us and we use the space better.
R: That's a good idea. I'm fed up with the mess in this room. We keep buying new things but if you ask me we haven't really got the space for them here, have we?
M: That's right, what we really need is a bigger office …
R: I agree with you. OK. Let's have look … Oh, you've put the photocopier near the door … I thought we might put it on top of that cupboard over by the plant. You see it does get rather hot, and I'd rather not have it too close to my desk.
M: Well, um, yeah, that's OK, we'll put it over there for now and see how the other things fit in to the plan, all right?
R: All right.
M: Right.
R: Now, what about the fax? That could go on the table between my desk and the door, except it makes such a lot of noise, it'd drive me mad to listen to that thing beeping all day long. Do you think we could put it out of the window?
M: I don't think the company would be very happy about that … but don't worry about the fax – I'm going to try and persuade Jill to buy a new one which is completely silent, they don't cost that much, so she won't argue.
R: Are you sure it would be completely quiet? (Um) Then that's the ideal place for it.
M: Um, I'll put it in pencil … Right, that's the table in front of your desk … new … fax … machine. Right. Now, the computer and printer.
R: Well, I need the computer as close as possible although I don't want it actually on the desk in front of me, if possible. It gets in the way when I'm talking to clients.
M: How about moving it to the table at the side of you? If we put it near the window then I'll be able to use it too without having to move you from your desk.
R: Well, that's a good idea, but the printer's there at the moment and the coffee machine, now I know I drink too much coffee but there's nowhere else to put it.
M: Now look, your printer's getting very old and it keeps breaking down every couple of weeks. I thought we could ask for a new one, you know, a laser printer, small and silent. Yeah, then you could have it on the corner of your desk, where the phone is now, the coffee machine … erm …
R: I could certainly use a new printer. Do you think she'll agree? I think they're rather expensive.
M: Well, so do I, but I'll see what I can do … oh, yes, right, the coffee machine can go behind the door on that little bookcase.

Listening scripts

R: Hm. That all seems OK, if you can persuade Jill to spend all that extra money on new machines …

Unit 8 Listening 3 Part 2

Jill: So, let me just get this right. You'd like a new fax and a new printer for the office?
M: That's it. I think we should replace both the fax and the printer. The fax is very old and it makes a terrible noise and the quality is so bad now that it produces letters and things which are almost impossible to read. I just feel it's not very good for business.
J: You've got a point there. We could do with one which made clearer copies. The other thing is that you can only put in one number each time you use it so it's a real waste of time.
M: Absolutely. If you ask me what we need is a new fax with a bigger memory and one which doesn't make much noise.
J: I think so too. The problem is finding the right model. Look, will you have a look around and see if you can find one which you think will be right for us? I think the best thing would be for you and Ruth to try a couple first and see if they're suitable.
M: Yes, so do I. I'll get on to that today.
J: OK. Let me know how much it'll cost and if it's not too much we'll go ahead and order it. Now, what about the computer printer?
M: Well, in my opinion we should replace it with a laser printer.
J: Why's that?
M: Well, I know we haven't had the present printer for very long, but it's just not suitable for the amount of work we do. What I mean is it's it's too slow and it often doesn't print very well and it's very noisy. Now, you see, a laser printer …
J: You've got a point there, we could certainly do with a faster machine, but don't we just need to buy a new part for the existing printer?
M: No, Ruth tried that and it didn't improve the quality very much and it was expensive. Now a laser printer …
J: Would also be expensive?
M: You do get much better quality with a laser printer and they're really easy to use and they don't make any noise. We need a new printer as soon as possible. I don't know exactly how much they cost …
J: Nor do I, but I know they're expensive. No, I'm sorry, I can't agree with you there. Look I've been thinking of replacing the whole computer system with a better model. Now I don't think we've got enough money to do that immediately, but in my opinion we should wait and then get a new printer which is compatible with the computer. (Ah). What do you think …?

Unit 8 Listening 4

Interviewer: Did you know that the time has come to throw away your diary and your address book, because this is the age of the Electronic Organiser. But first of all, what is an Electronic Organiser? Today we have with us Eric Newman, a computer journalist. Eric …
Eric Newman: An Electronic Organiser is a machine which functions rather like a very small computer. The Electronic Organiser usually has a miniature version of the computer keyboard and a little screen with maybe four lines on it. Now the main use of Electronic Organisers is, for example, you can enter all the names and phone numbers you keep in your diary into the organiser and it will store them and you can see an address or a phone number on the screen when you ask for it.
I: It doesn't sound very useful to me but let's look at a couple of models which you have brought along with you. This one's the Cherry, right?
E.N.: This is the best known organiser, and it's used in some big shops, you can see the shop assistants in department stores with these machines and they use them in quite an intelligent way – as a sort of satellite to the full-sized computer, which of course they can't carry round the shop with them.
I: It's not a very friendly size, is it?
E.N.: Well, no, it's not. It's far too big to put in your pocket and it's got a calculator keyboard which is not very useful if you can type, because the letters are all in the wrong place. It's also got rather a small screen – it can only show two lines, or four on some models.
I: And what can I do with it?
E.N.: People give these as presents or go out and buy them, and I think they imagine they're going to use them as an address book – for addresses and phone numbers. But I suggest they probably get as far as the letter M, maybe P if they've bought it themselves, and then they just give up and stop. Because the keyboard and the screen are just too hard to use.
I: Hm well, the next one is made by Blunt. Tell us about this one.
E.N.: Well, this Electronic Organiser is much more attractive. You can close it – rather like a wallet – to put it away or carry it around, it isn't very heavy, at all. (Ah) When you open it on one side is the keyboard, and it's a real keyboard, like on a computer or a typewriter, and on the other side is a screen. It's a good-size screen and the machine is quite easy to use, but it's still a bit expensive.
I: How do you put in a friend's address?
E.N.: Well, you just type it in – like on a typewriter. But there are things this Electronic Organiser can do which you can't do with a normal diary or address book made of paper. For example, what if you forget a name, you forget everything about this person, name, postcode, the lot, except that they live in, let's say Oxford Road. OK, if you have a normal paper address book you have to look through all of the book to try and find the right person. With this Electronic Organiser you can do the job immediately, you can do a search and ask the machine to find Oxford Road, or whatever, and get the information.
I: Well, I suppose it could be useful … although I can't remember being in that situation. Can it do anything else?
E.N.: Oh, I should point out that the Electronic Organiser will also give you a 'beep' at the right time, to remind you about all those important appointments.
I: What points should I consider before I buy one of these things?
E.N.: The important thing to remember is not to make a comparison between the different Electronic Organisers on the market, but compare the Electronic Organiser with a normal diary or notebook. (Yes). I'm a computer enthusiast and I don't use these things. I get them free and I just put them away in a drawer. If you are going to use the machine it must be of practical use. Now, here I've got a small machine, from California. When it's closed it's about the size of a video cassette and when it opens you have a good-sized keyboard and a good screen. This is like a small version of a computer. It's a bit expensive but this is the way forward. And if you can wait, it'll be around in a couple of years at a decent price. That's what I recommend.
I: That was Eric Newman trying to get us organised electronically. I don't think I'll be throwing my diary and address book away just yet, but anyway, thanks Eric. And next week we'll be …

Unit 8 Pronunciation

/h/

1 Listen and decide which word, A or B, is being said.
1 arm   6 eat
2 hill   7 eye
3 had   8 hate
4 old   9 his
5 hair   10 am

3 Listen and repeat these sentences.
I haven't heard from Harry for ages.
I hate eating in the heat.
I hear that Mrs Hill is ill.
Is this his hat, or isn't it?
You can hold my arm if you don't hurt it.
Had he hurt his eye? Yes, he'd hit it with a hairbrush.

Unit 8 Listening 5

1 You will hear part of an interview with a woman who has carried out a travel survey. What kind of travel is she talking about?
A coach travel
B air travel
C train travel
Interviewer: So, what were the findings of your survey, Patricia?
Patricia: Well, we're still getting about 20% of passengers saying they wouldn't recommend the company to others.
Interviewer: So what do people complain about?
Patricia: Interestingly, it seems to be comfort these days. It's legroom, how comfortable the seat is, what the in-flight entertainment's like and also the meals service, of course. We get a lot of families travelling abroad and people generally are going intercontinental more than they did and I think they are generally looking for a better in-flight experience all around.

2 You will hear Mary, a secretary, complaining about a new computer system she is using. Who is Mary talking to?
A a computer engineer
B another secretary
C her boss
Boss: Hello Mary. How are you?
Mary: Well, to tell you the truth, I'm not at my happiest, actually.
Boss: Oh, really?
Mary: I'm sorry, but I can't get on with this new system – it's been down again this morning – just when I'd got all my documents on to the disc, and if it's anything like yesterday, I'll have lost the lot and have to start again.
Boss: Well, there are always teething problems at the beginning with any new system and I'm sure that in the long run, this one's the best for us, you know.
Mary: Well, I can't take much more of this, if things don't improve, I'll have to start looking round for something else.
Boss: I'd hate to lose you, Mary. I mean, the place couldn't run without you, as you know and …

3 You will hear an advertisement for a place tourists might like to visit. What type of place is it?
A a shopping centre
B a restaurant
C a museum
Come and experience the superb fish and unique atmosphere which can only be found at world-famous Harry Ramsden's in Guiseley.
Harry Ramsden began the business with a modest shop in the town in December 1928; but by 1936 his fish and chips were in such demand that he opened new dining rooms with cut-glass chandeliers, stained-glass windows and wall-to-wall carpets.
Today Harry Ramsden's still enjoys the same success, decor and reputation, serving over one million customers a year. Harry's also appears in the Guinness Book of records, having served an amazing 11,964 platefuls in one day. So come and visit Harry Ramsden's and experience the unique atmosphere for yourself.

4 You will hear a woman talking about her dishwasher. How does she feel about the dishwasher?
A she regrets buying it
B she wishes she'd bought it sooner
C it took time to get used to it
I don't know how we managed without one for so long. It's amazing how quickly you come to depend on it. I just stack all the cutlery and plates in it after meals and then switch it on, usually in the evening, and the things are completely clean the next day. To think for years I said I didn't want one in the house, I must have been mad! I don't think I could ever get used to a sinkful of bubbles again.

5 You will hear someone talking to a group of students about an exhibition centre. What's special about the exhibition?
A it's all about music and sound
B you can touch the exhibits
C people explain science to you

Now, one place you should visit is the Science Centre. It's the largest hands-on science exhibition in the country, in fact, and it's got 140 exhibits on two floors, and everything is hands-on from lasers to lenses, bridges to bubbles. You can even make a bridge to stand on, touch a tornado, find out what makes an ice-skater spin faster and how a colour television works. There's a temporary music and sound exhibition on at the moment, and they've got the world's largest guitar for you to see and play. So it's a really fun day out, even if you're not that interested in science.

Unit 9 Listening 1   A B C C A C

You will hear people talking in six different situations. For questions 1 to 6 choose the best answer A, B or C.

1 You will hear part of a radio programme about fitness. What type of programme is it?
A the introduction to a report
B part of an advertisement
C a sports commentary

+ 9.000 ptas

Behind closed doors, Britain's overworked and overweight are paying a small fortune to keep themselves in shape. The health and fitness trade is seeing an increase in demand for personal trainers who provide one-to-one tuition in body maintenance, for fees of up to £45 an hour. But what are the advantages of having a personal trainer and is it worth the money? Lorna Todd went to a West London fitness club to find out.

2 You will hear a man talking about a trip he made. How was he travelling?
A by balloon
B by boat
C by bicycle

Irish

We left London around ten in the morning. The wind was getting up, but otherwise it was a fine day. Lois felt a bit nervous about the trip, but I was soon getting practical advice from our two trainers on how to avoid running into other traffic on the river. It only took us about an hour to reach the estuary, actually.

3 Listen to this telephone message from a businesswoman to a client. Why has she phoned?
A to suggest new ideas
B to turn down an invitation
C to propose a change of plan

Hello, this is Monica Fareham here. It's about our meeting next Tuesday regarding the London Marathon and our sponsorship of your entrant. What's happened is that I'm going to be delayed in Cornwall by a rail strike, so can we postpone our meeting until Wednesday at the same time? Let my secretary in London know if that's OK. Many thanks. Bye.

4 You will hear a woman talking about her job. What is her job?
A a doctor
B a nurse
C a dentist

Welsh

The people who come in here are often nervous and, of course, sometimes in pain and really upset. I try to make them as comfortable as possible. I keep smiling and talking to them although it's no good asking them lots of questions because they can't reply apart from making the odd noise. The work can be quite hard physically as well, which people don't always realise, but when people get out of the chair and look so relieved and grateful to be out of pain, it makes it all seem worthwhile.

5 You will hear an advertisement on the radio. What is being advertised?
A a restaurant
B a shop
C a pub

The last thing anyone wants to do on a beautiful summer day is slave away indoors over a hot stove – especially after a long day at work or a tiresome journey home. So that's exactly when you should pick up the phone and call Carlos's. In the time it takes you to put your feet up with a long cool drink, we can have one of our summer special takeaways delivered to your door. You're assured of great taste, great service and great savings - don't delay, call Carlos's now on 0171 ....

6 You will hear two people, Rob and Jane, discussing a course they have seen advertised. How does Rob feel about the course?
A He refuses to go.
B Jane convinces him to go.
C He is not keen to go.

Jane: It says here you can learn safely and confidently in a week.
Rob: Yeah, but it can't be the same for everyone.
Jane: Oh, come on – the package includes all the basic training necessary to control a horse and the lessons take place indoors – so you're not going to gallop off into the distance in lesson one.
Rob: But why, Jane? You know I was hopeless at skiing, and I've never even really learned to ride a bike properly – and they don't bite and kick!
Jane: But think of what a lovely feeling it must be, once you do get out in the open air.
Rob: Really Jane, I don't ...
Jane: ... and the price is all inclusive, you only have to buy a hard hat.
Rob: Couldn't I just hold your coat while you go?

Unit 9 Listening 2

Sue: 83670?
Jenny: Hi, Sue, I'm home.
S: Jenny, hi. Did you have a good time?
J: Well, OK.
S: What do you mean OK? That card you sent made it sound wonderful. I was really jealous. It made me wish I'd gone with you, after all.
J: Yes, well I wish you had come with me, Sue, then I might not have been so stupid.
S: Tell me more Jenny. What have you been up to?
J: Oh Well, I was really stupid, Sue. Before I went I meant to buy some sunscreen or lotion or something, but I couldn't find the one I wanted so I thought 'Oh, well I'll buy it there', you know?
S: Oh dear, I can guess what's coming!
J: Yes, so the first morning I got up and we were miles from the shops, and the hotel didn't sell anything like that and these people I met on the plane invited me to the beach with them.
S: And you got sunburnt.
J: Well, you know it doesn't feel that hot and I only meant to stay for an hour or so.
S: Oh, Jenny, no! But everyone knows how hot the sun is on those islands.
J: OK, OK, I know. I had the chance to regret at my leisure.
S: Was it really bad?
J: I couldn't sleep. I couldn't wear half my clothes because they rubbed and of course I couldn't go back to the beach for four days for fear of making it worse so I missed all the fun.
S: Oh, Jenny. What did you do?
J: Well, I wish I'd taken a few books with me because there was nothing to do there. I'd seen the island in a day and so I just had to sit in the hotel all day watching everyone else having fun.
S: Well, you must be brown at least.
J: You're kidding. I was bright pink for about four days and then it all started peeling off. I look a real mess. I wish I'd stayed at home.
S: Oh, Jenny, you can't mean that. It must be better than coming to the office.
J: Yes, but if only I hadn't been so stupid! Anyway how are you ...

Unit 9 Listening 3

Tony: And next on the programme, the subject of wills. They always say it's your last chance to get your own back on your family or reward someone for loyalty and kindness. With me is Laura Seagrave, who teaches law at Wickham Polytechnic. Now, is that generally the case Laura? Do people use wills to get back at their relatives?
Laura: No, not generally, Tony. Most wills are pretty ordinary and boring; people making sure their immediate family will be looked after financially should they die and that sort of thing. But there was an interesting case recently where the family were very disappointed.
Tony: Oh, yes. Yes. The millionaire who left everything to an aromatherapist.
Laura: That's right. This man, Edward Grey, left over a million pounds to a young woman who runs an aromatherapy centre, and only derisory sums to the members of his family.
Tony: And why was that, Laura?
Laura: Well, the will was quite explicit. He wanted the money to go into aromatherapy because he'd got a lot of relief out of it in his last years, and the money was left to promote aromatherapy in the area where he lived.
Tony: Oh, right.
Laura: But the interesting thing was that he was also very specific about why he didn't leave much money to his family.
Tony: You mean the will actually said as much?
Laura: Exactly. For example, Norman Grey, his nephew, received £50 only, to use to pay off his debts. And the reason for this, apparently, was that he had owed Edward Grey the sum of £50 for a number of years and had always refused to pay it back.
Tony: So, in other words, if he'd paid back the £50, he would have inherited a much larger sum?
Laura: That's the idea. Similarly, Edward Grey's sister, Mary, received £100 to spend on second-hand furniture, because she's been in the habit of coming round and measuring up the furniture in Edward Grey's house.
Tony: Because she thought she might inherit it?
Laura: Exactly, she couldn't wait for him to die. If she'd been a little more patient she'd have got the furniture and probably more money as well! And then, worst of all, the will actually stated that Cecilia Grey, that's old Mr Grey's daughter, should have £200 to keep her in her old age.
Tony: Well, that wouldn't keep her long.
Laura: It certainly wouldn't. It appears that Edward had asked his daughter to come and look after him as he got older and she had refused.
Tony: And so this was her punishment.
Laura: Oh yes. The will said that if she had agreed to come and look after him she would have inherited the house and a lot of the money.
Tony: I bet the family were none too pleased.
Laura: That's right, but there was nothing they could do about it. He'd been of sound mind right up to the time of his death. I'm afraid he just didn't like them.

Unit 9 Listening 4

Mr Fields: Camford 24689.
Louise: Hello, could I speak to Mr Fields, please?
Mr F: Speaking.
LP: Hello, Mr Fields, my name's Louise Platt and I live next door to your aunt, Mrs Grey, in Newton street.
Mr F: Oh, is there something wrong?
LP: No, no. Well, there isn't an emergency or anything like that. But I would like to talk to you for a moment about Mrs Grey. I'm very worried about her, you see.
Mr F: Is she ill?
LP: No, it's not that. It's just that I went round to visit her because, you know, she lives alone and I've just moved to the area and well, I want to be neighbourly, you know.
Mr F: I'm sorry, but what's the problem?
LP: Well, that's it you see, I said she should give me a number to ring, if ever she was ill or if there was an emergency. You know, someone in the family to get in touch with, because she's an old lady, you know ...
Mr F: Look, Mrs ... er ...
LP: Platt, Louise Platt.
Mr F: Look, Mrs Platt. I don't mean to be unkind and I'm sure you mean well, but ... if my aunt's well, I really don't see why you are phoning me. I'm a very busy man but I do go and see my aunt quite regularly and you seem to be suggesting that she's neglected in some way, and really I can assure you that's not the case. She's a very independent old lady and she

115

Listening scripts

won't thank you for interfering.
LP: Yes, but the problem is Mr Fields, that that old house is so dangerous. I'm sure there'll be an accident if nothing's done.
Mr F: Dangerous? In what way dangerous?
LP: Well, the electricity for a start.
Mr F: What's wrong with the electricity?
LP: Well, apart from the fact that it's all so old and needs rewiring there are certain things that are really very dangerous.
Mr F: What, for example?
LP: Well, she's got a socket right above the kitchen sink and you know that's so dangerous. The flex from the toaster trails across the washing up water. It's dangerous to touch plugs or sockets with wet hands or splash them. That socket should be taken out at once.
Mr F: She's lived there for thirty-five years and nothing's ever happened.
LP: That doesn't mean nothing will happen. She's also got a socket in the bathroom, which is not a good idea at all. And all the sockets are so old that they don't have switches and you know switch sockets are so much safer. And, of course, there aren't enough sockets in the living room and then she's got so many appliances working off one socket that I'm sure she'll overload the system. She's using old adaptors with three plugs in – all the flexes get mixed up and tangled together and that's such a dangerous thing to do, you know. And then upstairs the live flex is just pinned to the wall …
Mr F: OK, OK Mrs Platt. Listen, I'll go round and check these things if you like, and if my aunt wants something done about them, maybe I can help her in some way.
LP: Well, really the whole house needs rewiring, it's the only answer. And by the way, do tell her not to put wet clothes over the electric heater, won't you?
Mr F: As I say, I'll speak to my aunt …
LP: Anyway, my husband's an electrician, so if you want to get the work done cheaply, because these things cost such a lot of money, don't they?
Mr F: Thank you very much, but I think I'll let my aunt decide about that. Thank you for calling. Good bye Mrs Platt.
LP: Well … Why don't you just have a word with him, hello … hello …

Unit 9 Listening 5

1 I just couldn't remember what the next line was and, you know, I'd just read it in the dressing room and I thought, Well, I'll have to go out there and apologise to the audience and say, "I've made a big mistake." I've never been so frightened in my life. I was looking for fire alarms to set off so the show would have to be cancelled that night. But once I was out there, I was OK; it was all in the mind, after all, just my nerves getting the better of me for a few moments.

2 To a large extent, what you need is some kind of here-and-now practical help. For example, imagine what success would be like, imagine the goal and imagine being the great success. This combined with positive self-talk, which is telling yourself little encouraging things like "I will concentrate on the work and enjoy it and not worry about those people and how they react." There are some relaxation techniques which are also useful, even being fit, aerobic exercise can be a way of relaxing.

3 There are drugs which block the effects of stage fright, they stop the heart racing, they prevent the body from shaking and also decrease the level of anxiety. But do be careful; the thing is, if you're under pressure and you're doing something which is really important, and if you suffer from terrible stage fright, drugs can make you feel better. They're not to be advised, however, as dependence may be the result, and the real cause of the problem doesn't go away.

4 The one that sticks in my mind most of all is Jack Armstrong. I was once in a play with him, and it was the opening night, and I couldn't believe it. He was so absolutely petrified, standing in the wings, that he had to be literally pushed onto the stage. And I'm talking about the latter part of his career. At one point he did forget his lines and what he did, he turned to me and said, "What do you think?" and gave me the problem. A mean trick really.

5 You can change your life. You don't have to be the victim of your biography. A good example is Jan Paderewski the noted pianist and composer who was always nervous before a concert, and who was chosen to be the first Prime Minister of Poland when it became independent again after the First World War. So he was prime minister for a few years and when he went back to being a concert pianist, to his absolute amazement he wasn't nervous. Well, why? Because he had become confident in another way, his whole success as a person was no longer tied up with playing that instrument.

Unit 9 Pronunciation

/th/ sounds

The spelling t-h is used to represent two different sounds in English.
1 Listen to the difference:
    A th (θ)   B the (ð)

Unit 10 Listening 1

1 I like it because you can have a good look round and take your time without being bothered or talked into anything. You can try things on without feeling you have to buy them afterwards.

2 You needn't go to London for style and exclusivity. We can offer that something special, a really personal service. Our trained and experienced staff are on hand to advise you on the perfect outfit for every occasion.

3 Price is our main advantage, of course. People come here because they know they can get the same stuff cheaper. We don't have to pay high rents, heating bills or anything like that, so our prices are lower.

Unit 10 Listening 2

This is a customer announcement. In the Food Hall on the ground floor, our range of in-store bakery products has now been reduced. We have a full range of white and wholemeal, soft and crusty loaves and rolls now at reduced prices in the food hall.
Don't forget on the third floor we have 20% off all soft furnishings. This offer lasts for today only. We have a range of beautiful sofas, armchairs and other comfortable furniture. All at 20% discount, in the furniture department, today only.
You can buy two for the price of one this week in the Hardware Department in the basement. Buy any Brighthouse cleaning product and you will receive an extra one free. We have an exciting range of carpet shampoos, bathroom and kitchen floor cleaners and similar products to brighten up your home. So that's in the Hardware Department in the basement all this week.
Lunch is now being served in the restaurant on the top floor. Choose from the a la carte Penthouse Menu or take the set lunch for only £3.20. Today we have a choice of warming soup or salad followed by chicken and chips and trifle. So hurry up to the restaurant to be sure of a seat for lunch.
In the Book Department on the first floor, best-selling author Joyce Bakerson is signing copies of her new novel *The Miltons*. So if you'd like a signed copy of this wonderful new book and a chance to meet Joyce Bakerson, go along to the Book Department between two and three o'clock this afternoon.
We are giving away a free tie with each suit bought or ordered from the Menswear department this week. This offer includes both made-to-measure and off-the-peg suits. We have something for every occasion from the formal dinner to the Caribbean holiday, from the family wedding to something for the office. And with each suit a free tie of your choice from the Menswear Department on the second floor.

Unit 10 Listening 3

Anne: That's a lovely top you're wearing, Liz. Where did you get it from?
Liz: Oh, guess!
A: Somewhere expensive, I suppose?
L: No, no, it came from Ferguson's, actually.
A: Oh, really, I'd never have guessed!
L: Well, they have nice things in there, you know.
A: I never think to look … because they don't let you try things on, do they?
L: No, but you can take them back and change them if they don't fit.
A: Oh, yes, and then they make you buy something else from the shop instead.
L: No, no they don't, Anne. They let you have your money back, without any argument. It's their policy. (Oh). You're not allowed to try things on in the shop but you can always change them or get your money back.
A: Oh, anyway, they always make you pay in cash, that's the other reason I don't go there. I don't carry much cash about. I like to go to places where they let you pay with a credit card, or something.
L: Oh, well, I've got a Ferguson's card. It's not a credit card exactly, but it means you don't have to pay all at once. You're allowed to pay it off so much per month.
A: Oh, really? Like a charge card?
L: That's right, so whenever you see anything you can buy it, even if you don't have the cash on you.
A: But they only sell their own stuff, don't they? I mean, everything's got their label on it.
L: Yes that's right, they don't let the people who make the clothes put a label in. They make them put a Ferguson one in instead. But it is a guarantee of quality, Anne. No one else is allowed to sell Ferguson clothes, you see. So you have to go to Ferguson's to get them, and you know they'll be good.
A: Oh well, I'll go in and have a look around next time I'm in town. There you are, you've got me interested now. Do you think they'll let me have one of those cards?
L: Oh I should think so, if you've got a credit card already. They make you fill in a form, of course, and then you're only allowed to spend a certain amount per month before you start paying it off.
A: Oh yes, of course. Oh, anyway, it's a lovely top, Liz. (Thanks) I'd better be off.
L: Thanks, Anne. Oh, bye.
A: Bye.

Unit 10 Listening 4

Assistant: Good morning, Sir. Can I help?
Customer: Yes, it's about this pullover I bought here a couple of weeks ago.
A: And what seems to be the problem?
C: Well, the first time I put it in the washing machine, it lost its colour.
A: Did you wash it at the correct temperature?
C: Yes, of course I did. Look it says on the label 40 degrees.
A: Hm. And you say that the colour came out? That seems unlikely.
C: And it ruined two other things that were with it.
A: You are sure it was 40 degrees centigrade? Maybe you made a mistake.
C: Yes, of course I'm sure. I'm not stupid, you know.
A: Well, perhaps there's something wrong with your washing machine.
C: Look this is ridiculous. There's something wrong with this pullover, and I want my money back.
A: Have you got your receipt?
C: No, I haven't. I threw it away.
A: Well, I'm sorry. Without the receipt I can't do anything.
C: Oh, really! But look, it's got your label in it!
A: I'm sorry. It's company policy. We never give money back without a receipt.
C: OK. In that case I'd like to speak to the manager.
A: I'm sorry, I'm afraid the manager's on holiday this week.
C: Then I shall write him a letter, and what's more I shall tell him how unhelpful you've been.
A: It's a her.

C: Pardon?
A: The manager is a woman, Sir.
C: Honestly! You haven't heard the last of this. Goodbye!

Unit 10 Pronunciation
Word linking

1 Listen to these examples.
It's next week   She's finished, has she?
I went last night   Who asked the question?
I prefer baked potatoes   I'll leave it for you
It's stopped raining   Don't talk about it

3 Listen to these phrases and mark the letters that have joined together or been lost.
 1 You can't do that.
 2 He didn't throw it
 3 I'm going next year
 4 Do you want a small glass or a big glass?
 5 I'll look for him outside
 6 The problem with this exercise is…
 7 He asked the teacher a question
 8 She looked through the window
 9 I like boiled potatoes
10 He isn't taking the exam

Unit 10 Listening 5

Andy: And on today's programme we're talking about wishes – give me a ring, Andy Scott on Oxton 279053 and let me know about the things you wish you could do, or things about yourself you'd like to change, or things about other people. Don't forget there are free tickets for next week's Folk Concert for today's most original wish. So the lines are open now, and our topic is wishes. And here's our first caller, Jenny from Redhill. Hallo Jenny.
Jenny: Hi Andy. I wish I could ski.
A: You wish you could ski? Why's that?
J: Yes, all my family are off on a skiing holiday in January and I'm the only one who's never done it.
A: So are you going to have lessons?
J: I suppose so. But I wish I could do it now. It's the lessons I don't fancy. You know, falling over and looking stupid. I wish I could just get on the skis and do it, you know?
A: Well Jenny, I don't think I can help you much there. But if anyone's got any ideas, give us a call. Meanwhile Jenny, I wish you luck with your skiing.
J: Thanks, I need it!
A: Next on the line is Pam from Romford. Hi Pam! What's your wish?
P: Hello Andy. I wish I was really rich. (laughs)
A: Don't we all, Pam.
P: No really. I wish I had so much money I never had to worry about it again.
A: But what would you do with it, Pam?
P: That's not a problem, Andy. No, really I'm phoning on behalf of Cancer Research. If I was rich I'd give all my money to Cancer Research. So, you know, if any of your listeners have got lots of money and they don't know what to do with it …
A: OK, Pam. We've got the message. If there's anyone out there who's rich and wishes they were poor, Pam's got the answer.
P: Thanks Andy, bye.
A: Next on the line is Rob from Burton. Hi Rob.
Rob: Hello Andy. I wish I was an England International.
A: What … football, you mean?
R: Yeah, yeah. I wish I could play for England.
A: Do you play football now, Rob?
R: Occasionally, yeah. But I've always wanted to play for England.
A: Do you score many goals?
R: No, no. I never score goals.
A: Well, come on. Why don't you score some goals? You might be able to play for England.
R: I shouldn't think so, Andy.
A: Why not?
R: Well, firstly, I'm a goalkeeper and secondly I'm 38. So I think my chance has gone now, don't you?
A: Oh well, never mind. Next on the line is Rachel. Hello Rachel.

Rachel: Hi Andy. (laughing)
A: Well, what's your wish?
R: I wish you'd take me out to dinner one night. (laughing)
A: Well that's a wish maybe I can make come true. I think we'd better play a piece of music before my wife gets on the phone. (laughs)
R: It's my birthday, you see.
A: I see, and how old are you, Rachel?
R: Ooh, you're not supposed to ask that!
A: Well, let's wish Rachel a happy birthday. But honestly Rachel, if you want dinner, you'll have to tell me your age. Come on, how old are you – 21, 22?
R: Ooh, I wish I was! No I'm 72 today, Andy, and that's the truth.
A: Well, it looks like I've got myself a date. I hope my wife's not tuned in. Here's Stevie Wonder – I Just Called to Say I Love You …

Unit 10 Listening 6

1 The first drink-dispensing machine was introduced in this country about a century ago. But, of course, vending goes back a lot further than that – it's reputed to have been invented by Hero, who was a Greek mathematician, way back in 200 BC – and he invented a machine which stood outside the temple, and as you were going into the temple, you dropped a coin into the machine and a little holy water came out.

2 Times are changing. We travel more, we move about more – even in food and drink, we snack more: people on the move – and vending machines are convenient and hygenic – well, as long as they're cleaned and changed regularly, you know. If you see a cheeseburger in a vending machine and you want it, you can buy it, but just the idea of putting some money in and seeing what you get out is somehow tempting as well, isn't it? Even if you've got shops you could go to instead, people still use them, don't they?

3 But what do you do if your money gets stuck or nothing comes out - you can bang on the machine, because that sometimes works. But how are you placed if the money does get stuck? Or if you're unhappy with the product you've purchased? There's nobody there to complain to, but you'll find on every vending machine there'll be the name of the operator, a telephone number, and you'll be able to ring them and they'll refund you without question.

4 Now, we've moved over to one of the other machines, this one actually sells you a pair of reading glasses – they cost five pounds including the case. Who on earth would want to buy glasses out of a machine? I mean, surely you'd want to try them on! But of course, they are just magnified reading glasses, I guess this machine's here for that sort of person who's just got off the train, they're on the way to the office and and suddenly realise – Oh no, I haven't got my glasses! Whatever am I going to do?

5 There used to be a petrol station in North Wales, I remember, that had machines dispensing fish and chips! Really, chips coated in hot fat in those days, not oven chips like you might get today, and they were horrid, and really, thinking about it it couldn't have been the safest of things to have in a petrol station anyway. So that's an example of a vending machine that never caught on – I wonder if you've got any examples of mad vending machines that were short-lived for one reason or another – give me a call on ….

Unit 11 Listening 1

Young woman: At first, I thought it was a good idea – the air's vile. When it's hot and muggy you can hardly breathe. But I found that people avoided my gaze as I walked through London's Covent Garden. There wasn't much point in smiling back. After an hour I was desperate to take it off because I felt ridiculous. After two hours, I felt vaguely sick. Frankly, I can't see them catching on.

Unit 11 Listening 2 Part 1

Bob: So, don't forget, if you'd like to have your say, phone me on 2483692 and the lines are open now. That's 2483692 and the subject we're talking about is air pollution – smog – and how to prevent it, how to live with it, how to avoid it. First on the line is Lidia from Milton. Hello Lidia.
Lidia: Hello, Bob.
B: Fire away, love.
L: Well, Bob, I don't have a car. I can drive but I choose not to. When I really need a car I can hire one, but otherwise I get the bus or train. I think more people who can drive MUST use public transport instead.
B: Right, thank you, Lidia. And over to Les in Calford. What do you think of that, Les?
L: Well, that may work OK for Lidia, but it's a bit silly for me. I live in Calford and there aren't any trains or buses into Milton, where I work. People will not stop using their cars until there are improvements in public transport.
B: OK, thank you, Les, and before our next caller, here's a piece of music from …

Unit 11 Listening 2 Part 2

Bob: So now on the line I've got Malcolm from Milton. Hello, Malcolm.
Malcolm: Hello, Bob.
B: So, just to recap, Lidia said that she thought more people who could drive had to use public transport instead. She said that might be OK for Lidia but that people would not stop using their cars until there were improvements in public transport. What do you think?
M: Well now, that's an interesting question. You see I remember when I ….

Unit 11 Listening 2 Part 3
Part 3

Bob: Great. And now on the line we have Gordon from Newton. Hello, Gordon.
Gordon: Hi, Bob. I'd just like to say that I would be happy to use my bicycle all the time in town. But we should make special routes for cyclists – with parts of the road on those routes reserved for cyclists only. And then they could keep out of the traffic.
B: Right. Thanks, Gordon. Mary from Milton. What do you think of that idea?
Mary: I would like to ban cyclists from main roads, actually and cyclists ought to be made to take a test, like car drivers. That might lead to fewer accidents.
B: Well, thank you, Mary. And just before the commercial break, here's another piece of music from ….

Unit 11 Listening 3

Announcer: The time is seven-thirty and here is Nick Gregson with the motoring programme.
Nick: Well, you've probably heard the old joke about Henry Ford, who said 'You can buy a car in any colour as long as it's black'. Well, today green is the in-colour for cars – and that's not talking about paintwork either – green in the sense of environmentally friendly cars, that's what we hear about these days. Most cars, it seems, are recyclable. 75% of a car is made of metal and that gets melted down and used again when the car is scrapped. Well, the car manufacturers have been working on that remaining 25% – the other parts that maybe don't get used again. Jenny Wilson of Green Car magazine is here today to tell us more about the latest advances in car recycling. Jenny, are there other parts which can be recycled?
Jenny: Well, we're looking at the plastic parts at the moment, Nick. The first thing to make sure is that the same plastic is used on the various parts of the car. That means going back to the design stage and looking at research into plastics, and choosing one type of plastic that will suit all the jobs that the plastic parts do on cars. That is just beginning to happen on new models.
N: Are we talking about bumpers and things like that?

Listening scripts

J: Not only bumpers, but let's take them as an example. When a car is involved in an accident, new bumpers usually get fitted and the old ones can't be repaired, so they get thrown away. Well, what's beginning to happen now is that your local garage will send the damaged bumpers back to the manufacturer who will reduce the plastic into small particles that can be used again.
N: And are the particles used to make new bumpers?
J: The best ones, yes. But only the best quality goes back onto making bumpers, about 20% usually, the rest are used for making the underfloor mats and other less visible plastic parts, like linings for the boot and that sort of thing.
N: Why isn't the car 100% recyclable?
J: Well, it may be one day. It means looking at designs and materials. Cars have to be designed with materials that can be recycled in the first place. And then of course it's got to be organised. Used cars or damaged parts have to find their way back to the factory or recycling plant and then the recycled materials have to be fed back into the manufacturing process.
N: Will we get more money back on our old cars?
J: I don't know about that, Nick. But certainly expensive parts like catalytic converters that contain precious metals, which are reusable, can be part-exchanged, so that reduces the price of the new one.
N: Jenny, thank you. So the message is – don't throw anything away – it may be useful to someone.

Unit 11 Listening 4

Interviewer: There seems to be increasing evidence that we are coming close to answering that age-old question – Whatever happened to the dinosaurs? Why did a complete race of prehistoric monsters suddenly just die out? I've got with me today Dr Valerie Marshall of the University of Worcester, who's been researching into this area. Valerie, welcome.
Valerie: Hello.
I: So what happened to the dinosaurs? Was it disease, climatic change or, as has been suggested, something from outer space?
V: Well, the first thing is that it's becoming increasingly clear that the extinction of the dinosaurs and most other species around at the time, by the way, occurred at very much the same time. It didn't take millions of years, it happened very quickly.
I: So something dramatic happened?
V: We think so, yes. And although it could have been a giant volcano or something like that, evidence points to something from outer space. Not spacemen, of course, but something big hitting the earth.
I: Like a meteorite.
V: Like a meteorite or asteroid, yes.
I: So what evidence is there?
V: Well, large quantities of iridium have been found in rocks dating from that time, about 65 million years ago – and iridium is much more common in meteorites and asteroids than in earth rocks. We've also found glass spheres – round pieces of glass – that contain almost no water. Now, glass made on earth, by volcanoes, nearly always contains water, but glass found in meteorites doesn't.
I: So a large meteorite hit the earth – but why did it kill all the dinosaurs?
V: Well, probably it would have made a large crater and thrown up a lot of dust that could well have blocked out the light of the sun for years. This would be enough to destroy the food chain on which all the animals depended.
I: So they all died out very quickly, did they?
V: Oh yes, in a matter of a few years.
I: But not all over the world, surely?
V: In a large part of it certainly, and we can't rule out the possibility of a number of meteorites falling in different places. They often travel through space in groups and do cross the earth's path fairly regularly.
I: But where is the crater, or craters? If it's that big we should be able to see it, shouldn't we?
V: Well, a lot of material will have been deposited on top of it over 65 million years, and anyway it could be lost under the sea. Evidence points to the Gulf of Mexico actually.
I: But we shall never know for sure.
V: Well, layers of rock containing the glass spheres I mentioned have been found in Haiti, Mexico and the Southern states of the US. They were probably deposited on the edge of the crater and so give us an idea of where it might be. Often these layers are hidden under more recent rock formations, however, so you have to find places where they come to the surface.
I: So it was an environmental disaster which led to the extinction of the dinosaurs?
V: Oh yes, it looks like that. It shows what a delicate balance exists in a natural environment …

Unit 11 Listening 5

1
A: Oh what a lovely doggy – oh isn't he beautiful! Come here, good boy!
B: Don't get too close to that dog, he doesn't like strangers and he's got a nasty temper. He bit me the other day.
A: Oh, but he looks so nice.

2
A: It's our wedding anniversary next week. I'd like to go somewhere really special, you know. But there's nowhere near here is there?
B: I always go to that French place in the High Street.
A: Is it any good?
B: Oh yes, it's excellent. You get a decent meal there.

3
A: Did you see that competition in the newspaper yesterday?
B: The round-the-world cruise? Are you going in for it?
A: I've answered all the questions but I don't know if I'll send it off, you've got to have someone to go with, haven't you?
B: Go on, you go in for it. I'll come with you.

4
A: I don't know if I'll pass this exam. I haven't got time to study really.
B: Well, if I were you, I'd make the time. It's a useful qualification for getting a job.
A: I don't know. I'll have to think about it …

5
A: Are you all ready for the exam tomorrow? Now don't forget what I've told you: you have to take your passport and show it to the supervisor, OK?
B: Is an identity card OK?
A: Yes, if it's got your photo on. But as I said before, if you've got a passport, take your passport. Don't forget.

6
A: Well I'm going to have a cup of coffee. What about you?
B: I don't know. I've already had lots today.
A: Go on. Another one won't do you any harm.
B: No really. It keeps me awake at night.
A: But it's only four o'clock in the afternoon!
B: All right then, two sugars. But if I don't sleep tonight that's your fault.

7
A: But you were there, Sid, we know you were there.
B: I said I was there. But I had nothing to do with the money that was stolen.
A: Look Sid, somebody stole it. Somebody who was there. And you were there, weren't you Sid?
B: I told you before, I didn't steal it.

8
B: Oh there you are!
A: I'm sorry. I couldn't find it, and then there was a queue.
B: Sssh, the film's already started. Sit down and be quiet.
A: How about a nice box of chocolates for the interval?
B: Oh, Derek. Sit down and shut up, I'm trying to watch the film.
Others: Sssh!
A: Sorry!

Unit 11 Listening 6

Tanya: I'd like to begin by saying that in my view there are many things that could be done in this college to make a real contribution to the ecology movement. As a member of the Ecology Society, I would urge you all to put pressure on the authorities to change a few things. It's high time we became a lot more ecology conscious, not only as students, but also as an institution.
Firstly, there's the whole question of recycling. It's time this college woke up to the fact that a lot of resources are being wasted. For example, paper. The college produces tons of waste paper every year. Hundreds of photocopied handouts are given out to students every day. Often (they) are only printed on one side. I'm sure the teachers could coordinate the photocopying better, so that we had fewer pieces of paper and each one used to the maximum. And, of course, we should always be given handouts printed on recycled paper. Which brings me to my next point. What happens to all the waste paper? All the handouts that don't get handed out, the extra copies, the used worksheets and all the pieces of paper produced in the office. Well I'll tell you, they get thrown out with the rubbish – and there is no effort to separate the paper from the other rubbish. This is a scandal. It's high time all the waste paper from the college was recycled. If the college kept waste paper separate from other rubbish, it could be sold for recycling, thus giving an extra source of money to buy books and other facilities for the students.
And so to my next point. Why are the drinks in the cafeteria served in plastic cups? Why is the food served on plastic plates? This plastic is not recyclable. It's time we went back to proper china cups and plates that can be washed and used again or, if that's too expensive, then we should use disposable paper plates and cups made from recycled paper, instead of plastic, which themselves can be recycled.
And the same is true in the college shop where everything you buy is put in a plastic bag. If a bag is necessary, which it may not be, then why not one made of recycled paper?
Then there is the question of cleaning. As you know, strong detergents and cleaning products are a major cause of pollution. You can buy environmentally friendly cleaning products these days, but this college doesn't use them! It's time we made a big effort to convince the college authorities that it is worth the extra money to avoid using those products which are not biodegradable.
And lastly, a plea from the heart. What about the vegetarian menu in the cafeteria? It's high time a range of vegetarian meals was on offer at lunchtime, made from organically-grown vegetables and prepared without using animal fats. At the moment, there's only ever one vegetarian dish on the menu and there are a large number of students who would like a choice. It's time we had a balance of meat and vegetarian dishes on offer. Well, that brings me to the end of …

Unit 11 Listening 7

1 This is really a national problem because this beach has the finest stretch of seaside architecture in the country. They are going to ruin the whole feel of the area if they build this huge funfair. This is a conservation area and the law defines that a development in a conservation area must both conserve and enhance the area. This proposal does exactly the opposite. People like us have got to stand up for certain things or you might as well just forget the whole idea of the likes of conservation areas altogether. If Blackstone beach isn't safe, where is?

2 The council has prepared a report which describes the development as the expansion of a children's play area. I don't see how anybody can possibly claim that a children's playground like Toddleland can be expanded into a socking great funfair taking over the entire beach, ruining a beautiful conservation area and taking away a much-loved public amenity. If you ask me, we should be discouraging the young from going to funfairs. Our pupils often use the beach to do their environmental

projects and for playing sports, such as volleyball and jogging, so they'd lose out if this went ahead.

3 This is the only part of the beach we can use because of the access. There is a lift that goes down from street level onto the beach at this place. People like myself, or those with small children, or people in wheelchairs will be denied access to the beach if this site is developed into a funfair. I can't do all the 120 steps that there are down to the beach. The lift is a great boon for me and to many people of my age and to get down there and find a funfair awaiting you is not in the least what I want. All I want is our beach and it is <u>our</u> beach.

4 Blackstone needs a family entertainment area of this size. 40 years ago, there were 10 million visitors a year coming to Blackstone, we're down to two million now. The council is encouraging us to develop the whole sea front for the next generation and we're organising a series of public meetings where we will explain our vision of the sea front of the future to the locals and answer their questions as thoroughly as possible. But in the end, they'll have to agree that the funfair is just what Blackstone needs to brings in the tourists.

5 For those who don't understand why a funfair counts as being part of a conservation area, I should explain that the existing Toddleland playground was actually built before we designated this as a conservation area. So, it's not as if we're saying that it's a conservation area one day, then we're going to allow a funfair to be built the next day. The funfair is already there. We're looking at how the funfair can be improved for the benefit of local residents and tourists alike. This is, after all, the council's responsibility.

Unit 11 pronunication
Shifting stress

1 Listen to these phrases and mark the stressed syllable on each word in bold type.

John is unable to contrŏl that dog.
I can't **permit** you to enter.
It was a strange **object**.
The footballer got a free **transfer**.
Vegetable oil is one of our main **exports**.
I shall now **present** the winner with this silver cup.

3 Now listen to these phrases and mark the stressed syllable on each word in bold type.

I can't work the **controls** on this video.
I haven't got a **permit** to enter the building.
I **object** to the way he spoke to me.
I would like to **transfer** some money out of my bank account.
This country **exports** a lot of vegetable oil.
I got lots of **presents** for my birthday.

Unit 12 Listening 1

My name is Paul and I was born in London. But when I was two years old my parents went to live in Scotland, so I've lived in Scotland for as long as I can remember. At the moment I'm studying engineering at Glasgow University.My main hobby is travelling and I hope to get a job as an engineer in a third world country. Meanwhile, I've been studying French and Spanish at evening classes and I intend to take up a third language next year.
My name's Catherine. I was born in Leeds and I've always lived in Yorkshire. When I was four, I went to live with my grandmother in Scarborough for two months because my parents moved house, but then I came back to Leeds. At the moment, I'm attending a secondary school in Leeds. My favourite subjects are Art, Design and technology and I hope to get a job as a designer one day. I have been taking driving lessons for two months and I intend to take my test as soon as possible.

Unit 12 Listening 2

1 You will hear someone talking to a group of people about taking a driving test.
What sort of people is he talking to?
A teenagers
B parents
C driving instructors
When taking the driving test, they should dress to convince the examiner in the first crucial seconds that, although they may only be seventeen or so, they are middle-aged at heart. Boys should get a haircut, wear a jacket with clean jeans and very sensible shoes. Girls should wear a skirt and flat shoes and avoid dangly wrist jewellery. But nothing too expensive, in case the examiner thinks you're going to dash out and buy them a sports car if they pass.

2 You will hear the introduction to a radio programme.
What type of programme is it?
A a medical programme
B a scientific documentary
C a cookery feature
Whatever the scientists say, we all know that breakfast is the most important meal of the day. You should start the day with a good nourishing meal if you want to find the energy to face the morning and keep going until lunch time. It is well-known that people who skip breakfast do not perform so well at work or school and tend to be more irritable too! We have all had those hunger pains mid-morning that lead to chocolate bars, cakes and headaches by lunch time. So fill up with a good, wholesome breakfast before you start. A low-fat dairy product, a high-fibre cereal plus a piece of fruit is the ideal combination, and on the programme today we have some mouth-watering suggestions of how to put them together.

3 You will hear part of a report on a consumer programme.
What is the subject of the report?
A new fashions in food
B new hair care products
C new types of pets
They used to be something you washed down the plug hole; now the varieties preferred by teenage girls simply wouldn't fit. Youngsters are investing in spiders, some as large as dinner plates. Sales of tarantulas and other exotic arachnids have quadrupled at the Pet City Superstore and the bulk of the buyers are teenage girls and young mothers. For those with the stomach, tarantulas start at around one hundred and fifty pounds.

4 You will hear a conversation between an employee and a customer.
Where does the conversation take place?
A at a hotel reception
B in a travel agency
C at an airport check-in
Receptionist: Could I have your name, please?
Mr Jones: Jones.
Receptionist: Just a moment, Mr Jones. Ah, yes, now, you've booked a single, haven't you?
Mr J: That's right.
Receptionist: With a reservation on the airline shuttle in the morning?
Mr J: That's it, yes.
Receptionist: And a deposit was paid by credit card, wasn't it?
Mr J: Uh, hm. I can pay the balance with my credit card, can't I?
Receptionist: Certainly. Now, did you want dinner this evening?
Mr J: But it's included, isn't it?
Receptionist: Oh, yes. it's just to let the kitchen know, because it is rather late.
Mr J: Oh, I see. Then yes, right away.
Receptionist: Thank you, could you just sign here, Mr Jones?
Mr J: Oh yes.

Unit 12 Grammar 1
Question Tags

Exercise 3.2 - Listen to check the question tag.

a You're Joe's sister, aren't you?
b It's a lovely day, isn't it?
c She's finished her course, hasn't she?
d You went to that party, didn't you?
e He always drives to work, doesn't he?
f You can give her a lift, can't you?
g You won't forget to ring Lesley, will you?
h Let's play Scrabble, shall we?
i You've met Mr Simpson, haven't you?
j You don't like tennis, do you?
k You haven't done your homework, have you?
l You'll have time for a cup of tea, won't you?

Unit 12 Listening 3

Host: Right, Julie's team, your turn. Here's your picture. Now, you remember the rules, don't you? I'll read you some biographical notes about the person and you press that buzzer just as soon as you think you know who it is. So, in your picture this famous person is 9 years old. He'd been born in 1756 in Salzburg in Austria, son of a violinist. By the time that picture was painted he'd already established a reputation as a child prodigy, making his first professional tour of Europe as a pianist at the age of six. it was already clear that he was going to become a brilliant musician. In fact, he went on to become a prolific composer and traveller. He was to be concert master to the Archbishop of Salzburg for a number of years, before resigning in 1781 and moving to Vienna.Julie, right, so you think you've got the answer. So who do you think this young man grew up to be?
Julie: We think it's Beethoven.
Host: No, I'm sorry Julie, it's not Beethoven. So, this is a chance for Erica's team to get two extra points, and remember you don't have to buzz; you can hear the whole piece. So, to continue, our young man was to move to Vienna in 1781, where he wrote two of his most famous operas before becoming court composer to Joseph the Second in 1787. In his rather short life, he was to write over six hundred musical compositions, including a requiem mass intended for Count Walsegg. Our composer was to die before this mass was finished, however, in 1791, and his last work has come to be regarded as his own requiem. Now, Erica, who do you think it is?
Erica: Well, we think it's probably ...

Unit 12 Listening 4 *Part 1*

Interviewer: At the height of the season the queues to Madame Tussaud's go on and on. The waxwork museum is one of London's most popular tourist attractions. So, who was Madame Tussaud?
Historian: Marie Tussaud was born in 1761 in France. In her life she was to know the French Revolution and then Victorian England. Her interest in wax modelling began as a child. She lived with her mother who was a housekeeper to a doctor, who was also the owner of a wax museum, and he taught her how to model wax from when she was six.
Now, of course, all normal life in France was interrupted by the revolution in 1789 and in fact Marie'd been sent to the court of King Louis the Sixteenth to be the art teacher to his sister. Marie was actually teaching her to make little wax copies of her friends. But her friend, the doctor was in fact very heavily involved with the coming revolution, he knew exactly what was going on and he got her out of the palace on some excuse, and got her back to Paris a matter of days before the revolution broke out. Then, she was immediately enlisted, I mean there was no choice for her, by the revolutionaries, to make wax works for the sake of the revolution – so, having been a state artist in the court, she was overnight the state artist of the revolution and of the terror. She was asked by the revolutionaries, as far as we can tell, to model the decapitated heads of the aristocracy and these were used to show people the events of the time. She herself was not a great supporter of the revolution, she just felt she had to do it in order to survive.
After the terror, Marie Tussaud escaped to a new life in England, even though she was parted from her

Listening scripts

family. Completely on her own, she created a travelling exhibition of waxworks.

She spotted that there was money to be made in England. There was enormous interest in England in the French Revolution and everyone wanted to know what had happened in France and, of course, she came over with this perfect wax work display. She had the French royal family, who she had known personally, she had the heads of the aristocracy, and so everyone was fascinated.

Her waxworks were so popular that a permanent exhibition was set up in 1835 in London. Although Marie Tussaud died in 1850, you can still see some of her original models in the famous waxworks in Marylebone Road in London.

Unit 12 Listening 4 *Part 2*

1 She was caught up in the French Revolution, but she was complex, she was ambitious, you can't pin her down, and so she was a wonderful, heroic revolutionary woman. You know, she played both sides; in a way she was almost like a double agent. She was furiously independent, hugely ambitious and completely driven by her work.

2 I went backstage at Madame Tussaud's and I dreamt how they modelled it. The wax is the end result of quite a long and complicated process and I became quite interested in that a lot of sculptors work at Madame Tassaud's and I saw the artists, the actual artistry of it.

3 I can understand Marie's fascination for wax, it infected me too, because I think this thing of how wax changes, how it can actually change its form, it melts and then it, sort of, re-solidifies, and how you can make something look lifelike – using wax, but it has kind of, rather alarmingly, dead quality at the same time.

4 I think that, for me, because this was very much how Marie looked at her work - that it was both real and not real – that it was make-believe, but trying to, sort of, persuade people that perhaps something might just move. There's a strange world between reality and unreality.

5 I see her as a survivor and I see that the surviving cost her quite a lot, she left her husband and one of her children behind when she fled to England and I think that must have created in her a tremendous sort of guilt, probably covering up a very deep sense of distress.

Unit 12 Listening 5

Interviewer: Apparently over half of office romances end up with the sound of wedding bells. So, if you met your current partner at work, you could be well on your way towards marriage. It's all come out in a romantic survey today put together by the Recruitment Consultants Company and manager of their Manchester branch is Lorna Telford and she's here with me to explain it. Lorna good morning to you.
Lorna: Good morning, John.
Interviewer: So, how does it happen, romance in the work environment, is it love at first sight?
Lorna: No, I mean, in our office in Manchester three out of the five people met their partners through work, and they all stress it was friendship first and then it turned into something different, but it depends on age and personal circumstances, of course.
Interviewer: It seems almost like a pair of shoes, doesn't it, in that you wear them in and then you become comfortable in the relationship. Whereas if you meet people in a bar or disco, then it's all a bit more difficult.
Lorna: Yes, you're very right there. I mean the time we spend at work has a strong link with the relationships we build at work compared to those we build with people we meet in public places and situations like that. You do get used to somebody and you get to know their ways and then, suddenly, love takes over and your feelings are so intensified, one would imagine, that it changes the whole thing.
Interviewer: I must ask, do you have personal experience of this?
Lorna: Yes, but it was through work, rather than at work. My husband was actually a client of mine but we'll say no more about that
Interviewer: But, of course, it can be a problem, I would have thought ,as well, because couples have an argument and you're still in the same environment eight hours a day – Oh I can see problems there ...
Lorna: You do find that. From the survey, although not many people were asked to leave their jobs, more females than males did decide to resign and I think it's because it became intolerable to be in the same environment – not only if a relationship had broken down, but can you imagine being with your partner 24 hours a day? I mean, no thanks!
Interviewer: What else did the survey show up then?
Lorna: One very important point was that managers didn't seem to be at all bothered, according to those having relationships, but we found that, in fact, managers do mind and they do not like relationships at work, regardless of the fact that nothing's ever said about it, they don't like it and so it can have a negative effect on your career. Another interesting fact that it did show up was that according to the individuals who were carrying on a relationship, their work didn't suffer. However, when their colleagues were asked, they felt that yes, work did suffer. So, there's a misconception there of how well you're doing at work and how others see you.
Interviewer: So, presumably the other people will think that the relationship is going to get in the way of work?
Lorna: Exactly, and it seems it does get in the way of people's ability to actually do the job properly. The people having the relationship don't realise this, but those who are observing do.
Interviewer: Well, if you're in love, you're happy, everything is great, doesn't that make you work better?
Lorna: I think you feel like that , but with all due respect, what actually happens is that you're not really concentrating on your work, and it is noticed.
Interviewer: What about secret relationships? Does your survey touch on those at all?
Lorna: It does, yes. What we found was that people ...

Unit 12 Pronunciation
Contractions

1 Listen to these pairs of sentences.
1 I can't stand jazz music.
  I cannot stand jazz music.
2 Please don't be late.
  Please do not be late.
3 Mary didn't remember to call me.
  Mary did not remember to call me.
4 John won't come to the party.
  John will not come to the party.
5 My work hasn't been affected.
  My work has not been affected.

2 Listen and repeat these contracted forms.
1 can't	2 couldn't	3 couldn't have
4 won't	5 wouldn't	6 wouldn't have
7 shan't	8 shouldn't	9 shouldn't have
10 oughtn't	11 oughtn't to have	12 needn't
13 needn't have	14 mightn't	15 mightn't have
16 mustn't	17 mustn't have	

Unit 12 Listening 6

1 Well, it's really quite, it's better now than it was with, well, say, the first one, because this time we're not actually bothered about having a, I mean we'd love a hit, but we're not desperate to have one. We've had all our hits over fifteen years or so and so by now we're kind of more relaxed about it. The first time it was like, "Goodness, I hope it gets into the charts," so well, it's a bit more relaxed this time.

2 We didn't actually sit down and work out an image, we never have. The media kind of put an image on to us and people, sort of, believe that, reading it in the paper and all that. I mean, when we went on TV we wore what people persuaded us to wear. They were making us... like the first time we were ever on TV, we wore these long, full-length, satin bottle-green dresses and they were absolutely awful, but ... after a while we didn't actually like what we were wearing and so we started wearing what we would like to see other teenagers in at the time.

3 No, I went through a stage from about, I don't know, twelve to fourteen where I really, really didn't want to join the group. I was very much into horse riding and looking after horses and spent my life working at a stables and being with my friends and I thought, "Oh, I really don't want to do this," you know, and I told my dad and he was brilliant, he said, you know, "You do what you want to do, don't feel that because the rest of the family did it that you have to do it." And then it came to, like, fifteen and I spent all summer with the girls, and I went with them every night and by the end of the season I couldn't wait to get out there - it was really strange, all of a sudden it was the only thing I wanted to do.

4 It's difficult, though, to feel that you are an individual, you know, we're The Daltons, we're good sisters, we have to be perfect and the same. I think that when we are at home in our own environment then we're individuals, but when we're working it's very very difficult to be an individual because people all put us into one barrel. If someone says something in an interview, for example, instead of saying Anne said this, or Maureen said this, they said The Daltons said this, so one person's opinion gets, kind of, put on to all of us and that is really difficult and nobody ever knows our first names, we're just one of The Daltons. So that's a bit annoying at times.

5 There is talk of a UK tour if this latest recording really takes off. We've all expressed doubts about touring now that we're married and have children of our own. But when we recorded the song we all said that if something did happen then we would promote it - so I'm afraid, yes, I'll have to really. I left my two-year old screaming this morning. He was stuck to the window like one of those toys you buy for cars. Yes, it will be a problem and I can't even think about it at the moment - but, like I said, we've committed ourselves now.